A REAL LIFE

"*Like Mark Twain with Drag Queens*"

A Memoir by
Perry Brass

author of *Carnal Sacraments, The Manly Art of Seduction,*
and *King of Angels*

Belhue Press

Belhue Press First Edition

Copyright 2020 by Perry Brass

Published in the United State of America by:

Belhue Press
2501 Palisade Ave., Suite A1
Bronx, NY 10463

Cover photo: The author (right) at 19 in 1966, with his first lover Dick Farnsworth in Central Park.

ISBN-10: 1-892149-29-X

ISBN-13: 978-1-892149-29-9

Electronic ISBN: 978-1-892149-30-5

Library of Congress Control Number:2019949893

For the memory of my parents Helen and Louis Brass, and for the memory of my friends Jeffrey Lann Campbell, Rod Michaels, and Roger F. Krentz, PhD, a lover of books of all kinds and knowledge in general, and all of my brothers and sisters who have died in the HIV epidemic. And also for Hugh Young, Ricardo Limon, Darrell Perry, Jonathan David Smyth, Rob Ritter, Bill Crist and Gary DePasquale, and all of the other people who have taken this journey with me and offered me their hands and hearts.

A Note about the Subtitle

People have often asked me what that first year away from home was like, when I hitchhiked from Savannah, Georgia, to San Francisco. I tell them: "It was like Mark Twain with drag queens."

Chapter

1

I was seventeen years old and on a quest: to find myself and to find love, although I had very little idea what either of them was. The only thing I knew for sure was that what I was—the deepest, central core of me— was forbidden. The year was 1965. Lyndon Johnson was president; John F. Kennedy had been killed two years earlier when I was a senior in high school, and the country was still roiling from the specters of racial integration, rock 'n' roll, teenage sex, and other threatening forms of "Commie subversion," including the one that I knew in truth included myself: I was attracted to boys.

I was born in the Deep South, in Savannah, Georgia, and grew up there in this polite, beautiful, azalea-filled coastal city where people like me were routinely murdered, if they didn't kill themselves.

I had tried to do that at fifteen, in the summer of 1963—driven to it by constant bullying at school with a hate-filled whispering campaign in the halls; and at home, by my mother, Helen Landy Brass, a once tall, strikingly beautiful woman who had looked like a 1940s movie star. Later, as an often-hospitalized "mental patient," she had been subjected to repeated electroconvulsive shock treatments administered in tandem with various highly addictive prescription drugs. The result was that for several years she had been determined to destroy me. I was the whipping boy, the stand-in, for all of her failings and psychiatric problems, and the final problem: we were both *queer*. She a secret, totally self-hating lesbian, a fact that I would not come to grips with for several more years, and I . . . both of us were cowering deep inside that labyrinth of shame that people in Southern towns erect to keep the black-and-white monstrosities of their own fears hidden. So there I was, dripping from sweat at the scalding dawn of summer break (after my self-described "Year of Incarceration" at the *un*surprisingly *redneck* University of Georgia, in Athens near Atlanta, where, as a too-"aesthetic," painfully shy *pansy* I'd had repeated death threats in my freshman dorm room), hitch-hiking from Savannah to . . .

San Francisco.

The Emerald City.

A place "crawling with queers," I'd been told —like *me*—though I could barely breathe the word, taboo as it was; still it was true. I was a good-looking kid with clear skin (except for a few minor acne breakouts), full, soft lips, intense blue eyes, curly, dark brown hair, and beautiful legs (those I got from Helen): when I wore shorts, people looked at me *seriously*. I had packed a small canvas suitcase with a few shirts, fashionable Levi "wheat" jeans, some nice pants, and a tie and a jacket. You needed them in those days. And of course a Boy Scout sleeping bag. It was a different world then: you saw kids hitchhiking all the time.

It took four days to the West Coast. The country was truly vast then— and varied, not all shopping malls endlessly repeating themselves. People were usually nice, stopping, taken with my Southern accent, politeness, and innocence. A young couple in the Ozarks invited me to go skinny-dipping with them in the dark. I begged off. And I'll never forget a fat, Southern, good-ol'-boy-type girl already pushing middle age who propositioned me with the question: "What do you hitchhiker fellers *do* at night?" There was a dirty old man outside Tulsa who tried to feel me up—I jumped out at the first stoplight. And two rawboned cowboys in the black, empty depths of a star-spangled Arizona night who talked about murdering "queers, homos— and what d'ya call 'em?—*impersonators?*"

I crouched down in the backseat, terrified.

I lucked out and got a long ride from the Grand Canyon to Los Angeles with a clueless recent college grad in engineering who admitted, confiden-tially, that he was still a virgin but was intent on changing that. I kept my mouth shut.

It was a short trip from Long Beach up to San Francisco. I rode into town in the rear of a pickup truck, gazing up at the magnificence of the city, its steep climbs and endless vistas, its dizzying streets, feeling San Francisco's famously bitter summer wind biting at the back of my neck. I got out at a decrepit YMCA on the edge of the Tenderloin district. I had about $50 left in my pocket, enough to keep me there for barely a week. The Tenderloin was a teeming warren filled with prostitutes, muscle-bound male hustlers, down-and-out SRO hotels, and sailor bars. I had never seen anyplace like it. I was at once shocked, scared, and fascinated. My first night, I listened to the wind howling outside my small room, and realized I was alone. Completely. What was I doing there? Or *going* to do? How could I at seventeen claim an existence of my own with no money, no family, or real ideas?

The next morning I went to the California State Department of Labor, where I had heard you could sign up for casual daywork. I didn't realize that thousands of young people were already going to San Francisco, hanging out in North Beach and Haight-Ashbury, trying to figure out a way they could stay alive. A nice, balding older man at a window, cigar clamped to his mouth, told me to "Keep comin' back. Maybe something'll come in as a dishwasher, or at a factory." I looked in the paper and saw big listings for private job agencies on Market Street. I hoofed over to them, but they all wanted money up front, before they'd even send me on an interview. I'd had no experience except for working at a couple of campus jobs in Athens, Georgia. But San Francisco was beautiful. I loved walking up the hills and down to Fisherman's Wharf.

A day or so later, I was on the cable car going into North Beach when a good-looking, well-dressed young man in a suit, seated with a large wicker basket on his lap, looked at me curiously. Suddenly, I just asked him:

"What you got in there, a snake?"

It looked like the basket Cleopatra's asp had arrived in.

He grinned. The seat next to him became empty. He told me his name, Michael, and asked me what I was doing that Sunday. I shrugged.

"Why don't you come out to Sausalito? Some friends of mine are going to the Golden Lantern, about 6. Just ask for it. Everybody knows where it is."

I took the ferry over on a beautiful, sharply bright afternoon. Sausalito with its steep, winding streets of country houses overlooking the bay was quaintly enchanting until evening fell, dragging a dark, cold sting with it. I easily found the Golden Lantern, but felt funny about going in. I was underage, and had no idea what kind of place it was. But once inside—past a vestibule with a bouncer who gave me a quick once-over—in a roar of California pop music, I knew.

It was a gay bar. And not just *any* gay bar but a popular one—like, it must have been *the* place to be on that particular Sunday evening. It was so crowded no one even noticed I was there. There was a stage, and on it were several black singers as well as several girls prancing around (whom I guessed to be men, just dressed as girls). Immediately below the stage, I spotted Michael inside a small clutch of people.

"You found us!" he said. "What are you drinking?"

I told him a Coke. I didn't want to try ordering alcohol. He introduced me to several of his friends and a young, very hip-looking woman close to his age in a leather jacket.

"Val," he said. "She's my sister."

Val smiled at me, and Michael said, closer, almost in a whisper. "She's a lesbian. We're both *gay*. See?"

Actually, I didn't. This world was so new to me. I felt like I was about ten years old, entering a foreign country. A few minutes later, they all decided to leave and asked me if I wanted to go back to San Francisco with them. We piled into Val's compact car and drove over the Golden Gate Bridge in the glittering dark. I was squeezed in next to Michael in the back seat. I had to ask him, but it was difficult.

"How'd you know I'm gay?"

Gay. It was still a hard word for me to use.

He chuckled.

"You asked me if I had a snake in the basket. How *phallic* can you get?"

So that was it? Val stopped the car, and we got out somewhere near Pacific Heights, in one of those beautifully "normal" San Francisco neighborhoods. That is, it was simply beautiful by itself, just for being where it was. Two of Michael's friends were a couple. I had never met a gay couple before. Val parked, and we went *up* into their apartment—in San Francisco, everything seemed *up*. The two guys were in their late twenties. They seemed so utterly sophisticated to me, a scared kid from Georgia who didn't believe anyone could be anything *less* than terrified about being gay.

Gin and tonics were offered, and we sat in a small living room and watched TV. Bronze-tanned George Hamilton was on, wearing white shorts. He had been dating one of President Johnson's daughters, Linda Bird, and was more famous for that than for his acting. My two hosts were snuggling on the couch. One looked up at the screen and sighed. "He's so pretty!"

I left soon after that. My head was spinning. So this was what things could be like in San Francisco—with young men exclaiming about George Hamilton, "He's so pretty!" I was happy. Deliriously so. I just had to find a way to survive, because it seemed like everyone wanted to be in San Francisco, even before the fabled "Summer of Love" hit in 1967. For the next several days I knocked on every door—all around Market Street, onto side streets, looking into small shops and big stores, snack bars and crowded restaurants, and walked out after being told over and over again, "No."

Discouraged, I returned to the State Department of Labor, with all the nervous-looking men anxiously pacing in a large, dirty room waiting for work. I registered my name again, and the clerk, the same friendly, dumpy man with a cigar said, "Lissen, there's really nothin' here f' you. You're just a kid. You really want t' work?"

I nodded.

"Then get the hell outta San Francisco! Go to the San Joaquin Valley. It's only a bus ride away. There are thousands of acres of fruit farms there, and right now they're lookin' for pickers. It's hard work, but you get paid at the end of every day. At least you won't starve."

I was now almost totally out of money. I had just enough to pay for my room at the Y, and a bus ticket to Modesto. At ten the next morning, I was on a bus filled with Hispanic dayworkers. We left the cold, fog-chilled summer air of San Francisco, and very quickly the temperature climbed to nearly 90 degrees. I watched the city give way to scrubby hills and then entered the valley itself, spread out in front of me, stuffed with its orchards and fruit groves, and endless fields of lettuce, cucumbers, beets, and other table vegetables. Modesto then was a sleepy small town; easily I walked to an end of it where the state highway began. People grinned at me, a really young-looking kid with a canvas suitcase and sleeping bag. I stuck out my thumb and decided to see what arrived next.

The first guy to pick me up was muscular and Mediterranean looking. There were a lot of Italians nearby who had bought farms decades earlier; he told me about the area as we passed groves of trees.

"You evuh heard o' Hershey Bars? Every time ya bite into one of 'em, you eatin' *ah-mans* from this place. Yep. See. It's the *ah-man* capital of the world!"

Suddenly I realized *ah-mans* were almonds.

After he dropped me off about twelve miles from Modesto, on a dirt road with farms on both sides, a very good-looking kid about my age stopped in his pickup truck. He asked me where I was going, and I told him I had no idea but wanted a job in the fields.

"Why don't you come to my place? We have a ranch, a few miles down the road. I'm Andy. Andy Weeks. What's your name?"

He had light, clear blue eyes, streaky blond hair, and the kind of open, friendly face you'd expect in a Walt Disney movie. He asked me about myself and told me that he lived with his mother not far from a small "fruit town" called St. Marco, a hamlet surrounded by ranches and orchards.

"Look what I picked up!" he said to his mother, who looked at me skeptically. "This is Perry. He's looking for a job in the fields."

She was a thin, sad, drawn-looking woman with gray hair pulled tightly back into a bun.

"You don't look like you can do much farm work," she observed. Compared to her son, I was puny. I knew it. "You can stay here for a day or so, till you find something. Andy likes having company since his father died."

She showed me to their spare room, and told me that they'd have dinner shortly. A few minutes later, Andy came bouncing in, overflowing with enthusiasm.

"You're all the way from Georgia—that's on the other coast, isn't it? I've never been anywhere—just Modesto and Sacramento. My dad died three years ago. Heart attack. Mom hates San Francisco. She says it's fulla beatniks and weirdos. So I never get to go there."

Uh-oh. I had to act cool now: I was one of those *weirdos.* I knew it. He was really nice to look at, with a silky-smooth, muscular body. I already had hair on my chest, inherited from my Russian-Jewish dad who had died of cancer when I was eleven. Both of us had lost fathers. I tried not to look at Andy too hard and pretended that I was just like him, without any kind of secrets or a concealable history. One of those nice "What-you-see-is-what-you-get" kids. He had a girlfriend named Ginger who lived on another farm near theirs. He asked me if I'd like to go out with him the next day to meet her.

"Sure!" I said and smiled.

The next day we drove off in Andy's pickup to meet Ginger, who looked kind of like Andy: brightly open-faced, engaging, except with freckles and red hair. She talked constantly, while Andy mostly watched. Almost nothing she said had anything at all to do with me. It was about the other kids in their school, who was going with whom, who would do what for the summer.

Suddenly she looked at me like I had just fallen in from outer space.

"You don't act like the kids around here," she said.

"That's because he's from Georgia!" Andy chimed in.

She suddenly gave me this guileful smile that came out of nowhere.

"No. You're kinda strange. I can tell."

"Ginger!" Andy protested. "That's no way to talk. He wants to work. Don't your father got a friend who's lookin' for someone to load boxes onto his trucks?"

"Shoot, Andy! Those boxes weigh thirty, forty pounds. Perry can't do that. Look at him?"

Andy looked at me. "Don't worry, Perry. You'll beef up soon. The important thing is you *want* t' work!"

Andy smiled at me directly, and I felt for the first time that he might be deeper than I had thought. Like he knew exactly what was up ahead: he'd marry Ginger and stay on the farm, no matter what. We went swimming in a man-made lake nearby. I wore a baggy swimsuit Andy lent me. He noticed that I had hair on my chest, and joked about it. Ginger's parents had a boat, and we went water-skiing. That is, I tried it for the first time and didn't drown. We had dinner with Ginger's parents, who were friendly but also looked at me oddly; like what was I doing there on their farm? Mr. Mc-Cloud, Ginger's father, talked to me about the job loading trucks—it would not be available for another month, but if I was still in the area, to come by and see him, and he'd connect me to his friend.

When Andy drove me back to his house, his mother met me at the door and asked to speak with me alone, while Andy did some chores back in the barn.

"I don't think this is the kind of life for you, Perry. Why don't you go back to the city, to San Francisco?"

I told her I couldn't find a job there, but I was willing to pick fruit in the Valley.

"This just isn't the life for you," she said, and opened her purse. She gave me a $10 bill. "There's a rooming house in St. Marco. Andy's going to drive you up to it. I'm sure something will happen for you. You're a smart young man, but I know this isn't the kind of place for a guy like you."

Chapter

2

Andy stopped the pickup in front of the rooming house. I could tell he was bothered.

"This is where Mom thinks you should be. A guy showed up at our door once and he ended up stealing her checkbook, but I don't think you're that kind of guy. You're just a kid like I am."

I wondered. *Was I?* He extended his right hand, and I shook it and then got out.

I didn't go into the run-down-looking rooming house, which looked a little too Norman Bates for my taste—real black-and-white horror movie material. Instead, I knew Mrs. Weeks's $10 bill could keep me from starving for a while, and as darkness gathered, out of sight of anybody, I rushed off into the closest waiting fields, now empty of workers. Hurrying, I zigzagged through various rows of waiting salad ingredients, and then came to a stream. I jumped across it. A short time later, almost hidden in the depths of a shrubby knoll, I found a small storage hut constructed of cheap plywood. The door was locked, but there was an accessible window, and I slid easily into it.

Inside were boxes of seeds, and equipment like buckets, hoes, and rakes. It was clean and warm with room for me to unroll my sleeping bag; I slept there for the next four nights. I got up at daybreak, rolled my sleeping bag, and then hid my suitcase in a tight crawl space under the hut, covered with brush. There were filling stations in St. Marco, and at daybreak it was easy to use one of their bathrooms, wash around, and brush my teeth. Sometimes I'd shower off in back with a hose, or wash in one of the irrigation canals that were basically clean.

I felt extraordinarily happy, completely free and yet settled in a wonderful way. I decided to call my new home the Seed House, and as long as I could get back to it after dark, I was satisfied. During the day, it wasn't that hard to find work; I would simply show up in the morning at a clearing near the road, and a work manager would give me wooden boxes to fill up with boysenberries, or strawberries, or peas, or whatever field needed picking. I was paid by the box, not the hour. The pay was low, the work backbreaking. Most of the pickers were Hispanics, but a few were itinerant whites, sometimes families of them, who had an extremely hardscrabble life right out of *The Grapes of Wrath*, which I had read in high school.

I learned from them that there were a few camps for pickers in parts of the area, and you could stay in them for less than a dollar a day. They had toilets, showers, and outside fire pits for cooking. Some actually had real cabins for families, but I knew I didn't want to be in them. One evening I retrieved my suitcase from the Seed House and hiked over to the closest camp. Almost all the faces I saw were white; the Hispanics seemed to be living out of trailers at the other end of the field. Two very butch-looking, middle-aged women spotted me and smiled. They invited me to come eat with them at their campfire. Their names were Pam and Lucy. They referred to each other as "Sister," even though they weren't. I had nothing to offer them, but there was a small grocery store and filling station close by. I trotted over and came back with some cheap cheese, very tasteless white bread, and something called "Sandwich Loaf," which was a slightly more processed version of baloney sprinkled with enticing of bits of sweet pickle relish.

Lucy and Pam had a station wagon that they slept in, and they invited me to unroll my sleeping bag out near it at the campsite that night. I agreed, and Lucy, who looked kind of like a tugboat captain, announced, "Well, Sister, looks like we done adopted ourselves a boy!"

For the next several days I hung out with them, which meant that we could drive over to distant fields that needed picking and come back at night to the same campsite. Like most of the people there, they were down on their luck—Pam, the more articulate of the two, had been a keypunch operator, and Lucy did simple mechanic's work on cars. Pam had become sick and ended up losing her house, located not far from there. "When we get back on our feet," she insisted, "We're gonna get us that house back!"

After several days, the Sisters decided that they wanted to drive off on their own, and said goodbye to me. This didn't bother me; I was getting somewhat tired of them, and soon moved on to another couple with a car:

a big, kind of blousy blonde named Judy and her sullen, sometimes explosive, greasy-fat redneck husband, Bill. They were traveling with their three-year-old daughter, a beautiful, very serious little girl with golden curls named Florence who amazed me. She never cried except when she was hungry. But routinely, it seemed, there was barely enough to feed her and keep gas in the car as well.

"If I gotta," Judy said defiantly, "I'm gonna go into town and hustle. But this kid ain't never gonna go hungry."

"Don't you say that," Bill said. "Not in front of the boy here," meaning me. He then promised that he'd pick even more the next day, and go into town—Modesto, usually—if he had to and get any kind of work that would pay him. During my brief but interesting sojourn with them, they managed to feed Florence and themselves, and put gas in the car and barely scrape by, but—truthfully, there were times when Judy simply disappeared and came back with money when the pickings got very low. Bill drank and could be mean when he got drunk. He and Judy would fight. Once she threatened to leave him for a "curly-peckered hog." I heard that and only laughed. Sometimes after work at the end of the day Bill and I would swim in our underpants in the irrigation canals that crisscrossed the area. It was at one of them that we met a tall, skinny, sun-wrinkled drifter named Tom, who waded up to me the next evening and whispered, "If you ever need anything, boy, just let me know."

I had no idea what he was supposed to do for me, until he started feeling me up under the water, away from Judy by the side of the canal in her bra, and Bill further down who made no bones about hating queers, or "fruiters" as he called them. I'd heard him talking loudly about bashing them in the face and very casually murdering them. After enough of that kind of talk, I decided this was no time to become more involved with Tom, Judy, *or* Bill. The next morning I moved on to another speck of a town in the valley, filled with pickers, truck stations, ranches, and fields of produce as far as the eye could see.

I was doing OK for several days, sleeping in the depths of the fields at night, finding water to bathe in and brush my teeth, and hanging out in the town square, drawing in a sketchbook I had picked up. Most of the people around me were Mexicans and they never bothered me. But one evening a group of the local white teenage boys decided to kill me. I was walking down the state road toward the fields when they drove up next to me.

"HEY FAGGOT!" they shouted, blew their horn at me, and tried to run me off the road as they passed.

I shot the bird at them, giving them the famous middle finger.

The car screeched to a halt, then backed up for about fifteen feet. They piled out.

I started running as fast as I could, while four football-player-sized kids chased after me. I spotted an alley and hid behind some garbage cans, but they soon caught up with me. I jumped out making as much noise as I could, and dashed to the middle of a two-lane blacktop road—a major thoroughfare around there—with this really big kid swinging his fists at me as I tried to flag down any car going by. Suddenly two local state troopers pulled their squad car to a stop.

They got out and looked at the boys.

"Wha's goin' on here?" one asked.

I started laughing suddenly, I guess from stress-induced hysteria. It was so pitch black out there except for the highway lights, that even the question seemed absurd.

"They're gonna kill me," I said trying to grab hold of myself.

"He shot the *bird* at us, Josh!" the big kid answered the trooper.

"No reason to kill 'im," the trooper said, his forehead wrinkling. He ordered the kids back into their car, and told me I had *exactly* ten-minutes to get my butt out of there. "There are fields all over here. Get lost in one and don't come back."

By daybreak the next morning, I was on the road to Los Angeles.

Chapter

3

Or Lost Angeles, as they called it.

It was certainly a great place to get lost.

I had no problems getting rides. This ultra-cute, deep-tanned, barefoot surfer kid, about a year older than I, with sun-streaked hair and genuine "surfer knobs"—thick fleshy bumps on his shins from surfboard riding—stopped. He told me what to look out for in LA. "The cops. They're murder. They'll pick you up for jaywalking. And the *queers*! They'll try to pick you up just waiting for a bus. So you need wheels of your own. That means you'll need to pick yourself up some coins, know what I mean?"

I didn't. But he winked at me, and I kind of got an idea.

I arrived toward sunset in scorching hot Downtown LA, an area I would describe as part skid row, part zoo. I spent my first night at a Christian mission for down-and-out geezers, then was released into the dawn with nary a clue what to do next. Till I realized that the surfer was right: the fact that I was seventeen and had become quite comely in the California sun was helpful. Men seemed to buzz around me at every point. That evening I found a particularly buzzy point close to the downtown YMCA. (The Village People would prove correct: the YMCA is "good for every boy.") I was blue-eyed and nicely tanned and trim from outdoor work; my curly brown hair had become honey-golden, and in a tight T-shirt and pair of jeans, I—

"What are you out for?" a man about thirty-two in a Corvette asked me.

Suddenly tongue-tied, I couldn't even say it.

"Why don't you get in?"

I did. He offered me a cigarette. I didn't smoke, but decided this would make me seem a little less green than I was.

He hit the gas, and asked:

"So? Is this going to be business or pleasure?"

Again, I was stone-silent. I just shrugged.

He smiled. "You *are* new at this, aren't you?"

He drove me to a respectable, family-style restaurant and bought me dinner. Hamburgers, french fries, and a Coke. I gobbled everything. At seventeen you are always hungry. Then we got back into his car, and he asked me where I wanted to go. I had no idea what to do next, so he took me up to Mulholland Drive. The view was gorgeous; we just looked at it. Suddenly I realized that, deep-down, this guy was probably as shy as I was, and I had no idea how to break either his ice or my own. He drove me back to the Y, and gave me a $5 bill.

"There's something about you," he said seriously. "You seem too nice of a guy to take advantage of"—then he drove off.

I had no idea how lucky I had been, but my whole adventure so far had been characterized by luck, except for the episode with the kids in the San Joaquin Valley. Part of it must have come from having good Southern manners and my accent: I didn't come off tough, like most hustlers I was sure did, even kid hustlers. I got a room for the night at the Y. In the communal shower, older men propositioned me. I had no idea how to deal with that, but had just enough money for my Y room for another night.

The next morning I walked back into Downtown LA around the notorious Greyhound Bus station and beyond that to Pershing Square, equally notorious for its street preacher crazies and its quite open male sex-market. Some men were out in the square already, open for business in standard hustler uniform: tight jeans and white T's; or denim shirts unbuttoned enough to show a bit of chest. Cops came in to poke around, glare, then leave. I got hungry, and explored some side streets filled with dirt-cheap greasy-spoon restaurants. All I could afford was a doughnut and coffee.

I was finishing the doughnut outside when a man approached me and started talking, like we had known each other forever. He was in his mid-thirties, short, muscular, with a thick neck and this awfully bleached platinum-blond hair that did not go with his face at all.

"I know," he said smiling. "This hair is *whore*-able, isn't it? I look like a whore, but it was for the last show I was doing. Ever heard of *Kismet*?"

I had. It was a musical based on *The Arabian Nights*; I had already seen the Technicolor movie with Howard Keel. *Kismet* also meant "destiny," and suddenly it felt like he—his name was Blake—was a part of that. He told me he was a professional opera-quality singer, from a good family in Miami, horribly down on his luck—but then, so much of Downtown LA seemed to be filled with guys like him: refugees of all sorts escaping from someplace else, drawn by some kind of perverse magnetism to this steaming concrete sinkhole, filled with hard-core Christian missions and side streets packed with cheap restaurants, all-night movie houses, and hustler bars. I was taken with him; I loved classical music and he was . . . God, a *real* singer of opera! I'd never met one.

He'd been up all night on the streets, not that long ago spit out of the bus station from Miami, living off coffee and cigarettes. He had no place to stay; I had nothing to lose. I snuck him back into my Y room, no easy feat, rushing past a big guard who turned his head. Blake was dying for a shower; we showered, and made love in my room. Like real *love*, as in, "Wow! This is what it feels like." I had never done that before, as in genuine, fantastic physical sex. Like something magical. His body was both hard and kind of pulpy—a genuine workingman's body, even though he was an artist.

He confessed to me, "You make me feel like I'm seventeen, too."

I didn't know what he meant; I was still an inhibited kid from the South, and felt funny about sucking his cock, and I couldn't imagine letting him fuck me. Then I realized we had the sort of nervous, shy sex you have when you're a schoolboy, but it was still amazing to me.

I asked him how he'd been making money.

He told me hustling.

"LA is filled with queens who'll pay for it. If they'll pay somebody like me, imagine what they'll pay you?"

I didn't want to imagine. But what else was I going to do? I had no money, real education, or family—when you come out *strange* by sixteen as I had, "family" becomes beside the point; it's never there anymore, except in isolated, usually disapproving ways. I was always outside the family: the sissy nephew, the queer cousin; the disappointing son. There was no way I could ask anyone related to me for a moment of help.

We spent the night together then got up the next morning, and I put my stuff in a 25-cent locker at the Greyhound depot where Blake had his. I was dead broke again, with just enough money for coffee and breakfast rolls for the two of us. We went back to Pershing Square, and I scored several times that afternoon. Older men (a laugh: older meant twenty-six, maybe even thirty) would pick me up and take me back to one of the numerous "trick hotels" in the area, where you could get a place for $4.50 or less. They would blow me or I would jerk them off. Since I was a teen "trade" hustler and very fresh meat, it was not expected that I'd do more. As evening approached, I met up with Blake back at the Square and we got a room together. I felt safe with him; I needed somebody—anything, really—and Blake was cultivated, artistic, and not nearly as phony as most of the people I met, although his story of operatic stardom back home in Miami and Chicago and other places never made much sense to me. If he were such a *star*, what was he doing on skid row?

We did this for the next several days. One problem with money that comes easily is that you never keep it. Despite an array of johns, we were always broke. I tried Manpower jobs, and worked for a day in a factory that bottled catsup. I hated the smell of the place; I got a job later cleaning a Japanese restaurant, but it did not last. Blake was sure that the owner, a young Japanese man, simply wanted to be seen downtown on the streets with me.

"You're young and handsome," he said. "Who wouldn't want to be seen with you?"

Those sun-filled days promised to last forever—hanging out in Pershing Square, and the quick, easy sex trade there—Blake, because he would do everything, got paid more than I did—and going to all-night movies, eating cheap, greasy food, and even taking the long, picturesque bus ride out to Will Rogers State Park, the famous gay beach in Santa Monica.

All of this was good. With Blake, I felt like I had some protection, thin as it was, from the sinister, rapacious world around me.

That was, until one day in Pershing Square I met *Rodney*.

Yes. Rodney.

He was my age—*exactly* seventeen—and the most beautiful boy I'd ever seen in my life. He was of normal height, but perfectly formed, as if someone had taken a pair of sculptor's calipers and created this creature from the most ideal proportions ever assembled, with rower's wide shoulders, a silken, creamy, honey-skinned chest capped with exquisite rose-petal-soft nipples, and perfect arms, legs, and face. He had a nose and brow you'd see on a statue of a boyish Greek hero, with greenish-blue eyes that truly melted time and an expression disarmingly innocent, yet capable of such defensive cruelty that it could, with perfectly aimed efficiency, destroy you. He was from Nashville, Tennessee, and had been hustling since he was fourteen. He came from a respectable lower-middle-class family (not one thrown into dire poverty as I'd been), and had started in local parks where older, often married men would meet him and either pay him or buy him anything he wanted, and then take him back to hotels. He kept small kid jobs, like babysitting, so that his parents would not ask how he had ended up with so much money for clothes or records or to spend on things that they couldn't give him. He had a deep, inviting, soft Southern drawl.

"I tell 'em from the start, 'Honey, I don't do nothin' but lay back and let you do all the work. And don't you even *think* about fuckin' me!'"

He had his shirt off in Pershing Square.

It was like a bolt of lightning had hit me, in the most delicious, almost mythically exquisite way, as though some teen-idol Apollo had just fallen out of the sky. Like Blake, his hair was also dyed—a kind of silver platinum color that strangely enough looked perfect on him. It made him look even more like an antique statue come to life. A moment later, the two of us were talking. I don't remember the first words we said. All I wanted to do was look at him and kiss him.

Another moment later, Blake took me aside, shaking his head.

"Perry, this is going to be a disaster!"

But when you are seventeen and in love, there's no way around it.

Rodney had been hustling in Hollywood. He knew exactly what to do, and where to park himself on the street. He invited us to come with him that night. The three of us took a bus out and soon stepped out onto Hollywood Boulevard: all bright lights and tourists and wide sidewalk spaces, with a park next to us.

"Look at this place," Rodney drawled. "Johns all over *heah*! Jus' waitin' for us!"

He was right. One immediately stopped for Blake, who was wearing a pair of jeans so tight they provided a National Geographic map to his considerable endowment.

This left me alone with Rodney. He suggested we go into the park. It was well-lit and still buzzing with tourists. Shortly afterwards, we saw a thick hedge of green bushes next to a wall. "Why don't we go there?" he asked.

We did, and within its depths, safely hidden from the outside clamor of tourist noise, with bits of moonlight glinting in his platinum hair, he kissed me.

I thought my heart would stop. His lips were luscious, soft, and moist. I didn't want to stop kissing him. I peeled off his T-shirt and mine too, kissing his beautiful chest and shoulders. I felt like I was already sailing off into the sky.

"We've got to stop this and make some money," he said, half an hour later.

Back on the boulevard, someone almost instantly—like, five minutes later—picked him up. The three of us had arranged that the next day we'd meet back in Pershing Square; I didn't have to wait very long when another car stopped for me.

In it was a polite, short, middle-aged man looking about as nondescript as possible, like some suburban housewife's overworked husband out for a drive. I hopped in. He asked how I was doing that evening. I told him fine. He asked where I was going. I hesitated. I wasn't sure what to say. Suddenly in the rearview mirror I saw his eyes narrow a bit, like he was thinking what to do next. Johns did that sometimes. The important thing with them was to stay in control, and maybe he wasn't.

"Suppose . . . ?" he asked slowly. "Suppose . . . I told you I was with the LA Vice Squad?"

I panicked. I thought about jumping out the car, but it was moving too fast. I started to sweat, then quickly drew a breath. Sure—this was no worse than being chased by those dumb-shit boys back in the Valley.

"OK," I said calmly and shrugged. "Then I'd ask *you* for every bit of ID you have."

I figured—maybe wrongly—that he'd have to stop to get his ID, and I'd jump out.

He looked at me and suddenly smiled this funny, sheepish grin. Like he'd been put back in his place safely now.

"Just joking," he said. "I didn't mean to scare you. You seem like a nice kid. I like the way you talk. You're from the South, I can see."

I wasn't happy with this. He put his hand on mine, and I removed it. He could tell he had pissed me off; he tried to make it up to me and took me out to eat—I was, as ever, hungry. I didn't know what his next move was, but I was broke and had to do what he wanted. I was very polite—you could say *Southernly*—eating my cheeseburger and the french fries he bought me. We returned to his car, and he didn't look at me, but just drove me back to Hollywood Boulevard and handed me $10.

I took the money and got out. I still wasn't sure what kind of game he was playing or why. Blake had told me that there were some men who just wanted to be seen with me. That is, in the company of an attractive kid. The fact was, strangely enough, they simply wanted to *be* with me.

"It's the Southern thing," Blake explained. "You make them feel good. Keep it."

I wasn't sure what to do then, but I couldn't just hang around Hollywood. It was too dangerous. There really was Vice Squad patrolling out there, and since they often worked under cover, you never could tell when you'd run into one. They could arrest you for being yourself, for simply even breathing. I guess being queer you weren't supposed to breathe—you could contaminate the very *air* the big bad straight world relied on. I strolled around for a while; it was getting later. Finally, about 2 AM, I found a bus stop with a bench, and sat down at it. It was in a pool of light surrounded by darkness and an eerie, jittery kind of silence. Three black men appeared. One of them with the build of a heavyweight boxer, strode over to me.

"Where you from, boy?" he asked.

"Georgia," I replied.

"They don't like us kind o' people in Georgia. They don't like no black people down there."

"Not everyone's like that."

"How I know you ain't? Why don't you act like a man and get up and swing at me!"

I was exhausted. All I wanted to do was get on the bus back to Downtown. Suddenly it arrived.

"You lucky," the man said. "You lucky you didn't swing at me. I wudda killed ya."

"Sure," I agreed. "I'm lucky." I got on the bus alone.

I spent the night in an all-night movie theater, falling asleep somewhere after King Kong met Godzilla. A couple of guys sat down next to me and felt me up, but I didn't care. The next morning, I met Blake and Rodney in Pershing Square. They had done well that night. Blake had made $20—he'd had to work hard for it, but he had made it; Rodney $30, for, as he put it, "just sittin' back and enjoying it."

But they were both impressed that I had made $10 without doing anything at all, and had been taken out for dinner as well. I didn't tell them about the suburban-husband's sick trick with the Vice Squad story. Frankly, I was embarrassed by it. It made me feel small.

After that, without any kind of formalities, Rodney joined us.

Sometimes the three of us would sleep in the same dumpy hotel room downtown; other times Blake would find johns of his own and stay the night with them. Rodney would not let Blake touch him, and I could not imagine going down on Rodney—after all he had a personal code, and guys who sucked him were johns. I was not going to be a john. But we would make out passionately until finally I couldn't take it any longer and would have to stop. At seventeen, my head was literally in the clouds. It was as if I were circling the world with him. Kissing him was like some kind of jet-propelled, out-of-body experience, fueled by teenage hormones and my own romantic impulses.

It went along with his beauty, something that men wanted to capture and pay for. I was aware that an endless wave of eyes would watch us on the street, glued to him, and then, as if by reflection, to me. I knew I was appealing, but he was light-years beyond that.

Rodney would do nothing but hustle. The idea of having any other kind of job seemed ridiculous to him; everything about hustling came easy to him with the perfectly generous hand of genetic "looks" cards he'd been given. Blake wanted a job, and started looking for one. Finally, he was promised one in a shop that sold records and sheet music downtown; he found out about it through one of his johns. I wanted a real job, too, but there was nothing there for me. I was too young and inexperienced, but, no matter what, I was not going to go back to picking fruit again.

Time went by quickly like money did, and yet, strangely, slowly too, because so many of my young feelings were tied up in Rodney, in just being with him or getting to look at him. Then, early one evening after Blake had disappeared into the first days at his job in the music shop, Rodney and I ended up on Hollywood Boulevard again. This time the johns weren't anywhere to be seen. Even Rodney could not attract anyone; we were lost in milling waves of tourists looking at the names of movie stars embedded on the sidewalk, with no one even looking at us.

Then, out of nowhere, a big, blond, Gidget-movie-surfer type with sun-streaked hair and mile-wide shoulders approached us.

"You guys like to go to a party?" he asked. "We got a car waiting."

Rodney hesitated. He was suspicious about it. This probably wasn't going to make us any money. But I just nodded. We were both hungry, but it would get us off the street and away from the constant threat of the Vice Squad and other cops. Why not?

The "party" ended up being in an empty beach house in Santa Monica; present were two older men, in their forties, and Tod, the young surfer, who had obviously been paid, in some kind of Jeffrey Epstein fashion, to procure for them—and of course Rodney, the *dish de jour*, and I.

What happened was very cool, "professional," even. Like wading out into an undertow. In fact, it shows why kid hustlers are often killed. The three of them were friendly at first, then everything got down to business—their business. After the two older men had pleasured themselves with Rodney and Tod had fucked me against my will, the two older men decided to dump us back on Hollywood Boulevard, at 3 AM, like discarded toys. I drew Rodney aside.

"Can you ask them for some money? We don't even have bus fare to get back to Downtown."

Rodney went up to up to Steve, at least that's what he called himself, and said something to him. Steve shook his head, disapprovingly, like he was shocked. He walked up to me. "You guys think you're hustlers? Shit! I work for the LA County's sheriff's office. If you try anything with me, I'll make a phone call and have you arrested. But I like you. Tell you what—I'll get you some sandwiches at the Hollywood Farmer's Market, it's where all the stars hang out at night, then let you out to get home."

I could only nod. At the brightly lit Farmer's Market, we ate the sandwiches in silence, and then were driven out to a quiet, prosperous-looking residential neighborhood soundly wrapped in sleep behind its locked doors.

"It's safe here," Steve said as he stopped his car. "No one's gonna bother you."

He hit the gas, and drove off. Suddenly I felt like I could hear a pin drop a block away. Like I was on an eerie movie set, and all the houses were only painted backdrops.

"What do we do now?" I whispered to Rodney.

He looked around. Except for a few parked cars, the streets were empty. Rodney exhaled. "Walk back to Downtown."

We were on a side street, when a cop car cruised by slowing, passing us.

Now we had to do something. We spotted a vacant lot with a house on it in the process of being constructed. We ran into it, taking refuge in a dark, unfinished basement.

I was so scared I could hardly breathe. A second later, flashlights were aimed in our faces. I ducked under them, then heard:

"Come out now, or we'll come in after you!"

I was so tired that everything instantly felt like a dream, or one of those nightmares that seem too real *not* to be real. We got up and faced two extremely beefy white cops who only grunted at us. We were handcuffed, shoved into the back of a squad car, driven to a local precinct, then pushed into a holding cell.

There a fat old cop stared at us.

"You two is real Hollywood, ain'tcha? Ya faggots, ain'tcha?"

"We're not," Rodney answered with complete dignity.

"Shut up, Fuckface! That hair tells me you're a queer. You think ya too good f' this? Take off all ya clothes. Every bit of 'em. Shoes and wallets, too."

It was freezing in the cell, basically just a concrete floor with two bunk beds, bare mattresses, and a hole in the floor for a toilet. After we were both naked, the same cop threw us two coarse Army blankets. I wrapped one around myself. I was freezing. For a second, Rodney pretended that the blanket was a mink stole, and started modeling it. We were both now punchy with sleeplessness.

The cop had woken up some other boys in adjoining cells. Why they were there I had no idea, but I didn't really know why we had been arrested either. Trespassing? Suspicion of hustling? Drugs?

The boys glared at us. "Hey, Faggots! Cocksuckers! Queers!"

They were white kids. Evidently we were in a totally white neighborhood.

The fat cop told them to shut up, and left. They quieted down, and went back to sleep. I managed to sleep briefly. Then the fat old cop reappeared.

"How old is you two, and how much edgie-cay-shun you got?"

We told him we were both seventeen. Rodney was in high school, but I had had a year of college.

"You lying," the cop said. "You only seventeen. You ain't got no year a' college, you lyin' faggot. We gonna separate you two and see if ya parents want yous back and'll pay for it. I need you to fill out these forms so we can contact them. Then we gonna put yous on a Greyhound bus to wherever you come from."

Still wrapped in a blanket, Rodney was taken into another cell. A few hours later, another cop, younger and simply more human, unlocked my cell and walked in.

"Your friend's parents agreed to have him sent back at their expense to Nashville. We haven't been able to contact your mother. You said you've had a year of college. Is that true?" I nodded. "Do you want to go back?"

"No," I said, emphatically. That was the last thing I wanted to do, to go back to my mother and her contemptuous family in Georgia.

"OK. If your mother agrees that you can stay, we'll keep you until your case comes up. Maybe you want to say goodbye to your friend. He's outside now."

Rodney, back in his clothes but still handcuffed, was led into my cell. We just looked at one another while the boys in the other cells stared holes into us. All we could say was, "'Bye." I felt like a piece of my heart had been ripped out.

He gave me one last look with his beautiful green eyes, and then the cell door slammed behind him.

I was kept in the holding cell for forty-eight more hours while my mother was being contacted by the State of California. Finally she agreed that I didn't have to go back to Georgia. The nice cop told me that she had said to him, after he phoned her, "If he doesn't want to come back, I don't want him."

I let out a sigh of relief. Anything was better than going back to that year of hell I had spent at the University of Georgia, that made even the kids in the adjoining cells look good; or going back to public housing in Savannah where we were the only Jewish family and I was beaten up and harassed constantly. That had happened after my father died of cancer at forty-two, and we descended—express, with no intermediate stops—into poverty.

During the forty-eight hours, I wasn't allowed to bathe or brush my teeth. Finally I was given my clothes back, and sent on a bus with other young offenders to Los Angeles's huge Juvenile Hall, home of thousands of other lost boys, some of whom were in for murder and armed robbery; others, like myself, for lighter offenses. At "Juvie," as it was called, I was given a freshly washed and pressed uniform, and finally told that I had been busted for being underage on the streets—against the law in California—and, of course, suspicion of male prostitution.

I was asked by a court officer if I knew anyone in Los Angeles who would vouch for me and would agree to be my legal guardian until I turned eighteen, the age of consent and legal adulthood, which would happen in September, a bare two months away.

I could only think of Blake. He was at heart an actor, an "opera singer." So I was sure he could pass muster as a responsible adult, and get me out. I remembered the name of the music store where he had just got a job, and gave it to the officer, along with Blake's full name.

"Is he a ho-*mo*-sexual?" the man asked with an emphasis on the "mo" part.

"No, sir."

"Then why is he interested in some kid like you?"

"He's just a nice guy," I answered.

The officer grinned. I was fooling no one, but at least this would be a way for the State of California not to have to feed me for a while.

Chapter

4

For the most part Juvie was a welcome relief. I was fed regularly, had clean clothes, and a place to stay. I was placed in unit of sixteen boys, of which about six were either openly queer or close to it. These boys were smarter, more articulate, and honest about why they were there. Mostly, it was problems with their parents. Some were declared "incorrigibles" by their parents, and sent to family court because they had talked back, or wore gender-inappropriate clothes, or got caught shoplifting makeup. We hung out together, playing cards, telling jokes, and supporting each other. Every one had a story about why he was busted, and what he would do once he got out—mostly never get involved with the law again. A few were real cross-dressers—one by the name of "Debbie" would not answer to any other name—but as long as they minded their own business, they were not bothered or bullied at all. This was totally different from the world I had left, stuck in poverty in lower-class Georgia, where as an often only too-recognizable "sissy" (certainly compared to other boys in a white Christian, dominant Southern-redneck culture), I'd had to hide every waking moment.

Our unit ate together and went to classes together, which were basically simply to pass the time, although some boys were serious about getting a GED. Because I'd had a year of college, the instructors were impressed with me and sometimes asked me to help other boys out with classwork. During the afternoons we were given time out in a large yard for supervised play. There the undisputable pecking order of Juvie made itself plain, and my queer pals made sure we stayed away from bigger, more aggressive alpha-butch guys who might attack us, although they were usually too busy challenging each other to bother with us.

There was also a defined racial structure with the black boys hanging out together and the SA's—"South Americans," or Hispanics—doing the same.

The SA's were more open about not judging the queer boys. Since nothing was in Spanish and they felt so alienated to begin with, their attitude, beyond *machismo*, was "You do yo' thing and don't bother me." The black boys were more sullen, their educational level generally lower, and they had not yet organized themselves around any kind of Black Pride. How you wore your uniform was important, and the black boys wanted theirs as big and loose as possible, so as not to be considered "stuff," or queer bait—not to invite any kind of looks. The SA's wore their uniforms a little sexier and sportier, and it was hard for me not to look at them. There were also, like I said, super-tough white offenders, and they were really scary. Some had been in Juvie for a year or so, and would be transferred at eighteen to California Youth Authority, the real prisons for young offenders where felons were sent. I had a run-in with a big blond kid like that named Steve who resented that the supervisors liked me; he attacked me with a fork at dinner.

I reported it, but was told, "Don't make a big deal out of it. He'll be shipped off to CYA in two weeks, and he's not looking forward to it."

At night we were locked into single-boy cells—about as big as a coffin—so that no "sex-play" could take place either between boys or between boys and adult supervisors. There was a strict rule that you were never allowed to be found alone with another person, even an adult. Any breach of this, I was warned, would be noted on your court papers when it was time either for your release or a transfer.

The first night I was locked in, I became claustrophobic and terrified. I rang the buzzer for the Unit Manager to come in.

He appeared outside. "What do you want, Brass?"

I realized there was nothing I could do or say about being locked into this confining windowless space. I asked if I could have some water, and he brought me back a paper cup and pushed it through a slot in the door. Each cell had a small sink, and I used that.

At the end of three weeks, I was told that the court had been able to reach Blake, and he had agreed to be my guardian until I turned eighteen. I felt really happy to be leaving Juvie, and yet strangely protected there. The social workers and adult supervisors treated me with a kind of respect and kindness I had not had in a long time. But being locked alone at night into that tiny cell was horrible—nightmarish really.

I showered and was given clean clothes to leave in. A court officer accompanied me to the courtroom, where a judge who meant absolutely nothing to me asked me if I knew why I had been kept. One of the social workers had coached me what to say, and I told him I did. He asked me if I'd obey all the rules of my parole, and stay in contact with the court through a parole officer until I was eighteen. I promised I would.

I was led into another room, and there was Blake, wearing a second-hand suit, his hair no longer dyed. He shook my hand, and we walked out together but I could tell he was not happy about what he was doing.

He had found a small studio in an apartment hotel on one of the better streets just outside Downtown. We got on a bus to get there. I had gained weight from all the starchy food at Juvie—every meal had some variation of potatoes, white bread, and rice in it to fill the boys up—and he immediately noticed it.

"You're going to have to get a job," he said. "I can't support you. And I want you to move out as fast as you can, because, well, I don't want you staying with me. I have a new life now, with a real job and new friends."

He did have my suitcase, rescued from the Greyhound depot locker, and I stayed with him for the next two weeks, sometimes sleeping on the floor. The apartment hotel, called The Windsor, was extremely gay. The manager, a smart English lady of a certain age who wore demure flower-print dresses and looked and acted like she came out of a W. Somerset Maugham play, just loved "you boys as long as you *behave* yourselves!"

Blake introduced me as his cousin, who'd only be staying a short while. Across the hall was a short, pudgy guy from South Carolina named Billy who worked in a big downtown hotel as a night manager, and during the daytime was a gifted shoplifter. Normally he was loudly Southern-queen-effeminate, but he could brazenly shovel it on even more when he wanted to. "If you're *really* super-loud and *nelly*," he told me, "all those people are just too darn embarrassed even t' look at you!"

He would march into swank department stores or pricey specialty shops with a big Saks shopping bag and after a few minutes start dropping things into it. He had a side business selling what he stole, usually to women he met at the hotel. Billy was taken with me, because we were both "Southern girls in tacky LA." He took me out for drinks and gave me presents that I'm sure came out of the Saks bag: expensive dark glasses, Charles of the Ritz face creams, etc.

On another floor lived tall, middle-aged Walter, who made a living going door-to-door soliciting donations for a church that he told me was a gay church in Hollywood. I'd never heard of it before, but he told me that it was totally integrated and most of the people who donated to it were black women. Walter was kind, and sometimes gave me a couple of dollars earmarked for the church. I had no money at all, my job search fruitless. My only way to eat was to go to Pershing Square during the day and get picked up by older men who'd feed me. I never asked money from them: I was too scared of ending up back in jail. One day, really starving, I sat down near a repulsive, wrinkled, toothless old geezer who leered at me ravenously. I managed to get lunch out of him, and then he expected something. Blake was at work, so I took him back to the Windsor.

Once inside, I invited him to make himself comfortable, and then I ran out and knocked on Billy's door. Luckily, he was home, I told him the story. He knew exactly what to do.

A few minutes later, Billy stormed through the door of Blake's studio as my psychotically jealous boyfriend, terrifying the old man as he threatened to throw him out physically. Since Billy was only about five-foot-four, he managed to puff himself up like a bullfrog to do it. Afterwards, we laughed.

I thanked him; he blushed.

"If you evuh want me t' do that again, honey, all you gotta do is jus' knock!"

Finally I found a job, just before my first appointment with my parole officer. It was in the Drug and Cosmetics Stockroom of the May Company, a pricey California department store on one of the better streets close to Downtown. It was a "fill-in" position; I was taking the place of another kid who had to go back east for a while. The pay was so small it was frightening, and I was warned that if I even "thought" about stealing anything, I'd be in handcuffs in thirty seconds. I did not tell them that I had been in Juvie, or that I was on parole. Since it was only a temporary position, they did no background check on me, but the important thing, as far as the State of California was concerned, was that I now had a *real* job.

Of course there were no real *drugs* in the stockroom except for some high-end cosmetics, and most of the stuff I handled were expensive imported soaps and bath supplies. The stockroom was in a dark area on a high floor, away from the main selling areas where the sales girls were charmed by my accent and the fact that I was so young. Many of them had never been east of the Mississippi and thought Georgia could have been in Russia—which is not so far off the mark, since Russia *is* just north of Georgia the country. When I told one pretty young clerk that I sometimes sat in Pershing Square, she said, "Why would you do that? Only *fruits* hang out there."

Since I was paid so little that even eating became a problem, up in the dark back rows of the stockroom I'd often open cans of Metrical and guzzle them for lunch. They tasted like flavored chalk, but kept my stomach from feeling empty. The good thing was that I was paid weekly, and after my first paycheck, I moved out of Blake's studio.

Things had become very difficult with us. For one thing, I started putting two and two together and went to the library and looked up some of the names of the important people he had dropped to impress me: a stellar line up of singers, directors, and even stars like Rudolf Nureyev and Franco Zeffirelli with whom he had chummed around back in his "glory" days in Miami and New York. A few of them, in fact, had been dead before Blake was even born, or residing in locations where he never could have met them. I kept this information to myself, and just stewed on it.

One day, when he had been really mean to me, telling me what a burden I was and how he had never wanted to come get me, I confronted him.

"You're a phony," I told him. "Every word you've told me is a lie."

His eyes and face reacted with fury and scorn. He had big shoulders and powerful hands. I thought he was going to hit me.

Instead, he sank on the floor in front of me, as if *I* had hit him. I was on the couch that unfolded into a bed. He looked up at me, crying.

I didn't say a word; I felt frozen watching him.

Finally he said, "I had to tell you that."

I looked at him; I had never seen anyone appear like that, so completely destroyed and hurt.

"Why?" I finally asked. "Why did you lie?"

"Because the real story is so ugly I can't live with it."

Chapter

5

Blake got up, and took out a small scrapbook from his luggage. "Here," he said, and sat down next to me, slowly turning the pages. There was a picture of him, younger, wearing farmer's overalls; one of an old couple who were wearing straw hats and overalls, too. Then I saw several of a pretty, young dark-haired woman and Blake. In one she was in shorts and a halter top; she had a very nice figure. There was a picture of the two of them looking like they are going out to a high school prom—he was in this crazy-looking summer white tux, with dark squiggles on it.

He laughed suddenly. "Can't believe I actually wore that."

Then pictures of two adorable little blond boys. They were alone; then Blake was with them, and the woman. And another of the old couple with them, on a farm.

"Who are they?"

"They were my family, back in Florida about six years ago. I was married to this girl, Evelyn. We had gone to high school together. Out in the sticks, near Tallahassee. Orange groves. Bean plants. Corn. I came from a farming family, very religious. In high school, I got involved with school plays. I wanted to dance professionally, but knew I couldn't. I couldn't even think about that. Evelyn came from a wealthier family in town. They weren't farmpoor like we were, but they were also very conservative. Her father agreed that I could marry her, because he felt that my folks had the right kind of values. We had these two boys. You can see them. Beautiful kids. All our folks were just crazy about them.

"Everything was going on OK, but I knew something just wasn't right with me. I didn't fit in inside; I went to community college—I listened to opera records. I could speak some French and German. Then one day outside of Tallahassee, I met this guy. He was a hairdresser"—Blake laughed. "What *else*? Sure, a hairdresser! And I started seeing him on the side, very,

very secret. Like so secret I couldn't even admit it, but I wanted to see him. I admit that. Then one day I read in the newspaper that there had been a bust of 'homosexuals and perverts' in a park not that far from our house. I was scared even to read the piece. My hands were shaking. Then I saw his name. They put his *name* in the paper. I felt horrible. I could never see this man again. I couldn't even go near him. I was so frightened that just the thought of it now makes me want to throw up.

"Then two days later I got a call from a local detective, asking me to come down to the police station. He told me that this man had named me as a 'fellow pervert,' and that the cops were doing a whole dragnet to rid the area of perverts, and that they could put my name in the paper, too, if I didn't cooperate with them *one hundred percent*."

He was shaking. His whole face became ashen, just remembering it.

"I had to say something to my wife. I told her lies had been said about me and I had to go before a judge. She asked what kind of lies, and I told her they were about sexual perversion. She looked revolted, like the idea was too disgusting for her even to imagine.

"'What can I say to my parents?' she asked.

"I told her I didn't know. But the two of us had to go before this judge, in some kind of 'mental hygiene court,' and he told me that I could never see my boys again. 'I won't have a recognized sex pervert around male children.'"

"What did you do?"

"What else *could* I do—I moved to Miami. I just left her; it was better to do that. I was really happy there for a while. See, I got involved with semi-professional touring productions of shows. They would hire the locals and bring in stars. I *was* in the chorus of *Kismet*—that's true, but that's not why my hair was that color. Why would you want a blond in *Kismet*? I had to have a regular job, too. I worked as a bookkeeper in the back office of an insurance company. Most of the time, nobody saw me. Then one day my boss called me in."

His face sunk, and his mouth twitched from nerves. Then he started speaking again.

"Somebody from Tallahassee had called him. An investigator. He had information about my boss's employees. One in particular was . . . 'a recognized sex pervert.' My boss asked me, 'Do you know anything about this.

Is any of it true?' I told him I didn't know anything. He said, 'We'll have to look into it.'"

"Did he?" I asked. "What did you do?"

"I left again. I packed a small suitcase—first I dyed my hair. I was scared they'd recognize me, some cop in Florida would already have a picture of me, and stop me. I had a little money. First I went to Atlanta, thinking I could start over there—not as a bookkeeper, they would ask too many questions, when you want to do that. But a waiter, maybe. I couldn't get anything; I didn't know anybody and I was running out of money. So I got a bus ticket to LA and arrived here dead broke."

He paused, then looked at me.

"That's when you found me on the street, Perry. I was barely eating then."

"Why did you tell me all those stories?" I asked.

"I wanted to, just to feel that I wasn't just nothing. Everybody here has a story, the whole place is full of them. Some are real, some aren't. The real story is I'll never see my boys again. Or my parents; they could be dead for all I know. You need to get out of this life, Perry. Go back to Georgia and get married and start a family. The gay life is nothing. It's just a bunch of cheap bars and drag queens and hustlers. That's all we have. That and lies."

"The worst lies are the ones told about us," I said. "You're not a bad person."

"Yes, I am!" he said emphatically. "I'm the worst. I gave up my boys."

"You had to, Blake."

"No." His eyes clenched closed for a second, then he opened them. "I didn't even have the balls to fight it. I just caved in and ran. I should have denied everything and fought it. Just fought it until they stopped trying to get me anymore. Then they'd get somebody else, instead of me."

"That's not right," I said. "That they just *get* somebody else. Did you love your wife?"

"I think so," he said, slowly shutting the scrapbook. "At least I wanted to. But I don't think I can love anybody. I think when you're a queer, it's programmed into you to lie and not to love. How else can you survive?"

He got up.

"I want you to get out of here, Perry, as soon as you can. I'm scared of the cops. They'll come back for me, I know it. We can be friends still, but you can't live here. I've done everything I can for you. That's all I can do."

I found a room in an extremely cheap hotel downtown. It was a dump with roaches and dirty floors, but I could afford it from what I was making at the May Company. The good thing was that it was mine, and I didn't have to answer to anyone. The idea that at seventeen I was living thousands of miles away from my mother and her very mercantile, closed-minded Jewish family in Savannah thrilled me. I felt like an adult, or a near approximation of one. I could sneak into bars and drink, pick up men when I wanted to, or be picked up by them—which was extremely easy in LA, even easier than catching a bus, I learned—and except for working to survive, I was making my own hours and life. Then in the heat of August 11, rioting started breaking out in the turbulent African-American area known as Watts.

I was in Pershing Square when I first heard about it; from the Square you could actually see distant fires and smoke. Cops started appearing all over the place, even in Downtown LA. The queers in the Square became happy. During the almost week of rioting, six days that resulted in the deaths of thirty-four black people, the cops could not focus their attention on "Vice." At the May Company, people didn't even want to talk about it; they felt it was beneath them to get involved with what "niggers" did. Watts could have been in another country.

I started painting again, doing watercolors and some acrylics. On the weekends I often went out to Will Rogers State Park, the gay beach in Santa Monica that I had gone to with Rodney. I would either hitchhike or take the long, slow bus ride out. Taking the bus, I became more aware of the riots, seeing trucks on city streets loaded with California National Guardsmen wearing riot helmets, who had been called in by LA's blatantly racist Chief of Police William H. Parker, who referred to blacks as "monkeys in a zoo."

Once I got to the beach, though, I could forget about everything. I took a sketchpad and could draw bathers. Having grown up in the Coastal South, I loved beaches, and felt hemmed in if I couldn't get to one. One day I was leaving the beach when a group of muscular surfers trooped up to the stairs, where I was waiting to use an outdoor shower.

One of them stared at me like I was something in a zoo myself, and smirked.

"Hey, faggot!" he said. "How'd you like it if I knocked out all your teeth?"

He was almost a head taller than I was. I had to look up to him.

"Is that a rhetorical question?" I fired back. "Or do you really expect an answer?"

The other surfers started laughing. I had got the best of their friend.

"Hey, leave him alone," one said, and they walked away.

I got under the shower and cleaned off, and two young men in their twenties who I could tell were gay approached me. They had heard what I said to the surfer, and were impressed.

"Most people are just scared of them," one whose name was Herb said. His friend Charles was a bit older, quieter, and really handsome.

They asked me if I had a car, and when I said no, they offered me a lift. We went back to Herb's small apartment on the outskirts of Hollywood, and had a drink. Charles, who was a sociology professor at one of the California state colleges, became really interested in me. He was doing research, he said, on young men of the streets who had experience hustling. I told him I wasn't a hustler; he said most hustlers said that. He asked me to fill out a research form, asking all sorts of questions about me, and I said I would. The next weekend the two of them met me in Pershing Square and we rode out to a big crafts fair in the San Fernando Valley. I found Herb interesting. He was an average-looking, very working-class guy who talked candidly about sex, especially anal sex. Most gay men could barely say anything about sex, except that it was bad, dirty, and scary if you got caught. Like me, Herb had been out on his own since he was really young, and the only thing that mattered to him was being happy and escaping his dreary job as a projector operator for a large corporation. He referred to his gay friends as "festive." He'd say, "I have to be careful with my 'festive' friends. Like, I can't mention them at work."

A few weeks later, the boy I was filling in for at work came back, and I was laid off as casually as you might discard a cigarette. I still had three weeks before I turned eighteen; I had decided at that point that I'd leave Los Angeles and go back to San Francisco. At eighteen I'd be more in a position to get a job than at seventeen and completely green to the world. I was soon dead broke again, and dependent on men I'd meet on the streets or Pershing

Square to help me. Often they bought me lunch or dinner, and as Blake said, they simply wanted to have me near them. The fact that I didn't act like a tough, dumb hustler was always in my favor, because there were so many of them.

The toughness thing was part of their draw: the fact that they were really "straight," and doing it only for the money. I met one once who was very attracted to me; he came out of central casting, with the cigarette pack rolled into his T-shirt sleeve and the kind of "Go fuck y'self" drawl that hustlers pulled out effortlessly. He did not have a good rep in Pershing Square, where the queens gossiped about everyone, including me. He offered to take me to Mexico with him; I shook my head, I wasn't even going around a corner with him.

Very late one night I was wandering by myself on the edge of Downtown when I saw this pale, sinewy guy leaning casually against the wall of an empty office building, with one high, black lace-up boot pushed behind him. He was all in black too, his shirt open almost to his navel, revealing his pale chest with some strange tattoos on it, and others on his bare arms. He smiled openly at me and I walked over to him.

"You're new here," he said. "Wha'cha name?"

I told him. He told me his name was Gwen.

"That's what I'm known here as." He lit a cigarette and offered me one. I didn't smoke but could do so "socially." It made me feel older and sophisticated. He had a lot of hair; it was piled up, teased, and dyed orange. I noticed the way he smelled.

"Shalimar," he said. "I always wear it. The johns love it. I guess it kind of reminds 'em of their wives. Or mothers."

He grinned. Suddenly a cop car came ominously cruising by, like a shark. Gwen suggested we move. We did.

"If they catch you just hanging around, they can ask you for ID. They act like they never seen a hair fairy before. That's what I am. I wish I was back in San Francisco. The hair fairies rule the streets there. They run around in packs; I had a pack and it was fun. Then I had problems with my old man, this guy who was taking care of me. He caught me dealing uppers and fucking other guys, so he threatened to kill me."

"Not nice," I said exhaling and trying not to cough.

He shook his head. "That's why I figured down here is safer and warmer. At least for a while. Being a hair fairy is neat. There are all these guys, mostly married, and they see you and they know what you are and what they can do with you, so they go right to you." He put out his cigarette. "You're like an All-American Boy type, but y'know, that never worked for me. I'm too kinky for it. This is the City of Night, y'know. You gotta show 'em exactly what they're gonna get."

Out of the darkness a car started slowing down in front of us. I knew what was going on, so I backed away and watched Gwen get into it.

I thought about the City of Night thing, and was walking back toward my hotel when a man approached me, smiling. He was built big, in his late thirties, black, and nicely dressed in chinos and a sports jacket.

"Enjoying the night?" he asked. I told him I was. He asked me where I lived, and I told him the name of my hotel.

"Never heard of it—I thought a guy like you would be in the Hilton or in Beverly Hills. Is your hotel around here?"

I told him it was.

"You hungry? I could take you back to where I live. I'm going to make a late snack. You look hungry."

I was hungry. The truth was I hadn't had anything that resembled real eating in a while. We got into his car, and drove off. I had this feeling that he lived close by, but he drove on for several miles, and then more miles. I had no idea where I was: it was just endless small bungalows that all looked alike.

Finally we got out and went into one by its back kitchen door. The place smelled like it had not been cleaned in months. He immediately took his shirt off and asked me to make myself comfortable. I realized then I didn't even know his name. He told me it was Jack. He smiled at me warmly.

"I'd like to feed you," he said. "But I think I'd like to go to bed first. Then we can have something to eat."

I was tired, and it was close to 2 in the morning. I forgot about even being hungry, and took my clothes off and got into his bed, which was very wrinkled like the sheets had not been changed in ages. With all his clothes off, he looked even bigger, much bigger than I was. He immediately went down on me, then stuck his cock in my mouth. I wasn't sure that I wanted that, and drew it away from me.

Jack became really angry.

"OK," he said. "You wanna play that game?"

I looked up and he pushed me face-down on the bed, pinning me with his weight. I kept trying to get off him, but he just bore down harder, slamming my legs aside, as he started fucking me, using only spit for lube.

"Don't," I cried. "It really hurts."

"Yeah. You like it. I know it."

"I don't," I said.

He stopped for a second, and pushed my shoulders down even harder.

"Listen, Perry," he said. "You gotta know how it is. My dick's hard and I'm gonna fuck you right now. I can fuck you now, or beat the shit out of you and then fuck you. So the choice is yours."

I exhaled, slowly, and he did it. Gwen had been right: this was the City of Night, right out of John Rechy's famous book. I had not read it, but people in Pershing Square were talking about it. There was no leaving now from Jack's place. If I had even tried to walk out into this quiet sleeping unknown area of bungalows, in ten feet the cops would stop me again. I knew it. It was late.

After it was over, I just fell asleep. That was all I wanted to do.

I woke up a few hours later, as dawn was coming up. Jack had made coffee, and I had some. He was dressed in a T-shirt and boxers. He smiled at me.

"That wasn't so bad, was it?" he asked. "You gave me a hard time, but you liked it, didn't you?"

I just drank the coffee and looked at him. He offered me some bus fare back to Downtown and I took it. Now that it was light, I wouldn't be in such danger from the cops. I got back to my hotel room, showered, and tried to sleep. For the next number of days... maybe weeks... even months, the pain of what he had done to me and the anger it unleashed inside would sneak back up on me. I heard his voice repeat, "I'm gonna fuck you ... or beat the shit out of you and then fuck you ... the choice is yours."

It joined other scenes. My mother hitting me, screaming at me, throwing me up against a wall, venting her rage on me; the kids at school whispering when I walked into the room. My terrible suicide attempt when I felt there was nothing ahead of me at fifteen. I would have to figure out a way to put it all behind me, to go on living and willing myself to live. I would do that, I knew, through the sheer joy of creativity itself, even creating myself as I went along.

A few days later, I saw an ad in the newspaper: "Clerk and counter boy needed in publishing job. Good pay and great office."

The address was out on Wilshire Boulevard; I had to take a bus to get there, and got there fairly rumpled, but looking presentable enough to pass as a regular teenager. At the outside office, there was a counter and a young man behind it. He smiled at me.

"You're here for the job advertised in the paper?"

I told him I was.

"Great. You're just in time. Come this way. We're expecting you."

I wondered how this could be, and he led me through a warren of cubicles where women on phones were all talking at the same time. Finally we arrived at a small conference room, where several boys my age or a bit older were seated.

"Good! One more!" A muscularly chunky guy in his early twenties dressed in jeans with a two-day beard said to me. He shook my hand. "I'm Pete. You wanna make some money today?"

What could I say? "Sure." I thought they were going to put me to work behind this counter and I'd do what was necessary to make it.

"Come with me. We're all ready."

He led us out of the lobby, to the parking lot where we got into three cars. I was with Pete.

"You didn't get to hear the first part of training, so I'm going to personally break you in. You're lucky. That doesn't happen to everyone. You're from the South, aren't you?"

I told him I had grown up in Savannah.

"Good. People trust that Southern accent. It's helpful. You have a good face. You don't have what I'd call a 'Surfer Attitude.' Nope, no way. But I think you can do OK at this."

We drove on for several miles. I still had no idea what was going on and asked him about the counter job in publishing that had been advertised.

"That job's been filled. We usually get some *faggot* to do it. Look, if you don't want t' do this, I can let you out right here."

The job was selling magazine subscriptions door-to-door, using a scam that was as old as the hills, but still worked in Southern California. There was a spiel and a choreography that went with it:

"Good afternoon. I'm just checking up on the boys we have working this neighborhood—they're giving out free samples of magazines. Did you get yours?"

This was still the era of nonworking mothers, and it was usually the lady of the house who came to the door. She would look at you completely confused. That was good. It meant she wasn't going to slam the door on you.

"Oh, sorry they missed you, but we're here to offer you a free deal today *only*, on your favorite magazines. *Life, Look*—the big picture magazines— or *Ladies Home Companion, The Saturday Evening Post*. All your favorites! Here's a list."

Immediately, you took out a full-color sales brochure with an address form on the back and pushed it directly at her like a torpedo.

Pete instructed me: "Stick it right into her *tits*. She's gotta take it then."

He went on with the sales pitch.

"These magazines are completely free because they want to increase their circulation in key areas like this one. All they charge you for is delivery. The only problem is that all they can give you is 48 months of them for free. That's all."

"But that's four years," the lady would usually say. To which you'd say, "Yes, we're sorry we can't guarantee you any more free copies, but that's in our contract. Some people want 60 months, but at this special deal, all we can offer is 48. And we can only do it today. Can you give me your complete address so I can run it past my manager to see if you qualify? Not all addresses here qualify for this special offer."

Of course they did. But if she demurred on this, you'd say, "Why don't you just see if you qualify? Not everybody does."

In the end, these "free" magazines would cost about $98 over four years, or to be more specific, $687 in today's currency, so they would be paying for the magazines many times over. Customers would have to commit to four subscriptions to get them "free," and go through a credit check that Pete would walk the suckers through. This included that you owned a car, and what kind of rent you paid, or job your "spouse," meaning your husband, had.

I went with Pete through this routine at four different doors; then he told me that I needed to start doing it alone, and he would watch. Though at first I was extremely nervous, I realized that it was all basically very simple—and a lie—just like the other lies I'd had to tell in order to survive in the world I was in. It was an act, and I could do it. I hated it, but could. I had no money at all; I was on the brink of being thrown out of the hotel I was in; I was barely eating. Like Pete said, people enjoyed listening to my Southern accent and trusted my fresh face. I would make $5 for every "free" subscription I sold. Pete told me that I could easily sell 12 a day, to make $60. I had been paid less than that a week at the May Company. $60 a day—$300 a week!—was beyond my belief.

I would also be paid at the end of every week. It was Thursday, which meant that I would not be paid until the following Friday. If I could just hold out until then, I'd be all right. I started knocking on doors and sold four subscriptions that first day. I could just see the money rolling in. The next day, I got up at dawn to take a bus out to Wilshire to start work. They gave us free coffee and doughnuts in the office: breakfast. Then Pete took me and another boy out in his car to the next territory we'd cover. I picked up things very fast; it was like my ears were completely open. Boys like myself were called "bird dogs." We'd go out and open up sales that had to be closed by Pete, my handler, or the office itself, his handler.

My first full day by myself I sold eighteen subscription, more than any other kid. Pete was beaming.

"You're a real hotshot, Perry. Keep it up. In a short time you'll have my job!"

I learned something about sales: the more you sold, the more confident you became and the better you were. There was always this feeling of luck— just hitting the right door, and making enough sales to make you feel confident enough to go on to more sales. There were times though when I hit a dry spell: sales just did not come. Then, as Pete put it, "In this business, luck is just one more door!"

It took a huge amount of energy out of me; at the end of the day, it was like something had hit me over the head. I was pooped. Just getting back on the bus to Downtown wore me out. As it got later, the buses came less frequently, and sometimes it would take me almost two hours to get back to my hotel. By the time we were through, it was dark, the sidewalks were empty, and sometimes I was alone at the bus stop.

One evening, I was waiting for the bus with two other people, both black women, when two men in plain clothes approached. They were big, and looked too serious to even try to avoid. One flashed a badge at me.

"Stand over here," he said, motioning for me to leave the bench at the bus stop. "We want to see your ID."

I had none. The only thing I could show him was my parole card. I knew he'd see it; in a minute he'd take my wallet out and see it.

He and the other cop looked at my parole card. They just stared at me for a second, and the bus came. I knew the next one would be in an hour. I asked if I could get on the bus.

They both laughed at me. The bus rolled off, and I heard a police operator voice in a walkie-talkie that one of them carried. They had phoned in my name and a description of me. They waited with me for about fifteen minutes until some kind of reply came. I was sweating bullets. I had no idea why they had even stopped me.

Then one announced, "OK. You're good. You just looked like the kid we want."

They walked away, without saying they were sorry or anything. I realized then my only "crime" was that I was a white kid waiting for a bus in the dark in LA. That immediately made me a suspect in the undeclared police state that Los Angeles basically was.

The week seemed to go by forever, but each day meant that I was closer to getting paid. Toward the end of the week, another bird dog was brought in for Pete. His name was Charlie, he was about nineteen, wiry, energetic, and black. In Pete's car, I learned that he'd been selling magazines door-to-door for three years. He had worked for other companies, in other territories, and now he was working for Pete.

Pete was not happy about it, but he had to accept him. We were let out, and then at lunch Pete asked me how I was doing. I was not having a good day, but hoped the afternoon would be better.

Pete looked concerned. "You better pick it up, Perry. Charlie's way ahead of you. He's a real hotshot. But y' know, who's gonna slam the door on a nigger? He makes a living at this, but they're never gonna make him a manager.

The problem is he just don't have the brains to be anything but a bird dog."

After lunch, things did pick up, but I did not do as well as Charlie did. We quit just before Pete was scheduled to pick us up. Charlie smiled at me.

"You seem like a nice kid," he said. "Too bad you're in this shit. I gotta be in it. I don't even have a high school education. I dropped out to take care of my family, then I got int' this hustle. That's all it is."

"Yeah," I agreed.

"Just be careful," he warned me. "They'll try to screw you out of your money. They do it to me all the time because, well, I'm black. It ain't no secret."

I asked him, "How do they screw us out?"

He told me that for every subscription I sold, I got $5, but Pete got $7. Pete had five bird dogs working for him, and the guy above Pete had 25 bird dogs and 5 managers: he got another $7. "The dude above him—he got the whole territory, so just imagine the kind of money he makes. They'll try to tell you that some sale didn't go through. Then Pete gets your 5, and his 7."

I nodded. I was glad to know the truth. The next day, Charlie didn't come out with us. I asked Pete what had happened to him.

"I traded him," Pete said. "For another bird dog, one I can train myself, like I did you. He's with another handler—who can deal with him. Charlie's OK, but the truth is he lies. He makes up sales, and then we gotta figure out what's really going on—you know how niggers are? His real sales are OK, but nothing like he tells you. He'll wash outta here in a couple of weeks, and then go to another company."

That Friday, Pete and I went over my sales. I had sold seventy-five subscriptions, and expected money from all of them. He showed me every sales application, and told me the stories of them, one by one. More than half the sales fell through: they didn't make either his credit check or the office's.

"You gotta be smarter, Perry. You gotta look at their lawns, like are the lawns taken care of? If they ain't, that's a sign that they ain't got enough money to pay someone to mow 'em. And their cars? Some of your sales didn't even have cars. But we like you. We can overpay you this week, just so you got a check from us that'll keep you coming back for more. I'm your handler, and I believe in helping my boys."

He handed me a check. It was for $93, after they took out taxes.

"Next week, it'll be a lot better, Perry. Don't you worry."

I thought about what Charlie said, and realized I had no option at the moment except to accept the check and hope that the next week would be better. Who was lying the most: Charlie, Pete, or myself, selling these stupid subscriptions?

I put the check in my pocket—it felt very good just to have it there. I took it out when I got to a check-cashing place downtown, near the area known as Skid Row. I handed it to the clerk inside the teller's window.

"ID?" he asked.

All I had was my Social Security card. I handed it to him, and he handed me back the check. I asked him what was wrong.

"It's made out to Perry Bass, not Perry *Brass*. Can you get the check re-made? If you can, I can cash it."

I felt totally deflated. I had no money now at all, and the check was worthless. I had no idea why the magazine sales company did that—was it just a mistake, or did they simply not want to part with the money for a few more days. There was only one thing to do, and I did it.

I went to see Blake.

He was not pleased that I was there. His life had really changed. He had moved out of the Windsor into a real apartment, with another man, a short, thin, very shy guy named Morris who also worked at the music store. They had become lovers, which only made Blake feel more insecure.

"Do you think Morris loves me?" he asked me almost as soon as I walked through the door. I had seen Morris before; he seemed a very straight-up guy, from a small town in the Midwest, the kind where all food was accompanied by macaroni and cheese as a side dish. I told Blake I didn't know, but he probably did.

Blake's face furrowed. The truth was I liked Morris a lot, maybe Blake could tell that. Finally, with Morris out of sight in the kitchen, I showed him the check and asked if he could loan me $5.00

Blake handed me back the check.

"OK," he said. "But I don't want to see you anymore. I don't want you to do this to me—come to me when you need money. You're a kid and you're

47

used to getting money off older men. I know that."

I took the $5.00 and walked out, feeling painfully hurt like my whole insides had been kicked. I wasn't going to hustle anymore; I was too scared of it. There was not only just the cops, but men trawling the back streets at night like Jack, looking for boys like me to fuck, if not rape. I realized Jack had all the right lines, and he had used all of them before.

But at least I could eat. I got a meal—Salisbury steak with french fries—at a very greasy café near Skid Row. While I was eating, two older queens stopped in. One was a linebacker-sized bleached blond, dressed in gray slacks and a woman's pale yellow angora sweater. The other looked kind of sheepish, like a middle-aged bookkeeper.

I could tell they were sizing me up. Then, like a TV game show host, the angora sweater announced to the whole place about me: "She's pretty, but she ain't gonna last here long. Her kind gets old *too* fast."

The next afternoon I decided to leave Downtown and go into Holly-wood. I was waiting for a bus when a man with a crane-like neck, about thirty-five, passed me in a car. He smiled, and I smiled back. A few minutes later, he had circled the block, then stopped in front of me.

"Need a lift?"

I told him I did; I was going into Hollywood. He asked me where, and I just shrugged.

"I live in Hollywood. Why don't you come by for a drink?"

We drove on for a while, then he parked near an attractive apartment complex. I did not find him especially attractive, just kind of plain look-ing. When he got out of the car, I realized he was the tallest man I had ever seen—like, I couldn't believe there was so much of him. I asked him how tall he was.

He sighed a second, like he was tired of being asked that.

"Just seven-one," he said. "My dad's even taller."

We went into his apartment. It was nicely, but blandly furnished. He asked me if I wanted a drink, and I told him no, but that I'd love lunch. He made a ham sandwich from the refrigerator, then his roommate came in. He was shorter, and he just kind of winked at the tall man, and disappeared. A few minutes after the sandwich, the tall man spread a bath towel over the couch, and started taking my clothes off. He did not take his off at all; he blew me on the couch. I never thought I'd get a blow job from a seven-foot-tall man who, aside from that, seemed so totally, blandly "normal."

After it was over, he drove me into Hollywood; I walked around for a while and then took the bus back. The next day I decided to go back to the beach at Will Rogers State Park. I did, and had a great time. I was waiting for a bus back to Downtown, when another man picked me up before the bus arrived.

He lived close to the beach and invited me back. He was of normal size, really nicely put together, with an English accent. We started kissing in his very smart apartment with all the lights turned down. I was very warm from the sun, and also horny. I came in about six minutes. He looked very surprised at me.

"Do you want to *pop* again?" he asked.

I looked quizzically at him.

"Climax. You know, cum?"

"Sure," I said.

"Let's have a drink first," he said. We were both nude and he made us some gin and tonics. I liked the way he looked, with a very English, sporting-guy's body. Like he could have been a rugby player. I sipped the drink, then realized I was really hungry, the way you get at seventeen. I asked him if he could feed me. He shook his head.

"I usually don't do that," he said. "But in your case . . ."

He ordered two fried chicken dinners to be delivered from a nearby restaurant. I was ravenous by the time the doorbell rang. He answered the door wearing only a pair of shorts, and not even bothering to tell me, naked, to cover myself. After the Mexican delivery boy left, I dove into my dinner.

"God, you are hungry," he said. "Horny and hungry. A perfect combination for boys!"

I ended up climaxing three times, then my English friend drove me back to Downtown. I knew I'd never see him again; there was just something about him that made me understand that.

On Monday, the week started again with Pete. I told him about the check, and he apologized and gave me a remade one. This time I checked the name, twice.

Now I knew that just getting through the week would be difficult. I made up all sorts of games in my head to do it. I was a visiting nobleman, a young doctor, all sorts of head games I'd play with customers to get them to believe me enough to sign the subscription forms.

Pete could see it. He asked me what was wrong. I told him that I didn't feel I was cut out for this kind of work.

"Who is?" he said. "You're a good bird dog, Perry. You have that Southern thing going for you. People in LA trust your accent and the way you act. What you need is a girlfriend. I could set you up with a girl. She'd keep you happy enough to keep you working all the day."

I realized suddenly I couldn't even play that game anymore.

"I like guys," I told him. "Maybe you figured that out."

He let out a small laugh, kind of like something from a cartoon where the wolf realizes that the pigs are never going to be a threat.

"No big deal. I've sixty-nined with some girls. So, you do it with guys! The important thing is I want you to keep making money for us. If you can do that, you can be what you want. Just don't make a big deal out of it—not all the managers are as decent as I am."

Pete was right. He was decent, and in a way I was lucky to be his bird dog. He had a decency that most of the other guys at the office lacked. Shortly after our talk, a very obnoxious guy named Steven Gold appeared at the office. He was the regional manager, two managers over Pete. He took Pete, me, and two other bird dogs out for lunch—hamburgers as usual at one of those Southern California restaurants with the standard plantings outside: papyrus plants and bougainvillea. Steve was from New York, and a Jew—he immediately caught on that I was a Jew from the South.

"You guys," he said, talking and eating faster than anybody at the table, "are more like *goyim*. I don't think you're real Jews. You're too much like Southerners. But Pete says you been keeping your sales up. That's all that counts."

He drove a silver Cadillac. Pete hated him; he called him the Silver Jew, because of his car, or sometimes Jew Gold—never to his face, of course. After he had dropped Pete and the other young guys off on their afternoon territory, he said, "Perry, I wanna speak to you."

We drove around a little more, with him using one had to tool down the street, the other to gesture to me.

"You ain't got what it takes here, Perry, but we like you anyway. It's like you're always someplace else. You gotta be *here* makin' sales all the time. You're a smart kid. When I first came to LA from the Bronx, I knew nobody. I had to live in a dump in Hollywood with queers all around me. Selling mags put me into a good area, gave me this car, made me feel like a man and not just some pushy Jew from the Bronx. Understand what I'm sayin'?"

I did. He was right. I was someplace else; I wanted to be painting pictures, or writing a poem, or at the beach. I didn't want to be lying to people and hustling magazines, which already seemed to me a worse kind of hustle than anything Rodney or I might ever do.

But for the rest of the week I worked, my sales added up, and I knew that very shortly I'd turn eighteen and be on the way back to San Francisco.

I still had some of the money from the $93 check, and was hoping that I'd be paid on Friday again, after my normal week's-end tally with Pete. I sat down in the empty conference room with him.

He looked at me seriously.

"Things ain't lookin' good," he said.

"Why, Pete? I've kept my sales up."

"No, Perry. That ain't really it. By *this* time, you should be aiming at my job. See, it's like this. You take my job, and I move up in the company. They need to promote one of my bird dogs so I can move up. We're firing you."

I felt like he had hit me—and also felt very stupid. A short time ago, it almost seemed like I could trust Pete. I'd "come out" to him, although that term was light-years away from usage.

He went over my sales. They were a disappointment. Too many people could not make the credit check. With my shoulders so tight they hurt, I asked if I could have a last check, since it was Friday.

"Sorry, we usually mail you your last check—since you're not coming back and there's no way we can take anything out for last-minute subscription cancellations. Just give us an address. After everything adds up, it's yours."

He smiled at me and shook my hand, one of those famous no-hard-feelings handshakes.

I left the office on Wilshire and realized I couldn't even leave LA. I had one last appointment with my parole officer that coming Monday, the actual day I turned eighteen. I was looking forward to it, but I didn't want to spend money on the rotten hotel I was in and decided, without even thinking, to check out of it and go over to Blake's.

Blake was even less happy to see me than before.

"What do you want now?" he asked.

I told him about getting screwed by the magazine sales company. I asked him if I could stay with him for the next two days, even on the floor if necessary. Morris came in.

"Let him stay," Morris said.

"Why? He's just a little hustler. Don't you have any hustler friends you can go to, Perry?"

"No," I said. "I don't have anybody."

"Jesus, Blake," Morris said. "You can't do that—just throw him out. I know you're bitter about a lot of things, but he's only a kid."

I had my canvas suitcase with me, and Morris put it next to the couch. He took my hand, and told me that he and Blake were going out for a Friday drink.

"We're going to do some serious drinking," Morris explained. "Come with us. You can have some sips from mine."

We went over to the Beverley Wilshire Hotel, which had an elegant bar. Blake and Morris had daiquiris, and I ordered a Coke since I was still underage and the waiter, a very proper kind of young queen, made it plain that he wasn't going to let me slip through. As Blake and Morris became more lubricated on their third drinks, they started talking about Blake's "talent." At first I thought they meant singing, then I realized it was that Blake was also clairvoyant.

"He can talk to the dead," Morris said proudly.

"When do you do it?" I asked.

"When I want to. Usually at a séance."

"Why don't we have one tonight?" Morris said. "I'm really in the mood for it."

Back at their apartment, Morris set up a card table, and Blake turned out all the lights and lit a candle that he placed in the center of the table.

The three of us held hands around it. I was skeptical, and also slightly scared—death frightened me. It really terrified me. I had already lost my father, my favorite aunt, both sets of my grandparents, and several friends to childhood accidents and illnesses.

Blake closed his eyes, and his hand squeezed mine tightly. Morris held my other hand, gently. We waited.

Finally Morris said, "Are you there yet?"

"One of us," Blake said, "Doesn't believe in this. He's a source of negative energy. Perry, you better not fuck up my spirits, like you fucked up everything else."

"Oh, Blake," Morris implored. "Don't blame everything on Perry. You just met him at a bad time."

"I want to see my boys," Blake said. "I want their aura to return to me."

"You mean," I asked, "you can contact people who are alive, too?"

"He can do anything," Morris said proudly.

"Then can you contact Rodney?"

"Sure," Morris answered. "But first let's contact someone dead. Who do you want to see, Perry?"

"My father. Can you contact him?"

Blake hesitated.

"Yeah," he finally said. "Easy. His aura is coming directly to us. What d' you want to say to him?"

Now I really was scared. Blake could feel it. He gripped my hand so hard it hurt.

"Ask him what he thinks of me."

Blake, his eyes still closed, moistened his lips with his tongue. I could see his face looking very tense, then relaxing. The next voice was not his at all. It was deeper and kind of hollow, like it was coming from a great distance. The sort of voice you'd hear in a deep tunnel.

"He's always proud of you. But he thinks you should be nicer to your mother. It's not her fault that she's been so cruel to you. She can't help it."

Suddenly I felt like my head was too heavy to be on my shoulders. It dropped to the table. I was crying.

"It's OK," Morris said. "People do that. Blake has contacted other dead people—some for me too."

Blake reduced the grip on my hand. His eyes opened.

"Sorry, Perry," he said seriously. "You don't know where the spirits are going to take you."

I raised my head. I felt better. Lighter. Blake lit a cigarette and blew the smoke over the table.

"The spirits like smoke," he explained. "We need to get some incense for this."

Morris nodded. Blake closed his eyes again.

"I see Rodney," he announced. "He's happy in Nashville."

I smiled. "Does he still love me?"

Blake's shoulders shrugged.

"He's forgotten all about you. All you mean to him is prison. He wants to leave all of that behind."

Now my face fell again. I didn't believe him. I would never believe it. But I didn't argue with him; I realized it was stupid to argue with Blake. I got up from the table. I couldn't sit there any longer.

Morris looked over at me. "Maybe he'll change his mind, Perry. He's only a kid."

"I don't think so," Blake said bitterly. "Perry has got to get used to the idea that he can't always get what he wants. I certainly did."

Blake smiled suddenly, then added, "Except for you, Morris."

On Monday, I went to see my parole officer, a tall, handsome, dignified black man named John White. His name struck me as funny, since he wasn't white; but then I wasn't made out of "brass" either. His office was next to the Los Angeles County Criminal Courthouse building, the one you see in the 1945 film *Mildred Pierce*. He got up from his desk, shook my hand, and smiled sweetly at me.

"I'm proud of you, Perry," he said, noting that I had not got into any other trouble. He didn't know that I was no longer working for the May Company, but I told him that I had been laid off and was going to return to San Francisco.

"That's your call. You can go anyplace in the world now since, you're eighteen. Just be careful who you associate with, 'cause you do have a record here in Juvie. Don't fuck up and you'll be OK."

He handed me a paper to sign. It said that I was now an "emancipated minor," and legal to live on my own. I realized leaving him that it was another way to track kids, and keep some kind of record on the tens of thousands of runaways who headed for California.

Chapter

6

Getting back to San Francisco was easy. I took a bus out to a freeway, and then on one of the on-ramps stuck my thumb out. A big truck driver living off stale coffee picked me up in a very large truck and took me all the way into the city's limits. Within an hour, I had located a hotel inside the Tenderloin area that I could stay in cheaply. It was called the Waterton Hotel; my rent was $15 a week, with a bathtub next to the room, but most important a small refrigerator and hot plate inside. I had enough money to pay for three weeks. It seemed like an immensity of security for me.

The Waterton was run by Mrs. Cook, the manager. She was amply, portly fat in a dark print housedress that she spilled out of from the top, with her hair crisply permed and dyed a canary yellow. Her fingers were stained with nicotine, as were her teeth. She invited me into her apartment behind the small lobby on the first floor. She had a little yappy dog, also looking nicotine-stained, that needed a good washing, and the whole place smelled of it. She asked me if I'd like a drink. I said sure, and she fixed me a sloe gin fizz, that is sloe gin, a slightly sweet dark version of gin, over the rocks with a little ginger ale in it. It was her favorite drink, and her cramped living room was littered with old sloe gin bottles.

"I gotta clean this place up," she said apologetically. "Now, Perry, what are you gonna do in San Francisco?"

I told her I didn't know, but I would get a job, and I also painted.

She beamed.

"Uh artist! We like 'em here at the Waterton. Just don't bring any strangers back, especially professionally. Know what I mean? I don't like that kind of stuff in my house, although it goes on all over the Tenderloin. My son Ray he watches out for it. If he sees somethin' that's just not right, he'll tell me and I'll have to throw you out."

A moment later, Ray appeared. He was very good-looking, with classic dark Italianesque features that must have come from one of Mrs. Cook's husbands—I gathered there had been several. He was also dressed in a completely recognizable hustler outfit: super-tight jeans and a revealing white T-shirt. He withdrew a small comb from a back pocket and assiduously used it, restoring the varnished splendor of his coal-black hair to a perfect DA—duck's ass—haircut, of which he was very proud. A fresh pack of Marlboros tucked into a rolled-up sleeve accentuated one of his smooth, tanned, bare biceps.

He wore heavy-smoked Ray-Ban sunglasses, and didn't smile at me.

"Hi, Ray," his doting Mom said. "This is Perry, our newest guest."

Ray grunted.

"You need anything, just let me know. And if you get into any trouble, I can handle it."

I thanked them both, and after a couple of sips of sloe gin went up to my room on the third floor. It was reachable through a series of back, very threadbare carpeted stairways that reeked of mildew. The whole hotel in fact did. I loved it. It felt like being in an English movie from the 1930s or 1940s, filled with character actors—and I was one of them.

I spent most of the next week just enjoying myself, walking around San Francisco, soaking up the warm air of September. I started ambling around Pacific Heights and the Embarcadero with my shirt off. It just felt like the right thing to do. Men on the streetcars looked at me and smiled; the warm sunlight of September in the hilly city itself seemed to smile at me. Finally I realized I had to find a job. The small amount of money I had was not going to last, and although I often hung around Market Street downtown where the hustlers gathered by the drove, I was not going to get involved in that world again.

At least, not in that way.

I got a newspaper and looked at the want ads. Many of the kind of jobs I wanted, entry level, were offered by Snelling and Snelling, which at some later point would morph into the world's largest job agency, but in 1965 the office was only a small walk-up off Market. I filled out an application; a pale-skinned, balding, rather chubby middle-aged man of medium height, who looked like he should have been sitting on a park bench reading a newspaper forever, winked at me from his desk. He came over, shook my hand, and led me back to his desk.

"Al Dimitre," he said. "What can I do for you, young man?"

I told him I was looking for a job, and had just moved to San Francisco.

He glanced at my application form that said I had had one year of college and had studied art, and then looked at me seriously. "Let's go out for some coffee."

We went out to a counter place around the corner, and Al began talking. He was from New York and had retained a kind of "caw-fee/chawk-lat" New York accent. He talked nonstop, a once-common habit of New Yorkers.

"I gotta tell you about findin' a job in San Francisco. It's hard here. Do you mind working around gay people?"

I told him no.

"Good. Some young guys do, so that's why I wanted to have caw-fee with you. You're a handsome kid. Anybody ever tell you that?"

I just smiled.

"I'm not coming on to you, but I just thought you should know it. I have a list of jobs that I think would be good f'you. They all pay the fee—Snelling doesn't charge you the fee, the client pays—but I want you to know I'll get a job for you even if there's no fee paid and I have to pay it myself. I'm just that kind of guy."

I blinked. I wasn't quite ready for that. We went back to his office, and I noticed that his office mate, with a desk next to Al's, was a tall, soft-bodied, bespectacled guy who kept grinning at me as soon as Al and I returned. We were introduced: Preston was from Alabama, but had lived in San Francisco for a decade.

"Best place in the world," he said. "If you like what's here. Has Al been treating you OK?"

"Don't try to steal him, Preston. He's mine."

Preston smiled. "I wouldn't think of it."

Al met me several times afterwards, always calling me first at my hotel with "Al Dimitre, Snelling and Snelling. Let's get together and have caw-fee." He told me that he was looking for the right job for me, and something was going to open up, although usually it didn't. Meanwhile, he got a chance to tell me a lot about himself. He had grown up in an orphanage in Pennsylvania, where he was roughed up a lot by older boys, some of whom, the tougher ones, he found extremely attractive.

The result was, he was a dedicated masochist.

"I love gettin' beaten up. It turns me on, especially by really tough guys. Do you think that's sick?"

"I don't know," I said. "But it's not something I'd want to do," I told him.

"Naw, you're too nice, Perry. I knew that when I first saw you. But I'd like to take you out for dinner sometime. No strings attached. *Really*."

I didn't believe him: after I had been raped by Jack in Los Angeles, the thought of beating up Al made my stomach turn. One day I came back to the Snelling office, and Preston met my eyes as I came through the door. Without Al seeing, he mimicked snapping a whip over his head. I guessed a lot of people knew about Al, who seemed so conventional on the outside, like a regular guy-next-door, Rotary Club businessman.

Finally, a real job came through. Al called me on the Waterton's hall housephone about it. Mrs. Cook knew every call coming in; she pushed a buzzer in my room to let me know about the call.

It was in the subscription department at the San Francisco branch of the *Wall Street Journal,* on the seventh floor of an old building on Market Street several blocks away from Powell, very convenient to my hotel. I would be opening mail, deciding who got it—a lot of it would be complaints about subscriptions not arriving—and also filling out and filing subscription cards. Mr. Alden, my boss, a tall suburban, white-bread Fred McMurrayish sort, barely looked at me during the interview. My predecessor had quit to go back to college, and he asked me if I'd do the same thing. I told him I had no plans to do that, and he shook my hand.

My pay was so low that it was breathtaking. I could barely afford to eat on it, but it was a real job in San Francisco. I could now live there, although it was strictly paycheck-to-paycheck, and there were very hungry weeks when I had to starve for a day before my weekly check was handed to me. There was a bar around the corner from the *Journal* where much of the clerical staff went that served an incredibly cheap lunch. Several noticeable queens worked at the *Journal,* at revoltingly menial jobs, making even less than I did. They were "screamers," obviously queer, and just a few dyed inches of hair away from being hair fairies; when they walked into the bar, other habitués would either ignore them or hiss obscenities at them.

I felt bad for them, and would talk to them outside the bar, but most of the time they didn't want to say much to me. They were closed and defensive, and had been hurt too much already.

Chapter

7

It was easy to discover the world of San Francisco at night. There were gay bars in the Tenderloin, and some outside of it, and they were for the most part not hidden away, unlike bars of this sort in many other American cities. They often featured full-scale drag shows, like the famous one at the Gilded Cage presided over by Charles Pierce, or the even more famous, sadly missed Black Cat Café presided over by José Sarria, the Empress of San Francisco. The Black Cat had already been shut down in February 1964, a year before I got to the city, after years of raids and other forms of harassment by the San Francisco Vice Squad and the California ABC (Alcoholic Beverage Commission). Despite its rep for permissiveness, there was very little love lost between the cops and the queens in San Francisco.

I met José one evening on Market Street.

I was sitting at an outdoor snack bar, and he came up to me with another older, stocky, very masculine man named Mel, who was a pimp. Mel introduced himself and immediately tried to recruit me—he decided I'd be perfect for his service. "You have to look butch—you can do that; and enjoy getting fucked. All my clients want that—a good-looking young man they can take out to dinner, say, and then fuck later."

"Mel," José interrupted, "I'm not sure this young man is right for you." He winked at me and introduced himself. He was pudgy, genial, and sweet. "You gotta be careful in San Francisco. There are all these old men here who'll pass you around like a box of candy. Then when they're through with you, they'll throw the box away."

Mel did not like the sound of this, and walked off from us.

José smiled at me.

"I think a young man like you is interested in real love. Go for that." He told me about his life with Black Cat, the "operas" they staged that were the first form of gay theater in San Francisco. How he had run for office, to be on the Board of Supervisors, back in 1961, and lost but put up such a good fight—I was amused. I had never met anyone like this. Then he shook my hand and, like a real politician, wished me good luck.

Hanging out on Market Street was something I did on the weekdays, when I had to be up early the next morning for work at the *Journal*. But the weekends were for more serious pursuits: the underground gay places where as a kid, still under twenty-one, the legal age for drinking in California, I could feel at home. On Market Street I learned about Pearl's, the coffeehouse behind the Gilded Cage that opened at 1:30 in the morning. I had already snuck into the Gilded Cage to catch the early shows, standing in the crowd until a waiter asked for my ID, so I knew where it was. Pearl's was never advertised, but the owner of the Gilded Cage decided there needed to be a venue for "kids," like myself, who could not get into the bars.

It was open only on the weekends, so the next Friday I took a nap after work and set my alarm for midnight. I showered, got dressed, and quickly walked to the alleyway behind the bar. There was already a line to get in: almost all of them were kids in their late teens or early twenties, with just a few older men thrown in. There was a small cover charge, maybe $1.75, for a first soft drink, and then we got in. Inside was a large back party room, elegantly decorated "San Francisco style": red wallpaper with black fleur-de-lis flocking, large crystal chandeliers and wall sconces, small cocktail tables. It was soon packed. I had never seen, or imagined, so many gay kids. I had been to a somewhat popular gay coffeehouse in Hollywood once, but this was body-to-body, with Barbra Streisand nasally belting out "Second Hand Rose" over a sound system and waves of young body movements mimicking her every intonation.

I was new, and kids came up to me; I made several friends that night who would be close to me only there. Many lived at home in the outer suburbs, arriving with friends who lived in the city, or closer in. Some, obviously, had had either to sneak out of a window from their parents, or make up crazy stories about why they were out so late. They were all prosperous looking, well dressed; no one was like me—completely on their own at eighteen. I felt sophisticated, grown up, and glamorous. I liked the feeling. By 2:30, most people had left—including the older men trying to pick up "chickens," that is, younger boys. I was approached by several of them, but found myself uninterested. Like José said, I wanted love—what I had found with Rodney. Someone I could go crazy over.

However—being eighteen, after all—that didn't mean that I would not accept a quicker substitute.

A short time later, one of my young friends from Pearl's told me about another place—the Chukker Club. It was an underground "speed" (that is, amphetamine) bar on Turk Street in the Tenderloin. It was in a basement, through a narrow, almost pitch-black, grope-your-way-through passageway, so just finding it was an adventure. Lots of kids hung out there, especially boys who went in for drag and drag hustling—that is, wearing some boy's clothes like jeans but also frilly female blouses, makeup, wigs, and earrings. The wig *de jour* was modeled after Streisand's dark, short "do": bangs in front, curls on the side; always teased up at the top and tapered to a short clip in back. In the Chukker you'd see about a dozen of them. These boys were not so much trying to "pass" as girls as to show their availability, like they had now intersected with another sex in this marriage of a targeted market (the johns) and capitalist availability (the "girls," who wore not heels but sturdy English-style boots with a zipper on the side: I guess if you are trying to outrun the law, the usual whore's come-fuck-me pumps just wouldn't do).

I became friends with a young drag named Sheila, who looked particularly fetching in her Streisand bob and sold Benzedrine tablets known as "bennies." They came packaged like something you'd buy at a movie concession stand—you know, like Necco Wafers or Life Savers: a roll of five in glassine paper, $3.00.

The Chukker was notorious. It was raided often, and cops would sometimes just walk in to intimidate the girls, or, as we might call them now, "transgirls," or nab them outside. At Pearl's I'd heard about a really nasty raid at the Chukker when several of the girls were smacked around and then arrested. It really upset the kids at Pearl's, many of whom were still in high school. I went down a few days later to see Sheila.

"Were you scared?" I asked.

"Naw," she said, popping her chewing gum. "I love this life. Johns, selling bennies. Freedom. When you play with fire, you're gonna get burned. If you're scared, it's never gonna work. I'm just so happy I'm not stuck at home with my parents. They never understood. My dad beat the shit out of me when he caught me once posing in front of a mirror in my bathrobe. I was wearing some of Mom's lipstick. I had to leave. I was in Wisconsin. I hated it."

I understood every word she said. There was something honest and real about being down in the basement at the Chukker that felt actually good. You were away from the "normal" daytime world that did everything it could to kill you. I understood that; it made me genuinely like Sheila. The only problem was, How do you survive in this night world that led to selling bennies, advertising your availability with a wig and lipstick to married johns, and working hard to protect whatever soul you had left?

The Chukker was managed by a short, aggressive Filipino queen named Carlos; I would see her all the time. Like the rest of the Chukker girls, she wore jeans, butch boots, a pert blonde wig, and flouncy blouses. She looked kind of like a Filipino Doris Day. She had a husband who protected her, who looked big, tough, and butch, but everybody understood that it was Carlos who fucked him.

"That's the way it is," Sheila explained it to me. "Femme on the streets and butch in the sheets. Most of these *bitches* are butches. They will flip you over and fuck you in a second."

I experimented with bennies a couple of times. They allowed me to stay up until 4 or 5 in the morning, but the crash later was exhausting, and they caused my adolescent skin to break out—a complete no-no to me. The gay world was a nighttime world, although there was also a daytime component to it—a few places where gays congregated, such as Union Square, which had an open cruising area, mostly for hustlers, and down by the Embarcadero, a small strip of sand by the water known as the "Bunny Patch." There gay musclemen in small Ah Men bathing suits paraded for each other. I didn't find it friendly at all. Most of these men were too self-conscious even to breathe. It was a silent pantomime of showing, preening, and seeing who could withhold the kind of friendliness that I wanted. It was middle-class, repressed homosexuality at its worst.

OK. Maybe not its *worst*, but certainly bad enough.

But in the wee hours of darkness, things just happened—impromptu drag shows in the backs of closed bars; or parties at Ronny's, a gay hotel at the edge of the tough Folsom district. I ventured into Ronny's a few times. Guys would keep their doors open, play records, and invite you in to dance—something hard to do in any place in San Francisco. There was sex, I was told, in some of the rooms, but you had to be careful about that, because the Vice cops could also walk in at any time.

I bumped into Al Dimitre on the street soon after.

"I heard you been goin' to Ronny's," he said. "You shouldn't. You can get a bad rep going there."

I asked him how he knew about it.

He smiled.

"I got spies. Y'know everybody in gay San Francisco talks about everybody else. Sometimes it's like being in a small town. Especially after New York. Wanna have dinner with me? You don't have to do anything for it. No strings. *Really.*"

I told him I'd think about it. The truth was I had started painting again, mostly watercolors and acrylics in my room. I loved it, and it kept me from going out so much. I did a really crazy painting called "Downtown LA." Hustlers, the Greyhound bus depot as an entry into hell, drag queens, and shy boys like me on the side. It was like German Expressionism. I found a gallery in North Beach called the Starving Artist and talked to the owner. He asked me to bring some work in, and I brought him "Downtown LA," some marine pictures I had done at the beach in LA, and some watercolor flowers. There was all manner of crap in the gallery, which looked more like a secondhand jumble shop, but my work looked good in it.

"You never can tell what's going to sell," the owner said.

Except for the pathetic wage, I didn't mind working at the *Journal*. I made easy friends with several other more-discreet gay men who worked there, older than I certainly but also in low-paying clerical positions. We had lunch together, sometimes splurging at a *hofbräu* on Market Street on schnitzel, wursts, and beer. San Francisco was still very much a working-class town, with cheap places for lunch downtown and a kind of tough-fun atmosphere to it. I discovered a place to buy high school student bus passes in the basement of a department store; I bought one without any questions, and so could ride the cable cars and buses for almost nothing.

My friends at the *Journal* were what used to be called in department stores "ribbon clerks," that is, "generic" fags from poor backgrounds with low-paying jobs. They were out enough and obvious enough that they weren't going to make it in the Big Man's World of Business, and most of the time even the thought of that was too terrifying, because for them it meant too much exposure. They did not want to make an issue out of being queer; they just wanted to get on with it. This meant working behind closed doors in the further back rooms of offices, where their friends were usually either other men like themselves, or female clerks of any age. They were never going to be in the big-ticket world of adult salaries, and would be "office boys" until they died.

One of them told me about Gene Compton's.

"You should go," he said. "It's a real scene."

I asked him what it was, and he told me that Compton's was a local chain of cafeterias. "They're all pretty queer, but some are *gayer* than others."

The one that he told me about I had to take a bus to—it was down Market Street in the area known as the Castro. I felt funny and uncertain getting off the bus; the area was tough, dark, dirty, and frightening the way the off-the-tracks underbelly of San Francisco could be at night. I approached fearfully; then the cafeteria appeared like a beacon of warmth with glowing plate-glass windows. I got a tray and bought some butterscotch pudding, then sat down at a long table with a group of guys whom I knew to be gay. There was no way around it. They were unapologetic hair fairies with yards of big, teased, dyed hair—as in Tequila Sunrise orange, Fire Engine red, and Screaming Canary yellow, that kind of stuff. The Chukker girls looked like ladies from Bloomsbury compared to these Compton's queens.

"Exactly *WHO* do you think you are sitting here?"

I peered up from my pudding. This tall, red-haired queen with menacing claw-fingernails and green eye makeup was glaring at me.

"Sorry," I said genuinely. "I didn't realize this was your place."

Her eyes narrowed.

"My name is Lulu, and I'm what they call a *bitch*. Who told you *you* could sit here?"

"No one," I said. "It's a public place."

Now I got really pissed, and turned my back to her, trying to enjoy my pudding even while feeling put upon.

A few minutes later, several really big bikers in leather walked in. My first thought was that there was going to be a fight between the bikers and queens. I was wrong. Lulu said something to one of the bikers who was built like a brick shithouse, and he walked over to me, grabbed me by my shoulders, and lifted me off my chair.

"You're leavin' now," he said. "Pretty boy."

I did. I looked at Lulu, shrugged, and walked out. The whole thing felt too pathetic and stupid. After being run out of that fruit town in the San Joaquin Valley, Gene Compton's seemed like a silly place to get bothered about. I found another one closer to me in the Tenderloin, where the queens were nicer and the straights more sympathetic to a kid like me. This was the Compton's where the famous cafeteria raid took place exactly a year later. That was one of the first times that LGBT people had ever openly stood up to the cops.

I told my friend at the *Journal* about what happened to me.

"Yeah, those girls! They're a tough bunch. If you had walked in with me, they woulda treated ya differently. The problem is, Perry, you still don't look like you belong here."

That was always a question—where did I belong? I was still a shy Southern kid on my own in San Francisco. Sometimes I found that answer on Market Street, not too far from Powell. There in the glow of evening I didn't feel alone, because it was filled with kids like me, hustlers and teen drag queens, or young gay men just looking for company. I became friends with a beefily built guy named Joey with very flat face and a bad overbite. He was a superb hustler, or at least wanted me to believe him to be. He sometimes worked for a service and other times "freelanced" on Market, seeing what he could bring in.

"You gotta have a specialty," he told me. "Like mine is straight guys who wanna believe I'm straight and what we do is almost nothin' but it's more than they're gonna get from their wives or girlfriends most of the time. Most of the time that just means I jerk 'em off, but sometimes I'll suck one if I have to, and there is more money involved. If that happens, it's usually because I get 'em so hot that they beg me to do it, and then I ask for, well, a lot."

For some reason, Joey liked me. I was his complete opposite, and he liked being so cocksure and instructive around me. It never occurred to me to go to bed with him, but one day, when I was very broke, he set me up with one of his "gentlemen."

That is, this older man started cruising Joey, then walked over to me.

"Hi," he said. "You look really out of place here. Can I give you a lift?"

His car, a big, late-model Lincoln, was parked close by. He was good-looking, in good shape with silvery white hair and a handsome, older Irishman's face—maybe in his mid-fifties. It started to rain hard, and he drove the Lincoln effortlessly through the slimy ruts and puddles of the dark Tenderloin. He asked me my name and where I was from. I told him.

In front of the Waterton, he said, "I'd like to take you out sometime. I don't live in San Francisco. I come in every now and then on business. I'm not a fairy or a pansy. I guess you can see that. You shouldn't hang around guys like that hustler. You're better than that."

I gave him my number at the hotel.

His name was Ryan Fitzgerald, and he called me about a week later and took me to a fancy European-style restaurant perched near the Buena Vista Café. He had reservations, and the maître d' had no problem that I was his dinner guest; however I saw that our table was in the back, in an alcove by itself, away from the crowd of well-dressed diners in the main room. Ryan smiled at me in my blue blazer (which came from a secondhand store) and tie as we sat down.

"You're a handsome young man," he said.

I felt nervous, then had a gin and tonic—no ID was asked—and felt less so. We both ordered steaks with baked potatoes. They were wonderful, but I ate mine with my head down most of the time while Ryan lectured to me on things a young man should know: that I shouldn't "associate with fairies, drag queens, and that kind of gutter trash you find in the Tenderloin. You should be living in a better place, with the kind of caliber you'd be proud to be seen with."

From time to time, I'd look up at him, smile glassily and nod. I had another gin and tonic. That helped. It would not have helped if I had told him I'd grown up with a violently unstable mother who was a repressed lesbian in a public housing project in Savannah, Georgia, where we were the only Jewish family and I was beaten up about once a week. But I could give a good impression. Actually, as a kid I'd been drilled in it—my mother's wealthier relatives had taught me how to eat at a fancy restaurant, what the salad fork was, how to handle a bread-and-butter plate, and other skills of that sort.

"You must think I'm an old fuddy-duddy," Ryan said after he had handed the waiter cash for the bill.

"No," I answered. "You're fine."

We walked around for a while and passed the Starving Artist Gallery, which was closed, but I told him I had work in it. Back at his Lincoln, I wasn't sure what we were going to do next—that is, what kind of sex would be expected for this night out. But none was. He simply drove me back to the Waterton, with a "I'll call you next time I'm in town."

I wasn't sure what was going on, but Mrs. Cook, who had her head out the window of her apartment, was impressed with Ryan's Lincoln.

"You got some friends," she said to me. Ray, who was next to her, only nodded at me and winked.

There were times when I loved being at the Waterton. With all sorts of hidden back staircases and levels of creaky floors left by decades of renovations and additions, it reminded me of being in some once-proud, musty old English establishment in a 1930s Alfred Hitchcock movie. It was humble, definitely. That was witnessed one moment when I woke up in the middle of the night and watched a line of mice racing across the foot of my bed. As long as they stayed at the foot, they didn't faze me. I became friends with some of the other residents. They included Jeremy, a short, pretty-faced young man and his girlfriend, Alice, who, like much of San Francisco, had relocated together from a small town in the Midwest. Jeremy was a drag queen, but he was a heterosexual transvestite. Mrs. Cook had no problems with this, because, at least, being straight he never brought back tricks to the rooms he shared with Alice, who often did speed and was completely compliant with her boyfriend's sexual inclinations.

They occupied a small "maisonette," or series of housekeeping rooms, in the hotel. Compared to me, they were quite prosperous, but almost anyone was. They invited me in for talk and to share some wine.

"Jeremy's the most wonderful guy I've ever met," Alice said to me. "He's sweet, polite, and loves me. I know about his dressing up. Look." She opened up a closet in the bedroom filled with very brightly colored clothes. "These are all his."

"I'm not queer," Jeremy told me emphatically. "I just like women's clothes and dressing up. It's simply kind of a 'normal' kick for me!"

I noticed that Jeremy had an English accent. I asked him if he were from England.

"No," Alice said. "That's just the way he talks when he gets excited and in a draggy mood. He has a whole personality change. You should see it."

I told her I wanted to, and a short while later, after Jeremy had closed the door to their bedroom, he came out in a strawberry-blonde wig and a beautiful crushed velvet purple evening gown with spaghetti straps. He was fair skinned with rosy cheeks that needed almost no rouge, but he did have a 5-o'clock shadow, and the wig needed some real taming. There were just too many stray hairs about it.

"You should do something about that," Alice said, stroking his jaw line.

He rolled his eyes.

"Mind you, I didn't want to go the whole route for Perry," he explained, sounding like a cheeky young Angela Lansbury. "Just give him a nice preview—like opening a show before the critics arrive."

"Not with your hair looking like this," Alice said, taking his wig off and giving it a good shake and then some therapeutic strokes with a comb.

"Women!" Jeremy said. "Y'can never please 'em!"

She handed him back his wig.

"Thank you, 'Leese," he said.

He carefully replaced the wig, smiled, and did us both a perfect little curtsy.

During the day, Jeremy worked in a tie and jacket as a travel agent's assistant. Alice did stints at various department stores as a clerk. She hated to work full time—she was actually more druggy and hippieish than he was. He told me he wanted nothing to do with San Francisco's hippies, bohemians, or the gay scene.

"I'm not gay, but gay bars are the only place I can go and get any kind of companionship, if you know what I mean. If I went to straight places, I'd get my head beat in. I know it. One of these days, Alice and I are going to leave here, and move out to the suburbs and have kids. I don't want any of them to be gay; I want them to be normal, regular kids. But they should be open to having a father who's different. That's all I can ask of them."

Chapter

8

Like Jeremy and Alice, I had also escaped to San Francisco from another place, where I was not a part of the "real" world. I was indeed part of another world, one as made up as the one Jeremy was in, and for the most part I felt that I was only suspended above it—at the moment, it felt that there was little possibility of me finding a "real" world of my own.

I felt that way at the *Journal*—no one I worked with, actually, had any idea what I did at night, or on the weekends. I was just a kid to them. There were several women in my department who lived in the suburbs, were married, and commuted in. They had no clue what went on in the Tenderloin, and even less interest in knowing. Sometimes they would let out catty, homophobic comments about the obviously queer boys who worked as clerks; the feeling was that these boys also did not exist in the "real" world of men and business: they were like cartoon creatures—definitely *not* "for real."

Occasionally I'd see, on the upper floors where the San Francisco office kept a news bureau, men in suits who I was sure were gay. There would be some momentary lightning flash of understanding between us, then it was gone.

They knew that I knew. But we also knew that we'd never talk about it. Certainly not at work.

Halloween came, the most festive day of the year in gay San Francisco. For one day out of the year, you could wear drag—legally. Luckily, it happened that year on a Saturday, so the entire day was dedicated to revelry. I saw girls in full drag on the Tenderloin streets out in the afternoon, screaming at each other:

"BITCHES' CHRISTMAS! IT'S BITCHES' CHRISTMAS!"

I had not heard the term before, but would soon get used to it. Pearl's was fantastic. I could not recognize half the boys in it, now dressed in the most impressive and amazing finery—like they had either robbed their mothers' closets, or been working on their own for months on these ensembles. There was a big drag ball that night in the Tenderloin, to which I would not be able to go being under twenty-one, but I did get to see lots of queens on the streets or in Pearl's.

Finally, Charles Pierce himself walked into Pearl's in a very chic Mainbocher suit, looking like a dead ringer for Bette Davis in *All about Eve*.

For a second, I couldn't keep my eyes off him. He saw me staring.

"Don't worry. It's only me, Dahling," he said in the best Bette voice I'd ever heard. In a white-gloved hand, he held out a cigarette.

"Got a light, Dahling?"

I told him I didn't smoke.

"Good! Young men like you should pick up their bad habits *considerably* later."

I thanked him and he walked on, while others bowed before him like he was definitely the queen he was.

A few days after Halloween, I got a letter from Ryan Fitzgerald. He told me that he'd be away from the Bay Area for several weeks, but wanted me to remember him. In the letter were two $20 bills. I was delighted. I was living so hand-to-mouth; my salary at the *Journal* was so low that there were weeks when I was barely eating. This gift gave me a bit of economic slack; I bought a couple of dark ski turtlenecks that looked great on me. They clung to my young body and made me feel really elegant. Feeling elegant in gay San Francisco was important.

I started wearing the turtlenecks with my sports jacket to Pearl's. The boys looked at me and smiled. I became close friends with a very elegant young man named Fabian who was around six feet and weighed about a hundred pounds. He was very spectral with a haunting, chalk-white face, deep-set eyes with rings of darkness around them, and a nose resembling an egret's beak. He was a strange bird indeed, and wore garments of stygian black, often with feathers attached as part of a cape or jacket.

"This is our *world*," he said, pronouncing the "W" very breathily, like he was blowing out smoke rings. I watched his very expressive mouth, with sets of dime-sharp dimples surrounding it. "You must respect it. It's very special. Most fools don't know it, but it is. It only exists when we are here, producing it. It is full of magic, like religion! Don't forget that, my young friend."

Fabian wore an onyx crucifix around his pale, thin neck. He went to services at various cathedrals and churches, and was especially fond of Glide Memorial, which had been a pioneer in actually recognizing the presence of gay people in their membership.

When I felt especially alone at Pearl's, I liked seeing Fabian, but I'd no idea how I'd deal with him in the daytime, when I had to appear conventional at work. I did see him late one afternoon on the streets near Union Square. He was in a light gray suit, not black, with no feathers attached. He nodded curtly at me, and walked on.

Going to Pearl's became very much a part of my world; sometimes I'd sneak into bars, but at Pearl's I didn't have to sneak into anything. The important thing was to be in this queer environment, where I and other kids like me could exhale for a moment—just relax—even though the terrible "rules of the game" made even these havens for us difficult.

One evening I walked in before the crowd arrived and, going up to the bar to get a Coke, saw a tall, nicely but casually dressed guy alone there. He was older than I, sure, but still good-looking, even youthful. He had a scotch in his hand. He smiled with this funny half-smile that suddenly broke into an expression of anguish.

I asked him what was the matter.

"Today's my birthday."

"Happy birthday!"

"I'm twenty-nine."

I nodded; that didn't seem so terrible to me.

"You don't understand," he said. "You're young. You've got everything ahead of you. Once you hit thirty, it's all over. Nobody wants you anymore."

I hadn't thought much about that. I wasn't even nineteen yet.

His eyes hit the floor. He took a big gulp of his scotch.

"I'm thinking about killing myself when I'm thirty. What else can you do? You become an old auntie. You know what that is?"

I had heard the term before. I shrugged.

"It's somebody who you feel sorry for. You see them in the bars, usually stuck in the back. They don't look young anymore. They can't hide not being young. Sometimes they pay for it. That's about all they can get."

"It sounds awful," I said, trying to be sympathetic, the way I'd been taught to be in the South. I had seen aunties before. Sometimes they came in in groups; they were bitchy and often drunk, and a lot of the guys my age made fun of them.

"This life is very cruel," he said. "I want you to know that. All we have is the bars—and the ones in San Francisco aren't always the nicest."

A few minutes later I left him and went over to talk to some friends my own age. But I thought about what he had said—that all we had were the bars, and about killing yourself at thirty. Later I learned that there were bars in San Francisco specifically for older men. They were sometimes called "wrinkle rooms," and hustlers habitually hung out in them. I also started to understand why queers in San Francisco, LA, and other places were always trying to look younger. To keep that mask of youth on, no matter how false it looked.

Some of it was to blend in, of course. To be a part of the "scene," which was so youth-oriented, and to feel that you wouldn't be made fun of, or felt sorry for, or simply ignored, if you could pass for a younger man. But later I realized there was another part too. As long as you were "one of the boys," you could deflect, at least inside, all if not some of the questions, stones, and taunts thrown at you by the daytime straight world as it aimed to contract your very being:

"Why aren't you married?" "When are you going to settle down, and have a family of your own?" "Aren't you tired of always being by yourself?"

And the worst, the one you most hated to ask yourself—"What's an old man like you doing in this 'gay world' full of boys?"

Because inside you knew you were never going to be an old man; certainly as long as you pretended not to be. But I would still see them: these old men nursing drinks in the corners of bars, looking furtively at what they weren't supposed to want, but always still did.

Early one morning at Pearl's, as it was near closing, another well-built guy in his late twenties walked up to me. He was good-looking in a very red-faced, rough way, and somewhat balding. He introduced himself—"Jim"—and asked me if he could buy me a drink. All I could have was a Coke, but he quickly came back with one and a real drink for himself. A few minutes later, we were on the way back to my hotel.

He had asked me if he could sleep with me, and I'd said yes. It was late, and I knew I was lonely enough, though not necessarily horny enough, to want him. There was something about him that I was not mature enough to find appealing, that is, he was like a real adult man, with no glitter or glamour to him. In my room we took off our clothes in the dark, though some morning light was already filtering in. He was extremely hairy on his back and chest, and his body looked beaten up, like he had been in a lot of fights or had been doing really hard manual labor. I turned away from him, and he suddenly hugged me so tight it hurt.

"Show some feelings toward me, Perry," he begged. "Please."

I didn't know what to do—feelings, they were difficult for me. At eighteen, my greatest feeling was simply for survival, except for those moments of extreme romantic flight like I'd had with Rodney, with whom I was still in love.

We had sex together, mostly fumbling and masturbation; afterwards, he started really trembling and got up. I asked him what was wrong.

"You don't know how hard this is for me."

I asked him why, and he got back into bed and told me that he had been in the Marine Corp for five years—all of the boys in his Irish Catholic family were Marines. He had hated every moment of it, but did it because . . . well, he had no idea that he could not. Suddenly he opened himself up to me and I listened. At several points he was close to crying.

The Marine Corps had been unmitigated hell; he'd had his nose broken in a fight, and several ribs broken in basic training. "The things they do to you, just to beat you down and then build you back up again. But I never felt that that had happened to me—being built back up. I just hated it. I got out early. I was going to crack up. The gay thing, it just terrorized me. If anyone had found out, I was sure they'd kill me. When I got out I became an airplane mechanic. I'd been trained for it in the Corps, and it pays well. I'm living with my parents now, down on the Peninsula, but I want to get a place of my own again. I had one, but lost it."

"Why?"

"It's another story. Can I see you again? I need to go back home now, but I want to see you."

I told him he could, and for the next several weeks, I didn't go to Pearl's, but only saw Jim. He had a wonderful two-seater sports car, and we'd drive all over the Bay Area, going to restaurants and bars. Since he made much more money than I did, he regularly picked up the check; but we always stayed in my hotel room, and he called me. I could never call him at home. Sometimes he would drop by after work in his mechanic's overalls, half-coated in engine grease. I liked the deep, sharp smell of the engine oil; I would peel his overalls off, and we'd bathe together in my bathroom, which had an old claw-foot bathtub in it.

He was extremely shy most of the time, and drank a great deal—more than I was used to, or could even understand. One evening we went out to a gay-friendly restaurant in Berkeley and met two of his friends there. They were both teachers, slightly older than Jim. They seemed to fit in beautifully in the restaurant, while Jim looked uncomfortable and soon had downed three scotches. I was getting nervous about him driving back. He went to the men's room, and one of his friends said to me:

"Jim's on the way to alcoholism. You can see it in his face. It's sad. He's a nice guy, but those years in the Marines just destroyed him. He was in Viet Nam—he never talks about that, I bet."

It was true, he didn't. I asked both of them if there was anything I could do.

"You could try to get him into AA, but I don't think that's going to work. Just don't get too involved with him. He's living with his family now, and that's even worse. Here he comes."

Jim sat back down. The two teachers smiled genially at him, like they were all just regular guys, and I felt bad.

A few days later, Jim asked me if I'd like to move in with him, that is, when he got a new apartment.

I finally asked him what had happened with his old one.

"It's a bad story," he said.

I waited.

"I had this boyfriend, Chris. He was kind of femmy. Sometimes people didn't know if he was a boy or a girl—he did drag a lot, and was really pretty as a girl. My parents never got to meet him; I just kept making excuses. Anyway, I had an apartment in the Sunset area over by the beach. I liked it a lot; it was quiet and I thought very private. He wasn't on the lease—there was no way he could be. One morning my landlady, this nosy old Italian lady, caught us in bed together. She acted like she had never seen anything like this in her whole life, and threw us out. She threatened to go to the police, and tell my parents. I'd used my dad as a reference, so she had his phone number."

"What happened to Chris?"

"He just split on me. He couldn't take it. I never saw him again, ever. Maybe he even left town. It really bothered him—suddenly being thrown out like that. There was nothing we could do. We had to pack up and get the hell out in a couple of hours. Mrs. Fugiari told us we had three hours to leave. 'You broke the lease! There's a morals clause in my lease, and you broke it!'"

The next few times I was with Jim, I felt even stranger, as if I couldn't really connect with him in any way. We had very little to talk about; I knew almost nothing about planes, and he was not interested in art or books. I started to feel lonelier with him than I did alone. I remembered a poem I had loved in high school by Sidney Lanier called "The Marshes of Glynn," which talked about how there were waters that were deeper than you could know or see.

Thinking about the poem in Jim's presence depressed me. There were too many things I could not talk about, like the life I had left in Georgia, and there were too many things he could never share with me, like his life with his family who knew really nothing about him. Finally he called me to make plans for the weekend, and I told him that I was busy, and wouldn't see him.

"OK," he said. "I understand. I do." He hung up.

I went back to Pearl's and immediately told Fabian about how I'd been involved with Jim for the past several weeks. At eighteen, several weeks is a lot of time; he smiled at me.

"We're so glad to have you back, Perry," he said. He shook his head sadly. "A *butch* in the closet! They are hard to be with, aren't they?" He smiled bravely at me, like he had been through the same thing before and knew firsthand how difficult it was.

Chapter

9

I had been hearing for some time about the Rendezvous, a bar on Sutter Street further up from the Tenderloin, not far from Union Square in a quiet, fairly high-toned shopping area. It was where all the "uptown men" went, the ones who had jobs and a "real" life during the daytime. Fabian didn't like it.

"It's the 'Wax Museum,' " he sniffed. "All those guys do is stand up and model for each other. They're straight during the day, and only come out a *little* queer at night."

I asked him if he ever went. He told me no. He had gone a few times, but the manager came up to him and told him to change his outfit before coming back. He was once escorted to the door. I was still curious, and got up my courage one Saturday towards the holidays to try it. I had some fake ID, easy enough to get, and dressed well, in a sports jacket and one of my turtlenecks. I figured that would make me look presentable.

The bar, hardly noticeable from the street, was on the second floor. I walked up the stairs about 10 o'clock. A bouncer sat at the landing. He glanced at me and didn't do a thing, so I continued up past another door into this large, dark, frostily over-air-conditioned room, accented with rosy theatrical lighting, and got ear-slammed by Frankie Valli and the Four Seasons blasting falsetto rockets into the air:

"Let's hang on—to what we've got!

Don't let go, girl, we've got a lot—

Got a lot of love *betweeeeeeen* us—

Hang on, hang on, hang on, to what we've GOT!"

It was like being hit by a wall of sound, cold air, and colder men. Tons of them, just "hanging on" themselves, already neck-deep in their own individual guys-night-at-the-gay-bar-appropriate, freshly pressed and dry-cleaned outfits. You could hardly walk more than six inches without bumping into another Brooks Brothers button-down shirt. Most didn't say a word. Maybe it was too early, or maybe I was just the wrong person. But then, precisely, what *could* you say above Frankie?

I went to the bar and ordered a tequila sunrise. I was enjoying it for a couple of minutes, and suddenly some of these button-down mannequins started staring at me. One approached.

"How old are you?" he demanded.

I swallowed some sunrise, then said:

"Twenty-two. *Why?*"

"'Cause I don't want this place to get closed down, kid," he said, almost spitting at me.

"He's twenty-two, I know," a tall, thin guy, who might have actually been twenty-two said. "I know him."

"OK," the first man conceded sullenly, then disappeared into a swarm of these cardboard cutouts all looking as starched, pressed, and folded as he did.

I peered up into the face of the tall, young gentleman who had come to my rescue: it was sweet, open, and endearing.

"That was stupid," he said close to me, leaning into my ear so that his breath warmed me and yet slightly chilled me at the same time. "Why was he bothering you?"

I shrugged and asked him his name.

"Jody. I'm new here myself. From Indiana."

He smiled at me. At that moment, I felt, no matter what people said about the Rendezvous, if somebody like Jody went there, it had to be fine. We found a place on the outside of the crowd, near one of the less-crowded side bars.

I told him that I was from Georgia, and had only been in San Francisco a few months. But I loved it.

"What do you love?"

"The freedom. I can be what I am here. I couldn't in Georgia."

"That's the thing. I'm not sure what I am. See, I'm married, but my wife's a lesbian. We met in high school in our small town in Indiana—farms every place. My dad and mom had one, and I was supposed to get married, so Karen, she and I decided to get married right after high school. Our friends got excited. We had an engagement party. Everyone was happy. Then a few days later, she said to me, 'There's something I have to tell you, Jody.'

"I said, 'What?' and she said, 'I really like women,' and I was so happy I almost cried. Because I was thinking about calling the wedding off, and this meant that we could keep all the gifts. Isn't that crazy? That was my first thought."

He looked at me, and his eyes—I couldn't even see their color in this dark—had a way of capturing all the phantom light in the room.

He asked if I wanted to go home with him.

"Won't your wife mind?"

"Naw. She's asleep."

He had a bicycle parked outside, and we both got on it; not easy riding up the hills in San Francisco with another guy on the back, but he had powerful legs, and soon we were at his apartment. It was a small one bedroom; his wife was asleep behind the bedroom door. There was a fireplace with gas logs in the front room. He turned it on, so that the glow from the logs lit up the dark. There was a couch that converted into a bed, and he unfolded it. We took our clothes off and got into the bed. He was all handsome legs and big chest and shoulders, with very clear, pale skin and light-colored hair. Now I could see the color of his eyes, a sparkling aqua blue, so beautiful to look into they were like swimming in clear water.

He was completely, ravenously hungry for me, and I was kind of awe-struck for a moment; the whole thing seemed so crazy. I had never made love to a guy with his wife in the next room, even if she was a lesbian. I somehow knew this wasn't going to last; it was just too hot and crazy to go on. I loved his very generous dick; it went perfectly with the rest of him, but too quickly we both climaxed and fell asleep.

The next morning Karen, who was very good-looking but darker complected than Jody, came out of the bedroom, and Jody introduced me, like it was just something he did. She was in a nightgown and went into the kitchen and made coffee. She brought it out to us.

"I'm glad Jody has a new friend," she said, yawning. "He's been lonely here. We just got here a month ago, and we don't know anybody. My girl-friend's in England—her name is Lynn and I miss her a lot."

"How did you meet?" I asked.

"That's another story! Jody and I spent some time in the UK after college. We didn't spend *that* much time in college in Indiana, but we both worked and had enough money to go over there. I met her at a museum where she was working. We lived with her for three months, and she's going to come over here as soon as she can afford it. Her parents are very cool—they had both been in the War, and nothing fazed them. They knew Lynn's gay and they didn't make a big deal out of it like our parents would—if they ever found out, it would just kill them! So Jody and I always put on this show for them when we go back home."

"It's not all a show," Jody said. "I love you. I really do. I'm so happy you're my wife. I'm really happy I married you."

"Let's don't go into that again, Jody. I love you too, but we know why we got married and why it keeps on working."

She smiled at me, and then at Jody. A few minutes later, I told her that I had to leave.

"You'll come back?" she asked.

I told her I would, and got their number.

I thought about Jody often, but I could never be in love with him: there was just too much between us, most of all, Karen. She was not like most of the lesbians I had ever seen, that is, she was not stridently working-girl butch or fluffy blouses and bouffant-hair femme. There were several lesbian bars up closer to North Beach, and I had been to one of them; all the women seemed to fall into one of those two categories. But Karen wasn't like that. There was something very appealing and sweet about her, kind of small-town-girl-next-door. Very Indiana really.

However, as I got to know this couple more, I started to see that this was not 100 percent true. They were both into drugs, Karen even more so. I picked up on this when I mentioned to Jody that I had gone several times to the Chukker and talked about my friend Sheila who sold rolls of bennies.

Karen was in the front room and her eyes lit up.

"We gotta get some of those. Some of my friends back in school were taking them. I loved them. Can you get us a couple of rolls? How much are they?"

I told her they were $3 a roll, so she gave me a $10 bill, and smiled. "Keep the change."

I went back to the Chukker a few days later, but Sheila wasn't there.

"Maybe she got busted," one of the other Chukker girls in yet another Streisand wig said sadly. "It happens too much nowadays!"

I asked her if she was selling bennies, and she said, putting on a very wide-eyed pout, "I don't sell to you. I only sell to people I know."

I asked her exactly *what* did she need in order to get to know me. "I want to buy three rolls."

"OK. That's a good way to get to know you," she said. "Deal."

I gave her the $10 bill with a dollar tip.

The next weekend I went up to Jody and Karen's apartment, and gave her the three rolls. Her eyes lit up. She cracked open one roll and popped one immediately, then gave one to Jody. She offered me one, but I refused. The three of us went back out later to the Rendezvous, walking there. The two of them were flying over the hills, giggling. On the way, Jody asked me if I wanted to smoke some pot. I had never done that before and wasn't sure I wanted to start, so he lit a joint, inhaled it, and handed it to Karen.

"This is going to be some night," she said.

We had no problems getting into the Rendezvous. I guess the fact that they looked old enough not to be carded helped. Once in, they had several drinks, and Karen started to get very loud. I went to a side bar to get a drink, and saw two young, very attractive-looking women, one of whom was blonde and the other was black. They smiled at me, and we started talking.

They were both straight, the blonde told me, but liked going to the Rendezvous because "all the men are so good-looking and none of 'em hit on us. You don't know how difficult it is for a woman to go to a bar and just be left alone."

Suddenly Karen sailed up to us.

"Hi!" she said, loudly. "I'm Karen. What are you two doing here?"

"I'm Geneva," the black woman said smiling. She did look like a model with really beautiful skin and facial features. "This is my friend Laura. We're just hangin' out for the evening."

"Sounds like fun," Karen said. "My husband's over there"—she pointed to a scrum of men across the bar in the loud darkness—"and I don't know what he's doing here *either!*"

Geneva's eyes suddenly popped out as Karen pushed up to her and started kissing the back of her neck.

"Hold off here," Geneva said. "This ain't my scene. I mean it. We only came—"

"I know," Karen answered. "They all say that."

She smiled at them broadly, out of a giddy haze of Benzedrine, marijuana, and alcohol. I grabbed her and got her away, but not before Laura warned me: "If your friend touches *me*, I'm gonna deck her!"

I told Karen I thought we had better leave. I left her for a moment to find Jody, but couldn't. He had just disappeared.

I went back to Karen.

"He does that," she explained. "It doesn't bother me. I mean, unless we're going to have fun with another guy or girl together, we sometimes leave alone."

I offered to walk her back to the apartment.

"It's OK. I know my way back. I think I'd rather be alone."

She looked for a second deflated—actually hurt—despite the Four Seasons pumping a nerve-pinching falsetto *"Sherry . . . Sherry baby! She-erry!"* over a sonic-explosion-loud bass through the freezing air-conditioned air. Why did the Rendezvous *always* seem to be playing the Four Seasons? Karen was obviously crashing already; I figured I shouldn't leave her. I walked down the stairs to the street with her.

Suddenly she started crying.

"I hate it when he leaves me like this. It's just so shitty. I miss Lynn so much. I wish she'd get here. I really made a fool of myself with that girl Geneva, didn't I? But, God, she was pretty!"

I walked her back to her apartment, in one of those slight, misty rains for which San Francisco was famous. She asked me if I wanted to come in, and I did. Jody was there, with a cute, short, collegiate-looking guy in another button-down shirt who suddenly looked too embarrassed seeing me and Karen.

"I think I'd better go," he said. "It's getting late."

He smiled at Jody and left. Now Jody looked like he was crashing too.

He made some coffee, and the three of us sat up for a while talking, with nobody mentioning anything. It was like we could have been back in a college dorm room. Then Karen went into the bedroom to sleep, and Jody asked me if I wanted to spend the night. I wanted to say no, but didn't.

I got up alone the next morning from the couch. Jody was in the bedroom with Karen. I snuck out by myself. It was still raining, and I walked through it feeling almost nothing except the cold rain itself.

A few days later I was facing another week of being close to stone broke. I was saving some money, and had about $30 in a savings account—for a genuine "rainy day." Suddenly, Ryan Fitzgerald called and asked me what I was doing. I told him nothing, and he suggested that he take me out for dinner.

I was delighted. I got into his Lincoln and smiled at him.

"How you doing?" he asked.

I told him fine, but broke.

"That's not good." He reached into his wallet and gave me a $10 bill. "This is just for you, 'cause you're a nice guy. You don't ask questions, that's good—anyway, it's not for services rendered, if you know what I mean."

I didn't say a word but put the bill in my wallet, and we drove out into the suburbs. This time we did not have dinner at the back table of a good restaurant but in the car, at a drive-in. I thought this was peculiar.

"There's some place I want to take you," he said. "It's not far from here."

I had a steak and baked potato. I was famished. Afterwards he started the car again, and we drove on about ten more miles to a wealthy gated subdivision with a guard at the gate who let us through.

We parked in a private, designated space. He had a key that let us into a building that backed onto a garden with a pool. An elevator took us up to the fifth floor, and an apartment for which he also had the key.

"Is this your place?" I asked.

"No, it belongs to a friend of mine. But I can use it on weekends. See, someone else used to live here."

The apartment was large, with light blue wall-to-wall carpeting, and the kind of generic Danish Modern furniture that could have been in a motel—although perhaps a good motel, like one with Picasso prints on the walls.

"How do you like the place?" Ryan said. "Would you like a drink?"

I told him yes—to both. I did like it; it was certainly an improvement on the Waterton, and I did want a drink. He poured a scotch for himself and a rum-and-Coke for me. Light on the rum.

"Let me show you around," he said.

He took me into the kitchen—fine—and the bedroom. He turned on one dim light. It had a large bed, and some suitcases. Then he turned on some more lights, and opened the door to a large walk-in closet.

It was loaded with beautifully hung and arranged clothes, all perfectly laid out in drawers or neatly pressed on hangers.

"Guess who lives here?" he asked.

I shook my head. I had no idea.

"A young man, like you, except he doesn't live here anymore. My friend, you see, was supporting him. He gave him a car, money, this apartment. He sent him to school, did everything for him. The boy, he had everything he wanted because my friend really loved him. My friend's married. He has another life, I can tell you that, but he did everything to make this boy happy. And he had *everything*. See these shirts"—he took out some expensive Brooks Brothers–type button-downs, and showed them to me. "He'd wear them once, that was all, then send them out to the cleaners to be washed and pressed again. He didn't even wear an undershirt with them. That's how spoiled he was."

I could see the anger in Ryan's face. I was sure Ryan was not the type of man to not wear an undershirt. I didn't say a word.

"Then this kid, well, he decided all this was not enough. He started playing around on the side. My friend couldn't be here all the time, of course. But he expected the boy to at least be faithful to him, to not embarrass him and hurt him. But he started to suspect things when he wasn't here—like when he came in, and the place was messed up, like a party had been going on.

"Then finally my friend caught him. He came in unexpectedly late one night and found him in bed with this other boy—and he threw him out right then. Those suitcases are his. He's going to come back and get his clothes soon—I'll have to arrange the whole thing. My friend can't even stand to look at him."

"I'm sorry," I said graciously. I had learned certainly how to be gracious in the South. "Your friend was very hurt. Maybe this boy just didn't understand that."

"I don't know what he understood. Would you like to live in a place like this? I could do it for you."

I didn't answer. Ryan turned all the lights off so that the only light that came in was from the parking lot below. He pulled me to him and started kissing me; he'd never kissed me before. There was something about his breath I didn't like; I realized he wore dentures. I knew what was going to happen, and just let it. He had a nice body, certainly for an "old man." It was trim and athletic. He wore old men's underwear: baggy boxers, a sleeveless T, and high, silk black socks, the kind I associated with lawyers. After he took his clothes off, he actually folded them and put them on a chair. I tossed mine on the floor. There was nothing about them I had to worry about.

I didn't know what to do, like I had no interest sexually in him. He took my head and pushed it toward his cock. Obviously he wanted me to suck him, but I couldn't stand the thought of it. I thought about the boy who had lived here, and realized there was no way in hell I could ever have been that boy. Then I thought: maybe there had been no "friend." Maybe this was Ryan's apartment after all.

I didn't know what to do with his dick. As dicks went, it was cut and acceptable, but as far as I was concerned, it was still on the wrong guy.

"Don't worry about it," he insisted. "It's clean as a whistle. Really. It's OK. It's clean. One thing I learned in the Army was to always keep your equipment clean, if you know what I mean."

I was completely unexcited; shriveled actually. He looked at me in the dim light.

"You're all played out, aren't you? You've given it to too many other men. I know boys like you. Let's just go."

We put our clothes back on silently. We hardly said a word on the way back to the Tenderloin. I felt bad. He was really a nice guy, it's just—I wasn't going to suck his dick and there was no way I could get excited over him. Maybe that was my problem. I wasn't that kind of boy; I *was* different, but now I was thrown into that world, that ugly, silk-black-socks world of men like Ryan Fitzgerald. Even José Sarria knew it: I was looking for something more than Ryan Fitzgerald could give me, and I was never going to be caged up in that apartment.

About a week later, I was in Pearl's and saw Fabian. He asked me how I was doing and noted that I had not been around for a while. I told him about going to the Rendezvous; his expressive mouth suddenly went southward.

"Oh, dear! I hope you got over that place! It's not for really respectable queers, you know that? It's only for those trying to respect something else."

I nodded. We sat down together at a small cocktail table, and he had a glass of wine and I a soft drink. The waiters at Pearl's were not going to be fooled by my fake ID. I needed to talk to somebody, and I told him about Ryan Fitzgerald; I felt embarrassed by it, but needed to get it off my chest.

A shudder went through him. He was wearing a black turtleneck and a black leather jacket with an array of sterling charms, some astrological signs, sewn onto it.

"Those *dirty* old men! All they ever want you to do is suck *their* dick. Or they want to fuck you. You deserve better, Perry."

I suddenly blurted out to him about Rodney, and that I'd been in love with him. "Real love," I said. "As real as it's ever going to get."

Fabian patted my hand, and smirked wisely to himself.

"He's all the way in Nashville, Perry. Just forget about him. That young hustler sounds like bad news no matter what. You need to go on with your life." He jumped up, so that his full very thin frame seemed to pop out at me like a 3-D picture.

"Got to run to the Boy's Room! I hate going here—first you've just *got* to go, then some horrid old man stares at you in the urinal, like they came equipped with a measuring tape. Don't you hate that?"

I nodded. It was true. There was something strangely tense about going to pee at Pearl's—the whole place had a kind of mock *piss* elegance to it, as if real human body functions shouldn't take place there. You had to be in control of everything, or else you would . . . well, there was no predicting what you'd do. Then I realized: it was also an ingrained fear of the cops. The john would be a perfect place for the Vice Squad to plant a guy and nail you. It made going to any bathroom in a gay bar, beach, or restaurant scary. Someone just had to look at you, and you looked back, and then, Bang! You could be arrested. Being gay was like belonging to a very private club, yet no one could ever tell exactly who was infiltrating the membership.

Chapter

10

After Fabian headed off for the men's room, two very wilted flowers sat down at the table with me. They were guys in their mid-thirties, I gathered, but they looked like every joint and muscle in them was at the point of exhaustion. One was about my height and weight, the other considerably pudgier. Both of them had very pale faces, and I noticed slight traces of makeup on them.

"We hope you don't mind," the pudgier one said. "We can't stand on our feet one second longer! It's not that late, and we feel like a bunch of old ladies already."

I told them they were free, absolutely *invited* to sit. Pearl's was getting super-crowded, it was full-blast cruising time, and I could feel that energy, if not desperation, in the air.

I told them my name, and asked theirs.

"My name is Mabel," the pudgier one said. "And this is my girlfriend. She's known as Goosey."

"Charmed," Goosey said to me, extending a very limp hand. "Are you in the *business*, too?"

Suddenly I swallowed hard. What *business* did she mean? For a second, I panicked. I was definitely not going to tell her I was a whore.

"She means *drag*," Mabel explained. "Goosey, does this young man with the complexion of a pink rose look like a drag queen to you? You must think every mother sends her daughter on the stage directly."

"No, I've never done drag."

"Oh, don't worry, you will," Goosey informed me. I asked them where they worked, and they told me it was not the Gilded Cage, but another, less savory bar in the Tenderloin called Whatever's Right. A lot of its customers were straight men who came in late to pick up the girls and be serviced by them.

"It's a tradition that goes back to Shakespeare," Mabel informed me seriously. "We don't hook that much. I mean sometimes, honestly, when it's the end of the month and the rent is due, we do. But basically we're artists, and," he sighed with genuine resignation, "drag is simply the form we use."

I became fascinated with them—except for the slight traces of makeup and looseness of joint (like their wrists could have used a good blast of hair spray to keep them firm), they looked extremely average, sort of like bank clerks in the back rooms who stamp checks, or those worn-out suburban husbands you'd sometimes see at parties who had given up everything so their kids could have a better life.

I told them I never would have guessed they were drag queens.

"I know," Goosey said, tossing her head back, slightly. "We're very plain, aren't we? That's the thing—beautiful men don't look that good in drag. You need a plain-looking guy whose face becomes a blank canvas. When we're in full makeup and wig, we just glow. You should see us!"

I told them that I'd love to.

"Just don't see *her* on a bad night," Mabel said, referring to Goosey.

"It *was* bad," Goosey intoned. "This horrible creature came in—"

"Your boyfriend!" Mabel spat out.

"No, not at all. But he *is* after me," Goosey admitted. "Looks like a cross between a dump truck and a garbage pit, but he's got the mean hots for me. He's sent me flowers—most half-dead—I think he got 'em from Woolworth's. He comes up after the show, wants me to do him, but the truth is, he smells. I mean like very, very bad. I can't bear a man who smells that way. I told him, 'Why dont'cha get some Right Guard or Jade East or something like that?' And he says, 'Honey, you jus' gotta like me the way I is.' What kinda way is that t' talk? I feel like I'm just bein'—"

"Listen!" Mabel broke in furiously. "She got so freaked out t'night, she tore her wig off like a damn whore, and her boob tape too!" Suddenly Mabel calmed down and asked: "Honey, you didn't rip off any skin, did ja?"

"I'm OK," Goosey said. "I jus' gotta have the manager tell this creep, name' Bob, we don't want him around no more." She smiled at me very sweetly, even shyly. I could easily imagine that the two of them had left some small town in Iowa where they had been best friends and bashful Sunday school boys, the kind who used to raise rabbits for a joint 4-H project. "When you gonna come visit us? I mean it."

About a week later, I did. It was on a Friday night, and late, between shows. I decided I should just see them. I managed to get in without any problems. In a bar as bedraggled and tough-looking as Whatever's Right, the bouncer must have figured that if I had the balls to enter, I must have been at least twenty-one, or close. It was densely smoky. The air reeked of cheap cigars, cheaper perfume, stale lipstick, and, like a faulty open toilet, the remnants of certain body functions. It was less than two-thirds full, unlike the packed Gilded Cage. Most of the customers were men, except for some thrift-shop drag queens and a few very sad, tubercular-looking hookers.

But Mabel and Goosey were *superb*. That's the only word for it, especially compared with most of the other no-talents, who merely lip-synced and tried way too hard to look comic book sexy or comic book tough. Instead, Mabel, packed into a fluffy Lana Turner sweater outfit (like a very big-boned Midwestern blonde: one of those never-as-easy-as-you-thought girls who used to date football players), and Goosey, who in drag easily out-swanned many classic beauties from the 1930s (the kind with a just a smidgeon too much nose, like Barbara Stanwyck or Norma Shearer), used their real voices—which, coming from actual "females," sounded wonderful.

"Oh, *daaaarling*," Goosey groaned, professing a genuinely tired place at the fag end of boredom. "So *hard* to find a man who knows how to treat a lady right. Don't you agree, Mabel?"

[Mabel, getting up and surveying the audience, Indian-scout style:] "So hard to find a man period. Any *hard* men out there?"

A roar went up.

[Goosey, demurely:] "Any *fairies*???"

Sudden pin-drop silence, as the "orchestra"—one rye-soaked pianist—went into the opening bars of "There Are Fairies at the Bottom of Our Garden":

"There are fairies at the bottom of our garden!
It's not so very, very far away;
You pass the gardener's shed and you just keep straight ahead—
I do so hope they've really come to stay."

I was hysterical; I thought they were really great *artists*, and they were certainly having more fun than anybody in the audience, who seemed either half shit-faced or blind-horny as they cruised or groped the various hookers and drag queens. One of Bob's truck driver brothers—he must have been—was getting ready to approach me when the show finished. Applause, mostly from waiters and bartenders, rang out. I jumped up to go through a door at the side of the stage that would lead me back to my friends.

Another burly character was waiting back there. He asked me what I wanted. I told him I was a friend of Mabel and Goosey's, and he led me with the lurching, top-heavy gait of Frankenstein's monster back to their dressing area, which had room only for a few beat-up chairs, a cracked mirror, and a mountain of beer crates.

"You came!" Goosey exclaimed. "How'dja like th' show? Cute ain't it?"

I told him I loved it.

"We feel like we're wasted here," Mabel said, bitterly. "But you gotta get into show biz one way or another. We tried out for other bars, and they said, 'Oh, this one's too fat and that one's too skinny—and they don't look so good in drag.' The goddamn liars!"

"She *likes* it here," Goosey explained, "'cause we're headliners. Truth is, we pack the house!"

OK, I found that one a little hard to believe. I grabbed a rickety chair, sat on it, and for a moment gazed at myself in the mirror that was half smudged with cold cream.

"We got one more show," I heard Goosey say, pushing me out of my self-gaze. "Wanna be in it?"

"*Whaaa?*"

"Come on," Mabel said. "It'll be fun! We'll dress you up—you can fit into some o' my costumes. All you gotta do is just walk on the stage, smile, and pretend to be, like, shocked. Drag is like life, you know? I mean all of life's like drag—it's just a big performance."

I thought about it—for one nanosecond—then said yes.

I was wearing so much greasepaint and pancake makeup I thought my face would crack. I was wearing a dark Joan Collins wig, nylon stockings, a corset, falsies, and this large dark-magenta rayon ball gown, like Bette Davis might wear, that covered up most everything else about me. They decided my name should be Pearlette, and Goosey was going to sing, in a very sultry manner, "Night and Day" as I stepped out on the stage and just vamped for the audience and for them.

We went over a few moves for me, and Mabel handed me an old-fashioned, black-handled fan, the kind of that snaps open and closed, as a prop.

"You're fabulous!" Mabel cooed. "Pretty as a picture."

I looked at myself in the streaky mirror, moving my face from full to profile, and wondered. I still didn't think I was *that* convincing as a woman, then realized: maybe a lot of women felt that way, too. That is, if they ever really thought about it.

I realized I was nervous, like suddenly pee-in-my-panties so. I asked about a bathroom. There was a toilet down the hall all the drags used.

"Hurry!" Goosey warned. "We're gonna be on in about three minutes."

I ran down to the john, which of course had to be in use. Finally one of the queens wearing only boy's briefs and falsies came out, and looked at me and started giggling. Now I really felt bad. I managed to get into the small john, and suddenly realized I had no idea how to pee wearing a dress, a corset, and stockings, too.

"How the hell do they do this?" I said to myself as I pushed my pelvis up, managed to roll down my stockings, pull up the dress, and lower my corset and briefs.

After holding it in, I had to let go; I peed, then redid everything.

The piano was playing, and Frankenstein from the backstage door marched up to me.

"They wanna know where you are, Miss. Come on. You're on!"

With that, he pushed me out onto the stage and into the lights.

Mabel, in black, opera-length gloves, had her arm out.

"And this is our cousin, Pearlette, just up from the country—Transylvania! Give her a big hand, Boys. She's a virgin and is looking for a *special* experience tonight."

"I'll give it to *uh*!" offered a booming cigarettes-and-beer-soaked voice.

"No, you won't!" Goosey said protectively.

"How much you wanna bet?!"

Immediately Goosey zoomed over to me, her face crushed with anxiety.

"That was Bob," she whispered. "Now he wants *you*."

I didn't know what to say. My mind went blank, as Goosey recomposed herself enough to start "Night and Day."

All the moves I was supposed to make evaporated; I was frozen. Then I realized something: if I could sell phony magazine subscriptions door-to-door, I could do this. I broke into a full smile, and manned up: using the snap fan as a prop, I became coquettish, flirty, and outright cute. I mean—flirty *cute*—I already knew how to do that. Some of the beefier men in the audience, who looked like longshoremen, were eating it up, grinning and aiming compliments at me, some shoving each other to climb onto the stage, while a few were less complimentary, as in "Who does that bitch think she is?" Or more directly:

"Take it all off! Show us what you got there, Girl!"

I'd already seen Natalie Wood transform herself from Baby Louise to Gypsy Rose Lee, but I was not going to expose my eighteen-year-old chest, hair sprouting on it, on this meager stage. Then Mabel gave me this very strange panicked look, like everything was falling apart in front of us, and Goosey, without any warning, started belting out "There's No Business Like Show Business," which later I learned was a fail-safe signal for the bouncer to call the cops when things got *totally* out of hand—meaning Bob was already stomping onto the stage about to grab her.

She stopped singing. The pianist went on anyway, as Bob *did* grab her, and began drunkenly tearing her smart little frock off, and grabbing at her stuffed brassiere. Then I saw them: four cops in uniform strode into Whatever's Right, and I knew just what I had to do.

Get the hell off that stage immediately.

I tore off to the dressing room, grabbed my clothes, and ran into the john and locked it. There was barely enough room to change, but there was tiny sink and some paper towels to wipe my makeup off. Finished, I cracked open the door. No one was left backstage. Out front they were probably all being lined up for the cops to question. I was underage, with an arrest record and a file in Los Angeles's juvenile court system. There was no telling what was going to happen if I was arrested again. I tiptoed back toward Goosey and Mabel's dressing area, and then saw Frankenstein, kind of lumbering around all by himself.

"Good, I saw yous," he said. "Lemme getchu outta here."

He took me by the hand and led me down a dark passage to a doorway that exited onto an alleyway. God only knew how many drunken sailors must have gone this way at some point. The alleyway was scary in close to pitch-black darkness, but I was very relieved to be free.

I saw Goosey and Mabel the next Saturday at Pearl's. Goosey had a black eye. I felt terrible for her.

"She always goes for the brutes," Mabel said. "And look where it gets her."

Goosey shrugged and tried to act unconcerned.

"So, I like a little man in my man, what's wrong with that? But this Bob—!" She turned to me. "How'd you like your drag debut? Wasn't it fun?"

"No," I said, emphatically. "It was horrible. It's hard enough being a gay boy, but being a girl, too—those men were awful."

Mabel smiled. "Obviously, Perry does *not* have a real appreciation for super-butch types. Y'know, the real McCoy? Truth is I don't either, but show biz sure makes you do strange things."

Chapter

11

The beginning of the holidays approached, and also darker weather, as the bright sparkling days of San Francisco in Indian summer simply disappeared, and I realized I was alone. The holidays do that to anyone, especially to kids on their own for the first time. As a child growing up painfully alone in Jewish poverty in the South, the holidays had never meant that much to me. My father had died in mid-December when I was eleven, and every December afterwards my mother descended both into depression and anger that she had been left alone with two kids and no money. We were the impoverished relations of wealthier people, once poor Eastern European immigrants who had made money in the South from selling dry goods, *schmattes*, mostly to poor black people. In truth, my mother's family had indeed worked hard to get where they were, and made doubly sure that you never forgot it for a moment.

But, in an even deeper truth, they had not worked any harder than the black people who'd worked for them menially in their stores; and when my parents, following one failed business attempt after another, spiraled down into indigence, accompanied by my father's cancer, her family looked down on us with what they felt was a justifiably earned sense of superiority. It was a superiority with a secret inside it—probably one of several painful secrets— that I was not to be admitted into until after her death: that early on my mother had been officially, medically diagnosed as a paranoid schizophrenic, one of the most severe forms of psychiatric illness. This explained those uncontrollable fits of violence she had, often directed at me.

Christmas was hell. My mother throwing things and screaming, or breaking down and crying, while my younger sister and I cringed outside her bedroom, hoping she would not call one of us in. Nancy would flee if she did, and I had to face Mother alone. She would then tell me how stupid I was; that I had no possibility of understanding what was going on; that all I was "good for was books"—I was, in short, a spineless, worthless sissy. Afterwards, she would grab my hand and demand I not leave her, holding on like a vise. Sometimes she would ask me to read to her from the Bible, mostly the Psalms, and I would, until eventually she might calm down.

Then there were those times when she didn't. The screaming, throwing things, and tearing up her bedclothes continued, until I would have to call her doctor, who was not a psychiatrist but would finally send an ambulance around. They would either take her in to the mental ward of the local hospital, or shoot her up with a sedative to knock her out cold. I learned later that she was put on Thorazine, a powerful antipsychotic that produces a zombielike state. As a kid—starting at eleven—I'd had to act like an adult. I'd learned how to cook, set a table, iron my own clothes, sew on buttons, and do all those things that my mother could not do. I'd stopped thinking about love, or shelter, or a home that felt like my own. I'd realized I would never get any of that, until I left.

Now, Thanksgiving meant no place to go. I didn't want to impose on Jody and Karen—they were a couple, after all. Instead, I stayed in my room and read for a while. I was reading Christopher Isherwood's *A Single Man*, and loving it. It was an actual book about someone like myself, though a lot older, but definitely queer and even actually "out," hardly hiding it really, just as I was. But George, the English, middle-aged college professor "single man" of the novel (based somewhat on Isherwood himself) was in the comfortable middle class, and I definitely was not. I could do an approximation of it somewhat, but I was always only too aware of what it was: an *act*, just like Mabel had said. A kind of drag really—like life was. That was all.

I decided around 7 o'clock to go out and get something to eat. As I passed Mrs. Cook's apartment on the first floor, she stuck her head out.

"Perry! Have you got dinner plans for tonight?"

I felt ashamed, but told her I didn't.

"Good!"

She opened her door and led me in. In the middle of her living room was set a table with a large turkey in the middle of it, with all the usual accompaniments, and her son Ray and several of his own friends nearby, as well as a small number of older hotel guests.

"I do this every year," she said smiling. "I want you boys to have someplace of your own at Thanksgiving."

I sat down at the table and almost cried. I had never felt so good about being with strangers. In fact, they were not strangers, at least at that moment. Ray came up to me and smiled. He was wearing his usual super-tight T-shirt and jeans.

"How ya doin'?" he asked. "You getting' enough of what you want?"

I told him I was, although the truth was, I didn't even know what that was. But San Francisco seemed to be the perfect place to look for it.

The time between Thanksgiving and New Year's floated by—or maybe I did, living as I was, so basically detached from the world. That seemed to be the only way I, and most gay young men, could live. If you were gay, you were not really a part of your own family; you could exist with them, but they would never *really* know about you. Ninety-nine percent never knew. You were the unmarried kid who remained a kid, or the eccentric uncle or the odd nephew. I had been in contact with my mother, I wrote letters to her and called her sometimes. She was living with another woman, Esther, a German refugee whose father had been Jewish, whom I hated. Esther seemed to bring out the worst in my mother, and they had a combative relationship with regular flare-ups of temper and loud proclamations of victimhood. My sister, who was twenty-three months younger than I, had already left home at the age of thirteen, putting herself voluntarily into the Savannah Home for Girls, a place for "abandoned girls"—a euphemism for girls who had strayed outside the usual moral boundaries set up for them, often involving crime, pregnancy, or both.

I had gone to visit her a couple of times there. I felt terrible for her. She had reached the point of no return with our mother Helen, whose own code of morality, as a shame reaction to her lesbianism, was wrapped in barbed wire. What I and my mother were was something neither of us could talk about openly; but she was furious about it. She loathed that I was queer—it revolted her. The unfaceable truth was: she had produced one of her own. My father, in his definite World War II way, had been "macho" and solid, a man who loved to talk but rarely said anything about himself. She often spurned his steady, tenderly secure masculinity, as she did everything else, but at least she could depend on it. When he died, she went into a torrent of guilt-laced grief. But I later learned that, even as he had become extremely sick, they were already on the verge of divorce.

They were both physically very attractive. My father had deep blue eyes, curly dark hair, and a very sensuous mouth. My mother was tall and in her youth had a wonderful figure; she was "statuesque" like Bess Meyerson, another gifted young Jewish woman from that period. People looked at Helen on the street. She knew how to dress in a kind of sporty, casual-chic way, which later I realized carried a lot of lesbian coding. When I was twelve or so, she would sometimes take me shopping with her, and the sales clerks would ask, "Miz Brass, why are you takin' that boy clothes shoppin' with you?"

She would say, "He has good taste."

It was true, though I wanted to be a "real" boy, just like she wanted me to be. But that never happened. Instead I became furiously rebellious, and by the end of my fourteenth year was in open conflict with her. She threatened to have me locked out of the house, or sent away to the Bethesda Home for Boys, an orphanage outside Savannah that was opened after the Civil War. I was scared of that, sure I'd be bullied even worse there than at the housing project or at school. But there were moments when I considered it; I would do anything to get away from her. We ended up genuinely hating each other; there was too much to deal with, too much baggage to carry, too much that could not be talked about.

Finally, by the time I was seventeen, both my sister and I realized she was a lesbian. There was no way around it. Even not talking about it did not make it *not* so. It took years for any of us to talk openly about it, but by then there was too much pain inside our family structure, too many lies that you had to tell in the South to preserve dignity, for the truth to make anything less painful.

Pearl's was fabulously decorated for the holidays, with greenery and ornaments all over the room, centered on an upside-down Christmas tree suspended from the ceiling, twinkling with metallic silver icicles and lights the size of small insects. It was like something glimpsed in a scene from a Nordic winter fairy tale. I was awed by it but told that it had become a tradition at Pearl's, one loved by the resident drag star, Charles Pierce. It symbolized the total inversion of the place, the bar attached to it, and then queer San Francisco itself, which existed as a kind of bizarre, sometimes dreadfully painful dream suspended over the city. The holidays were a difficult time for gay men. Most people recognized it—there was that sense of being divorced from family, as so many gay individuals in San Francisco had migrated there to escape the threating innuendoes of their roots "back home."

Drag itself became a little more acceptable at the holidays. There were so many parties, and many of them were "masquerade" ones, even if drag was not so much a masquerade as an inner revelation. You were showing your own female heart; that was the only thing that made sense. Drag was like an arrow, pointing to something most people could still not talk about honestly.

I remember many men that I had gone to bed with waking up in the morning and asking, "Perry, why do you think we're gay?"

I couldn't answer. There was the stock Freudian crap that the popular imagination liked, about overpossessive, close-binding mothers and distant fathers. But that did not seem to fit me. My father had not been distant and my mother and I had a hard time tolerating one another, even though we were both gay.

I decided the question contained a significance that we could not really understand. Heterosexuals didn't ask themselves, "Why are we straight?" And Jews certainly didn't ask why they were Jewish. Being a Southern Jew, a double outsider, I realized early on I could see things in a different way: all Southern Jews were really "queer," just in different ways, because they had to see themselves as cut out of another kind of material than the rest of the human stock down there. I remembered as a small boy riding in the backs of cars with Jewish friends and sitting on the laps of older boys: they just took it in stride. There was something about Southern Jews that still kept a patch of Mediterranean passion inside it, like a taste for something beside white bread and margarine—perhaps a need to use the brain itself as a sexual organ.

I decided that the "Why are we gay?" question was the queer equivalent of kids asking how babies are born. We wanted to know how we came out into the world, what strange twist of circumstances, of being itself, had brought us to this.

Or brought this to us.

Toward Christmas, a lot of servicemen started coming into the bars—I guess they had Christmas leave but didn't want to go home to their families, and San Francisco offered another kind of family, even if only one you had to pick up.

I met Robert, who was about a year older than I was and already had been drafted, at Pearl's. He was a small guy, about five-six, and he looked so fair-complected and fresh-faced that he could have passed for fourteen. He was of course out of uniform, and staying at the Presidio, the Army base within San Francisco. He went back to my hotel room, and between the sheets he was anything but fourteen: we spent the night in an almost constant round of nonstop sex. He knew he was going to be shipped off a few days later, possibly to Viet Nam where war was starting to boil up.

We had breakfast together at the Gene Compton's in the Tenderloin. I felt this huge tug, like I wanted to go with him. Suddenly I realized I had my elbows straight up on the table with my head resting dreamily on my clasped hands.

"Please stop that," he said.

I blinked.

"I never can tell who's going to be in here," he explained. "And you don't look like the kind of guy I should be hanging out with."

I got up a short time later, shook his hand, and he left. He wrote me several times; he did end up in Viet Nam. Then he disappeared. There was something very much like a child in him, trying hard to be a "real" boy, too.

Some of the women at work, realizing I was a long way from home, bought me a white shirt for Christmas, and I bought them bottles of cologne. We never talked about my personal life, although I told them that I went out to bars at night. Christmas Day I had the day off, of course, and I stayed in and painted; later in the early evening I took the cable car up to Fisherman's Wharf and walked around in the dark. It was empty, few people were out at Christmas. In the darkness, with the black water of the bay behind me, I felt like the whole world was out there, and it was waiting for me. I walked back to the Tenderloin, feeling very good.

On New Year's Eve I went to the Rendezvous. It was so packed that I had no problem getting in. Strangely enough Fabian was there; and so were Jody and Karen. Everyone was in this giddy, wild mood, talking to everyone else—unusual really for the Rendezvous, but it was New Year's Eve, a night to let your hair down, and unloosen your collar. Karen told me that Lynn was coming over from England.

"I'm so happy!" she said. "I feel like we're really going to be a family."

"I'm glad you are," Jody said, sullenly. He pulled me to him and started kissing me. He was high. I could tell it. On what, I didn't know. He asked me if I wanted to go home with him, and I told him I'd take a rain check. I wasn't sure if I wanted to go home with anyone at that moment: I was feeling too good, too crazily good—San Francisco at New Year's Eve, at the Rendezvous, with what felt like a thousand guys around me. As the old Gershwin song went, "Who could ask for anything more?"

Fabian approached me with a martini. He offered me a sip. I still wasn't sure about drinking anything that tasted so strongly of alcohol. I was stuck on drinks like tequila sunrises.

"It looks like you're having such a good time," he said wearily. "It's so good to be young like you. Wait till you get to be my age!"

I understood what he meant, even though Fabian was only about twenty-six or seven. I was still "chicken," instantly desirable in this bar culture that existed only at night. But I knew my expiration date was approaching faster than I could imagine.

"You're not so old," I said to Fabian. He lowered deeply set eyelids. His face reminded me of a Carnival mask with a beaky nose. Everyone else seemed to be so giddy, but he wasn't. Of course the Rendezvous was not his favorite place, but at New Year's it seemed like a different bar.

"Sometimes I think about killing myself when I turn thirty," he said to me closely, under the outrageous din of the noise.

"That's terrible," I said. I thought for an instance about the good-looking man I had met at Pearl's and also, inevitably, that I had tried to do it myself at fifteen. The thought was just too awful. I couldn't bear even having it for a second—suddenly I kissed him, like I had never kissed him before. In fact, I *had* never kissed him before. The bar was so jammed that no one cared; usually you could never kiss another man openly like that.

"Wow!" he gasped, and suddenly walked away from me.

I went after him, and asked him why he had left me.

"Perry, you're only feeling sorry for me."

"No," I said, and asked him if he wanted to go back with me to my hotel. He hesitated for a second, then said, "Sure. But let's wait until midnight."

We did, and I kissed him again and also kissed Jody, very quickly. He and Karen were going out to another party, and asked me if I wanted to go, but I had already spoken to Fabian. Jody gave me a very funny look, like why was I with this odd character? But I realized then that I needed to be.

Under all of his black clothing, Fabian's body was scarecrow thin, and so pale it was almost translucent. He was shy at first, then became really passionate, and I responded. I didn't like the way he smelled or his hair, which was coarse and unwashed, but I didn't want him to go off by himself feeling the way he did.

Afterwards, he asked me why I had asked him back to my room. I didn't want to talk about it, then finally confessed.

"I tried to kill myself at fifteen."

"That's so young," he said.

"Thirty's not a whole lot older."

He smiled. He had beautiful dimples really.

"I shouldn't have said that to you. I didn't realize it would bring all that up. My parents have never liked me. I think they hate me. I'm so strange to them; they're Italian immigrants and have a *finocchio* for a son. It's something they can't live with."

"Can you?" I asked.

He shrugged his thin, avian shoulders. It was interesting that he wore feathers. He was like a large bird with his deep, black eyes—wise, intuitive. "I have to," he said. "I don't have a choice."

"That's good," I told him. "That's really good."

I became closer to Fabian after that, although I had *zilch* interest in him sexually. I was not really mature enough to find a man like Fabian beautiful; I was still into preppy-WASPy, military-looking guys, as any Jewish boy from the South would be. I didn't know any other gay Jews. They seemed almost impossible to believe, and the kind of men I'd find at the Rendezvous or Pearl's were trying so hard not to stand out—and then get hammered down—that any kind of ethnicity in them, except maybe "black Irish," was totally repressed and squelched.

But I would see Fabian often at Pearl's, and we would talk while a whole parade of young men crowded around us, usually with older men chasing after them. Or, I would meet him on Market Street, near Powell, and we'd hang out and look at the hustlers and the flow of customer traffic around them. Fabian liked hustlers. He told me that even when he was fifteen and he used to sneak into downtown and try to get picked up, no one ever offered to pay him.

"I just don't have that kind of look," he said. "But you do, Perry."

I only smiled—my stints as a hustler were too horrible to think about. One night a group of four guys, all in their late teens or early twenties, came up to us.

One started screaming to Fabian:

"Hey MISS THING! WHAT YOU UP TO?"

He looked himself kind of like Fabian, dark, skinny, but with better hair, nicer skin, and better clothes. Fabian smiled and introduced the quartet to me.

"This is Dingey David," he explained ("dingey," meaning short for a "ding-a-ling") referring to the loud queen, "and David Pitts, he's Dingey's friend. Who are these new guys?"

They were taller and good-looking and could easily pass for "regular boys," that is, not eccentrics like Fabian or street queens like Dingey David.

They were Oliver and his boyfriend, Steven. They had just come to San Francisco from Boulder, Colorado, and looked it, with a kind of fresh-faced sweetness to them. After their first fifteen minutes on Market Street, the two Davids had approached them; they told me they had been looking for work and had been living in a Tenderloin hotel like I was.

"I'm going to try to find them a job," David Pitts said. He was short, kind of chubby, but dressed nicely in dark slacks and a pearl-gray cashmere sweater. He was a typist in a corporation downtown; he had met Dingey David on Market Street, and they bonded because they both loved classical music. Like a lot of gay boys, both of them had been piano prodigies as kids.

"It was Van Cliburn," Dingey said. "My mom wanted me to be him. She knew I was queer from the year one. She once said to me, 'I don't care that you're not like other boys, David. I just don't want you to end up like some of those fruits you see in Hollywood or San Francisco.' So of course I did!"

Suddenly, a beautiful, slim blond boy approached out of the surrounding dark. At first he looked about fourteen, but as he got closer to me under the streetlights, I realized he wasn't. He was closer to twenty, or even past it.

He walked up to David Pitts with his hands in his jeans pockets and smiled. David wrapped his arm around him.

"Everybody," he said, "This is Ray. Raymond. He's new in town also. He's from Texas, by the border, right, Ray?"

"My name is Ramón," the boy said. "It's Spanish. My parents were Basques, you see, that's why I'm blond. I grew up speaking Spanish. They live in a small town by the border. My sister's still there. They don't know I'm here."

"You mean they don't know that you're a hustler," Dingey David said. "This is David's new chicken—and he's not even a *real* chicken. He's older than all of us!"

"Shut up!" Pitts said. "Don't listen to him, Ramón. Come on, you can stay with me tonight."

The two of them walked off, and I was left with Oliver and Steven from Colorado, Fabian, and Dingey David, who had a constant need for attention that quickly bored me, although in truth he was smart. He had a part-time office job that paid very well, because he already understood a lot about computers before most people did. We had coffee at a small café nearby. I felt good about being with these guys; I needed friends. The gnawing, deep loneliness in me needed them.

Dingey told me about his job. "I figured if I can understand how to play the piano—you have notes; you know, that's like a code?—I can understand anything. I got my gig through a really good agency."

I told him I wanted another job. My pay at the *Journal* was so small I could barely eat on it.

"Just go there," Dingey said to me seriously. "You can pass for smart. I know it."

"But I know nothing about computers," I said honestly. "I'm terrible at math."

"That's not good," he said. "You gotta have some math. But go anyway."

He wrote down the name and address of the agency, and told me the name of the man to see there.

Chapter
12

I called the agency and was told by a receptionist to come in. It was up a flight of stairs on a small side street near Union Square, on a nice block. I had never heard of it before, and went on my lunch hour. The man I was supposed to see was named Jeremiah Leopold. I had no idea what he would look like, but thought he might be Italian or Mediterranean in some way.

The receptionist told me that Mr. Leopold was away, but would be back any moment. Since I had a limited amount of time, I became uneasy. I was given an application to fill out, and was doing it when I heard:

"You're Perry? Come with me."

I looked up. The man was of slightly below average height, very trim, and incredibly handsome, with striking Semitic features, an almost perfect nose, and very sensuous lips. He was also black. I smiled and went back with him to his office.

"You were referred by David Rogers?" he said. I nodded. "He's a smart kid, but a little crazy. I hope you're not going to be like him. He's at entry level for data management. Can you do anything like that?"

"I don't know," I said. I had no idea what "data" was, or how you managed it.

"I'll give you a test," he said. "It's only fifteen minutes. I can tell very fast if you can do this."

He led me to a small room for testing, then walked out. The test was awful. I could not understand most of the questions, and the figures were impossible for me to decipher. When he came back in, I was sweating. I knew I had failed it.

He took it from me, and frowned.

"Where are you from?" he asked.

"Savannah, Georgia," I said.

"That's nice. I like Savannah. Not a great place to be—for somebody like me, but I met some nice people there once." He looked at my application. "I see you studied art. That's what I was doing before I got into this." He handed me his card. "I'll find something for you, better than what you're doing. Would you like to have lunch sometime?"

I told him I would, and gave him the number of my hotel. A few days later he called me, and I agreed to meet him in North Beach where he lived. We had lunch at a small, bohemian restaurant that was frequented by lesbians. After we were seated, a tall, very sturdy blonde woman with short-cropped hair walked up to him. They shook hands, he introduced me to her—her name was Syd—they spoke briefly, then she went back to her own table with several other women.

Jeremiah looked at me.

"She's a wonderful painter," he said. "And a nice woman, not one of those stomping dykes you see in North Beach a lot. She doesn't stomp."

I could only smile. Compared to the women I knew in the South, who made an art form out of being shy and demure, she *did* stomp. Definitely. After lunch we walked around North Beach for a while, then went to his apartment that was on a side street filled with galleries and other arty places. I told him that I had been showing my work at the Starving Artist Gallery, and they had sold some of it.

"That's good," Jeremiah said. "I'm sure it doesn't pay your rent, but it's good. What do you want to do with your life?"

I didn't know. All I wanted to do was what I was doing: making art, being gay, and staying alive. The last two definitely did not mix in Savannah, or most of the South. All I could tell him was that I wasn't sure.

"You need to get some more training. You could become a computer programmer."

"But I'm terrible at math," I protested.

"You don't need math. It's another language. You just have to be good at languages, and I'm sure you are. There are several schools in San Francisco that teach programming. I can show you where they are. We can go up together to some of them."

He got up and showed me some of the artwork he had bought recently, including some small paintings by Syd of women and San Francisco scenes. Since he had stopped painting and was making money, he'd decided to buy art. He sat back down again, and took my hand.

"I really like you, Perry," he said. "I'd like to help you."

I felt funny. He was so much older than I was—probably thirty, at the very least—and he was black, although he looked more Semitic than Negro, like maybe his family had come from Ethiopia or some other exotic place. I was not used to black men—and there was that horrible thing that had happened late at night in Los Angeles.

I got up and told him I had to leave. He asked me if he could see me again, and I said, "Sure."

"Good. I'm having a party here next weekend. Why don't you come to it?"

The party was late in the afternoon on Saturday. It was a beautiful day, a bit chilly but beautiful, and I walked all the way up to North Beach to Jeremiah's apartment. It was in the back, on the third floor, and I was a bit out of breath when I arrived. His living room was packed with an assortment of people, many black, all of them kind of "arty," which made sense because Jeremiah liked those sort of people. Dave Brubeck was playing on the stereo, and people were swaying to the music. Jeremiah came up to me, smiled broadly, and introduced me to most of the people. Then he walked away for a moment to make sure there was enough ice and food. People smiled at me broadly but didn't say a word, and turned away from me as soon as they could. I felt very put down and hurt.

Jeremiah came back, and announced in a loud voice that I was only eighteen and was from Savannah, Georgia, and that I worked for the *Wall Street Journal*.

Everyone started laughing. I hated it. I wanted to leave.

I decided to have a drink first. There was a bar with ice, alcohol, and sodas. I had a Coke, and sat down in a corner by myself.

Jeremiah came by.

"Are you OK?" he asked.

"No," I answered. "Your friends are really rude. Why is everyone laughing at me? Is it because I'm young?"

"No," he said. "Come with me."

He dragged me into his bedroom and shut the door.

"They're all stoned out of their minds," he said. "You're the only one here who's not."

"I don't smoke marijuana," I said.

"Why not?" He sat down on his bed and pulled out a joint from a pocket, lit it, and gave it to me. I had no idea what to do with it. I hated smoking cigarettes—I usually just ended up coughing the few times when I did. He showed me how to keep the smoke in my mouth and swallow it slowly so that none escaped.

I did. Then I coughed. There was a knock on the door.

Jeremiah opened it.

"What are you two doing in here?" a very good-looking, nicely dressed woman wanted to know. "Don't you know you don't disappear at your own party?"

"Sheila, we're not doing anything bad—except I'm teaching Perry how to smoke boo. I think that if he's going to live in San Francisco, he should at least know that." He smiled broadly. "Sheila and I work together," he explained. "She's kind of like me, another hip person trying to stay alive in the business world."

"Oh, no, honey," Sheila said. "I'm not like you. You're way ahead of me." She turned to me. "Jeremiah taught me everything I know about headhunting. But I'm a good study. I did learn as much as I could—mostly, take the money and run as fast as you can."

"We'll be out in a second," Jeremiah said. After Sheila disappeared, he closed the door again, and pulled me to him.

"Will you stay after the party? They are all going to leave soon."

I nodded.

He kissed me on the mouth. He had beautiful lips. His mouth tasted like marijuana. I didn't mind it.

About half an hour later, everybody left.

"That was fun," Jeremiah said. He took his shirt off. He had a very handsome body; it was all beautiful muscle and reddish-brown skin.

"Where are you from?" I asked him. "I mean, where did your people come from?"

"Some were Cubans. I think way back they mixed in with Spanish and Italian Jews at some point. People say I 'look' Jewish, for a black guy. It's true, I do. But I'll tell you where I'm really from."

"Where's that?"

He smiled, like there was this whole devil in his face.

"I'm from some place where I wanna fuck you in the worst way."

He started to take my clothes off, and the rest of his as well. I didn't want him to do that, and I wasn't even sure that I wanted to stay. But I did stay, and he didn't fuck me; we had a very good time anyway.

I saw Jeremiah then at various times, sometimes we'd meet casually after work. Maybe I was looking for a mentor, and he enjoyed the role. He had lived in New York where he had gone to Cooper Union and studied art, and later he'd gotten a degree from Pratt. I asked him once why he had left New York and gone to San Francisco.

"It was a guy," he said. "I was in love with him. Another black man. Tall and really good-looking. He had family in Oakland, and I ended up following him here.

"What happened?"

He paused, like it was hard for him to speak.

"He was killed in Oakland. Murdered. It happens there, too much. I knew I wasn't going to live in Oakland. I had to live in North Beach, where my kind of people hang out—the ones who don't really care if you are black or white or gay or straight. It's different from the rest of the world. That's why I stay here."

We did go to a school that taught programming. It was in a building off Market Street, on the second floor. A receptionist told me that I could start as soon as I wanted to. "Most instruction is one-on-one. It's a two year program, but a lot of young people stay on for another year or so."

Jeremiah smiled. "I told you," he said. "It could be four years. But you'll get the money back when you start working."

"How much is it going to cost?" I asked the receptionist.

"We're very reasonable. About $3,000 a year. Considering that so much of our instruction is one-on-one individual—you can't get that at other schools."

My face hit the floor. I had no money at all. I walked out with Jeremiah.

"Can't you get it from your parents?" he asked.

I shook my head slowly. I didn't want to tell him: my father was dead;

my mother a violent, abusive schizophrenic who was in and out of mental hospitals; I had grown up in a public housing project—I had nothing. There was no money.

"I don't know what you're going to do, Perry," Jeremiah said. "I can't place you if you have no technical training at all. Your friend David has the kind of mind that works well with computers. You don't. I can't even get you an entry-level job that might lead to some training."

"What should I do?" I asked.

"I don't know. You should find some way to get yourself back in school. You'll really just descend down to kid hustler level if you don't. I've seen it happen a lot here. Young guys come here thinking the streets are paved with gold, but they end up *on* the streets—and it ain't gold, believe me."

I didn't know what to do. I just knew that I had to survive on a very day-to-day level now. Jeremiah seemed to belong in a world that I was locked out of—that world of the hip who could still make money. They were hustlers in their own way, too, but I didn't know that then. I really knew very little, except what I was looking for: a place to be myself, and find love.

Chapter

13

I knew there had to be some other way to make money, and I was just not going to end up hustling on the street. The next couple of weeks seemed to go by slowly. It was February, the slowest short month in the calendar, the one before spring happens. I was doing my mail-boy work at the Journal in my sleep, it bored me so much. In my hotel room I drew and painted and wrote poetry. Despite everything I felt very happy, free, except for the money thing hanging over my head.

I was usually paid on Wednesdays, and there were days when I simply ran out of money by the end of the weekend. This meant that the first two days of the week I'd have to carry some kind of lunch from home, often a hard-boiled egg or a bologna sandwich. There were times when I was light-headed with hunger by the time Wednesday came around. One weekend I was close to that state, but I decided to spend the last money I had washing my clothes at a laundromat a few blocks from my hotel.

I put my everything in a pillowcase, and trudged over there. I liked the laundromat; it was warm on a cold day and filled with Tenderloin characters—street hustlers of various sexes and genders, tough-looking sailors who kept to themselves, and a few elderly derelicts who had been in the Tenderloin all their lives, crammed into hotels like the one I was living in. I had started reading a book when a woman suddenly approached me.

She was a middle-aged, dyed blonde, but slim and vivacious.

"I would love to find some watercolors," she said.

Those were her very first words to me. I blinked.

How did she know that I . . . ?

"You would?"

"Yes, my room here is so drab, and I'd love to have some watercolors to put in it. You don't happen to have any, do you?"

"Yes. I do."

She smiled radiantly at me.

"Can you bring them?"

I ran back to my room and brought her a whole group of watercolors I had done. She looked at them, overjoyed.

"These are beautiful," she said. "But I don't have a lot of money."

"Neither do I," I said.

"Will you take $5 for one?"

I immediately said yes, and had her pick one. Then I threw in another for her as a gift. She took both of the watercolors, one was of flowers, very colorful, the other a scene from out my window, and disappeared.

I never saw her again, but I thought this was an amazing sign, like an angel had appeared in my life asking me for exactly what I had. I have always believed in the reality or believability of angels, and here was one of them. Her $5 meant that I could eat for a few days—I could really stretch it, until I got paid on Wednesday.

As February slogged on very slowly, I knew I had to look for another job. I started combing the papers and looking for work. Again the story was that either I was too young, or not educated enough, or that bosses were afraid I was going to be drafted immediately.

Finally I saw another ad that seemed to be perfect for what I was looking for.

Chapter
14

Ambitious young men sought to enter the exciting world of educational publishing. Will provide training, if you are the right man for the job.

I called and told the receptionist, a young woman, that I was applying for the job I had seen listed. She told me to come in the next day at lunch hour and speak to her boss.

The next day I nervously approached the office, which was a short walk from the *Journal*. It was on the second floor; the girl at a counter smiled at me, and then ushered me into a second room. There I saw five guys, roughly my age, seated on folding chairs, hunched over the writing pads in front of them.

A very well-dressed, fair-complected young man in either his middle or late twenties was addressing them.

"I want you to take down *every* word I say," he said forcefully, like a drill sergeant. "So pay complete attention. We call this the 'Invocation.' You'll learn every word by heart. It is what will earn you *more* money than you ever *thought* you could make."

A pad was handed to me, and I sat down too.

"Good evening, I can tell by your home that you really care about your youngsters. They are the hope of the future, and we know that you want them to have the best future available to them. You can scrimp on a lot of things in life, but their education is the *last* thing you want to scrimp on. We can tell you are not the kind of people who will shortchange their kids, after all you want them to have *everything* in life that they deserve. That's why we have picked your home as models for the rest of the community. We want to be able to tell other customers that if they have any questions about the value of our product, they can come to you, because you represent everything that is good about this neighborhood."

I felt lost for a second, and yet, strangely, not lost. Like . . . I'd heard all this before. The *spiel*, the pitch, the "you're-going-to-get-something-for-free" hook dangled before the gullible customers—yes, I had heard all of that before. So my first thought was: I want to get the hell out of here.

But my second thought was: I'm barely eating on what I'm making at the *Journal*.

I stayed, and wrote down every word. The fresh-faced young man came up to me afterwards, smiling and offering me his hand.

His name was Jim Hodges. He was from Ohio, recently married and new in San Francisco. He was very happy to see me and delighted that I was from the South and still had a heavy Southern accent.

I asked him what were they selling.

"We're not selling anything, " he said earnestly. "It's an *opportunity*. That's what we're offering. Have you ever heard of *Collier's Encyclopedia*? It's one of the great books of the world, after *Britannica* and *World Book*. What we're offering is a free placement of the books. You place a set in a home for free. They just agree to get the next ten years of updates, at only $20 a year, plus some small handling charges, and you get $40 for every set you place for free. A lot of our representatives place three sets a night: that's $120 a night. Do you think you'd like to make that kind of money?"

I blinked.

I felt like my breath had been taken away from me. I had been making about $50 a week, and barely able to eat on it. This was door-to-door, like selling those magazine subscriptions in LA, but these people didn't seem as sleazy as the mag guys had been, although the hook—offering people something for free—was always the same. I didn't want to think about it, but it was there: the constant sucker bait of the American Dream itself, endless as all those fabled dangling *opportunities* exposing themselves in front of you, like the great, endless landscape itself between Georgia and California.

"This *is* an opportunity," Jim said to me—there it went, that word again. I nodded. "I'll train you myself. You'll be my *guy*. Do you want it or not?"

I still hesitated. His eyes bore into me.

"Can I think about it?"

"No. This is more money than you thought you'd ever make. I like you, Perry. I like the way you look, and that accent is very nice. So it's either yes or no."

What could I say? No one at the *Wall Street Journal* had ever said to me, "I like you, Perry." I shook his hand, and told them I'd quit my job that day.

The next evening, I went out with Jim Hodges and about six other salesmen selling the books. We would start off at a California hamburger place, eating dinner. Jim bought me a burger, and I was excited to start. I simply tagged along with him as he rang doorbells and got rejected a lot, mostly by housewives, but he also managed to make several "appointments" for later in the evening.

The appointment, done usually after 8 o'clock, was the important thing. That was when you had both parents together, and you could "hook in" both of them. You would show them samples of the books, and give them brochures with charts that told them that homes with *Collier's* had fewer cases of juvenile delinquency, high school dropouts, drug abuse, and other social ills, and also their kids did better on those all-important college applications. The word "college" usually got both parents smiling. It was important to get both on board. You also told them what a deep honor it was to be the "models" on their block, with their free set of books displayed in a special bookshelf that would come with them, and also all that very important, neighborhood *prestige* the books afforded.

"Believe me, all your neighbors will look up to you," Jim promised.

At that point, once they realized that they'd get a "free" set of *Collier's Encyclopedias* for simply keeping the encyclopedias up to date for twenty years—"Some people want us to do it for thirty, but we're already losing money with this offer"—you could get them to sign, and I saw Jim sign up two couples that first night.

I was dazzled. I thought, this wasn't like selling mags in LA door-to-door . . . no, sir. This was definitely *above* it.

I went back to my dingy hotel room that night excited and also scared. What would happen if they found out (1) I was a terrible salesman because, deep down, I still found it impossible to believe in myself as well as these things I was selling? And (2) I was queer? There was only one recourse: I'd have to keep both of these characteristics of mine a very deep secret.

The next day I arrived early at the *Collier's* office—usually we were supposed to get there about 2 o'clock to be driven to a designated territory, but Jim told me to arrive at 1 so that I could meet his boss. Jim was there, and frowned at me.

"Don't you have anything better to wear?" he asked me. I was wearing a sports jacket, tie, and sweater. "You look like some college kid instead of a professional."

I smiled. "Maybe that's not so bad," I said. "I am eighteen."

"OK, but we want to get you into a suit as soon as we can. We—"

Suddenly this fat man in an extremely tight but only too obviously expensive-looking dark-gray, sharkskin suit came rushing out of a side office, slamming the door behind him. He had a puffy, fat-cheeked face like a large underwater leech. All you saw was mouth and eyes.

"Jim-boy! You got your newbie here for me?"

"Yes, Mr. Schtipting, this is Perry Brass. He's from the South. I think he's got real talent."

A viselike grip was extended to me, pumping my hand, almost crushing my fingers in it.

"I'm Jack Schtipting. Me and my brother Robert run this operation. Where are you from in the South?"

"Savannah," I said. "On the coast."

He grinned hard like Jackie Gleason did, like the way he shook hands.

"I know where Savannah is! I been there drinkin'. That's what everybody does in Savannah. It's a great drinkin' town. You gonna make so much money, young man! You're gonna be a winner! A winner! I can smell it! I know it! I love Southerners—that accent. It's almost like an English accent, y' know that? People love it. It's classy. It's got this . . . classy thing. Know what I mean? They just wanna listen to it!"

"Thank you," I said, smiling as much as I could. I felt if I smiled any more my face would peel off my head, but I had to keep up with the wattage of this guy.

"We're gonna treat you fine. You're gonna do *soooo* good. You're gonna crack *sooo* fast. I can see it now!"

I kept nodding and smiling, until Jack Schtipting disappeared back into his office.

"He's something, isn't he?" Jim said to me. "You know the Invocation by heart yet?"

I told him I was working on it.

"Good! I want you to start working on appointments with me today. Even if you muff the Invocation, you'll still get some experience doing it."

I lowered my voice.

"What did he mean by 'crack'?"

"That's when you crack open your briefcase, show 'em the brochures and the sample volumes, and make your first sale. We want you to crack *fast*, Perry. We know you got it in you."

He put his hand on my shoulder and kept it there for a moment, looking directly into my eyes. Then several other men approached, and he released it.

That day I went out with Jim and three other young salesmen in Jim's car. They were all about as new with the company as I was, all white, and mostly with no college. One, a redhead named Bob Howard, had already cracked. He was full of himself, preening and talking about it to impress Jim.

"I knew I got 'em when I told 'em I was about ready to get married and I'd make sure I had *Collier's* in my home even before I bought my first TV." He smiled broadly, showing a mouth full of big teeth. "I don't know what got to 'em more—that I was gonna get married or the TV thing? Imagine, you'd git these books before you'd even git your first TV set!"

I was in the front seat with Jim, while Bob Howard was in the back. I could see Jim looking at him in the rearview mirror.

"We don't like you guys to lie," Jim explained. "But you can certainly stretch the truth a bit."

"I am gonna git married," Howard insisted. "What d'ya think I am? Some kinda queer?"

Jim chuckled. He was completely in control.

"Nobody thought that," Jim said. "But keep that kind of language down. You can forget and end up saying something like that in somebody's house. Sometimes their kids can hear it, and the parents—well, nobody likes that."

"Yeah, I know," Howard said, sullenly. "We're in San Francisco. So no matter what, you can't even punch one in the mouth."

"Why would you do that?" a somewhat older guy next to him named Gerald Kennedy asked. Gerald and I had spoken to each other; I learned that he was a seminary dropout. He had wanted to be a priest and then realized it wasn't for him. He told me that he had no working skills at all, so the *Collier's* opportunity had appealed to him.

"Why??? What th'—sorry, Jim. I know I'm not s'posed to say stuff like that. S'pose one of 'em comes on to you? Like you're in the john and one of 'em starts acting funny around you?"

Everybody laughed.

"You been hanging around johns, now?" Jim asked. I looked at his face in the rearview; Jim's eyes darted toward me. I pretended to be a million miles away.

He parked the car in another suburban area, and then we broke into teams, kind of like Mormon missionaries. I was with Jim again, as he made appointments, and then he put me on my own.

Nervously I rang the first couple of bells. I thought my heart would stop every time someone came to the door. At first it was only the maids, then a wife appeared. I couldn't get anywhere with them. All the words would not come out. I was stammering, sweating. This was a lot more involved than the magazine subscriptions. There was more at stake, I knew. On my tenth ring though, I made an appointment. I felt like I could breathe again.

We met up for dinner, hamburgers again. Jim was very proud of my appointment, and told me that he would "bring it home," that was sales talk for complete the sale.

He looked at me, and smiled.

"I can tell you're not ready to crack yet, but you're on your way."

Bob Howard had made six appointments and was crowing about it. Gerald had made three, but seemed disappointed about it—like he had wanted more, and it just had not happened—while Jim tried to cheer him on and inflate him. The third guy in the car, Frank Oglesby, had disappeared. He came back to the restaurant a short time later with another man, who strode in beside him.

He was gorgeously dressed in a very expensive Brooks Brothers suit and a thick, camel hair overcoat. I was introduced to him: he was Alex Tournier, a district manager and Jim Hodges's immediate boss.

Alex grinned at me, like I was a puppy in a store who had caught his eye. He had beautiful, clear skin and fabulous dark hair that was perfectly styled, so that each thick lock of it knew exactly where to stay. He took me aside.

"I've heard you haven't cracked yet, Perry. Don't worry. It'll happen. Jim likes you a lot. That's important."

After dinner, Frank was to go off with Alex, to watch him close sales, and I would continue with Jim, Bob Howard, and Gerald Kennedy. As we were walking toward Jim's car, Alex grabbed my arm and led me toward his. It was an immense, new dark blue Cadillac. It looked like a yacht parked next to a bunch of rowboats.

"Just remember this, Perry. I didn't get this this car and this coat by being the world's nicest guy. Get what I mean?"

I nodded.

The next evening, I still didn't crack. Things were getting tense, and there was more pressure put on me. Even Jim, who had been really nice, was starting to ask me what was wrong. "Do you have your whole heart in this? You've got to have that, you know? People can tell it if you don't."

I took Jim's advice seriously. I went over every word of the Invocation until I could say it backwards. I studied all of Jim's mannerisms and movements, copying them whenever I could. He had a way, for instance, of taking one of the sample volumes of *Collier's* out of briefcase to show the couple, and dropping it. That way, usually the husband would pick it up, then would leaf through it on his own. The volume we were given had the see-through pages of the Human Body, and also a great display of color photos of the solar system. It looked really impressive. Jim would say, "Just keep it for a moment, Ralph"—or whatever the husband's name was.

That way, the husband has his hand on the book, and wasn't going to let go of it. In fact, Jim told me, "Don't even try to take it from him. Let him pass it to *her*."

At the end of Friday's work, I felt really bad. I hadn't cracked and I was sure that at any moment they were going to let me go. I had enough money saved for only another week or so at the Waterton, and the weekend before me didn't look good.

Jim drove me back into town, to let me off on Market Street not far from my hotel.

He parked for a moment.

"I want you to work out," he said. "I really like you, Perry. You can tell, some of these guys here don't have the brains you do. You just got to see this as the most important job in your life. That's what sales is all about. You've got to believe you can succeed before you *can* succeed. You've got to tell yourself you're a really *big* winner, and not accept anything else."

For a second or so, he just beamed at me. I could feel this positive energy of acceptance coming straight through him.

I nodded and thanked him. Suddenly he put his right hand on my hair and ran it through it. I had no idea what was going on. Jim was married—I knew that—and lived out in the suburbs himself, without any kids. I couldn't tell if he was making a pass at me, or just trying to keep me working because at that point, if I quit before they fired me, it would reflect badly on him, too.

I thanked him again, and left the car. He waved to me as he drove off.

I felt really good about going back to Pearl's on Saturday night. It was wonderful to be back in a queer environment that I knew to be so much more truthful that anything at *Collier's*. I saw my friend Fabian there. He smiled at me almost wistfully.

"Perry, where have you been?" he asked.

I told him about my job working door-to-door.

"It's a totally straight environment," I said. "I have to pretend every moment."

He sighed. He was wearing total black and a long cape; like he should have hailed from Transylvania, but on Fabian that Gothic look was normal.

"In that case," he said, "you need a good dose of the gay world. We should hang out on Market Street for a while."

We left Pearl's. Market Street not far from Powell was buzzing with hustlers, gay kids, and assorted johns. I saw Raymond, David's hustler friend, and then David Rogers, aka Dingey David, showed.

"Hey girl!" Dingey David screamed to me. "Where you been? Ain't seen you in a long time. Did you ever get it on with Jeremiah Leopold?"

I wasn't sure how to answer that. Raymond looked sullen. I knew that sometimes he hung out with Dingey David, just for company, but he always had a superior attitude toward him, which David would easily spit back into his face.

"Would you pipe down," Raymond said. "You're scaring all my customers away."

David laughed.

"Why don't you get yourself a real job before you turn into a fat old queen?"

Raymond didn't answer him, but just walked away, then turned back to him.

"Screw you," he said softly, then disappeared.

Suddenly David Pitts showed up.

"Where's Raymond?" he asked Dingey David.

"*Ramón*, you mean?" he asked, parodying Raymond's supposed Spanish roots. "She'll be back. One way or another, she'll be back. There are so many johns out here tonight, and they all like her type: boy-boys. Not that Raymond really is one."

"I told him I didn't want him coming out here. You know I can take care of him."

I felt bad for David Pitts. He had a big crush on Raymond, or Ramón. There was something so appealing about him. He had a genuine aloof but vulnerable James Dean quality to him. It was true, even if most of the rest of him was just an act.

The two Davids walked off, and I, looking at the hustlers on the street, thought about that for a second. All of them had an act, pretending to be straight when they weren't, or pretending that they hustled only for the kicks of it, and not actually to pay the rent. Suddenly I realized that a car had been circling the block and slowing down in front of me.

It was a small black compact, and in it was a middle-aged, dumpy-looking guy, balding with glasses.

"Want a lift?" he asked.

I got in and smiled at him.

"What's your name?" he asked.

"John," I said. "John Wilkes."

"Like Booth?"

I smiled. "I'm from the South," I said, then it just came out of me: "I'm in medical school and I need some money for textbooks. Do you think you can help me?"

"That depends on if you help me."

He grabbed my hand and put it on his crotch.

I told him that I wanted $20, and he asked me what I'd do for it, and we negotiated the whole thing. He was staying in a motel out of town, and we went there. I made sure that he paid me first, before I got into bed with him. He was short, kind of stubby down there, and he smelled bad. I hated doing it—but I was getting so low on money that I was glad to do anything.

Very early the next morning, before sunrise, he drove me back to Market Street, which was all boarded up. We didn't go through any of the protocols of exchanging anything beyond my fictitious name. I slept through most of Sunday, but at least I had enough money to carry me through the week.

Chapter

15

Monday was a special day in the Collier's office. When I got in, Jim Hodges informed me that there was a regional sales meeting that we'd need to go to later in the afternoon. "It's at a hotel out of town. You'll love it. They have one once a month—the company buys you dinner. Not much of a dinner, but that's not the point."

I noticed that there were a lot of guys coming in for the meeting whom I had never seen before. They were older, many in their early to mid-thirties, dressed very sharply. Jim introduced me to several of them. Bob Howard appeared and gave me his usual big, toothy smile. I could tell Jim was put off by him but had to pretend to like him. When he was out of earshot, Jim said, "That guy takes up too much oxygen, even for a salesman."

I smiled. I noticed that Gerald, the ex-seminarian, was not around, and asked about him.

"He went belly-up," Jim said, using the term for when you ran out of balls, or the determination or stomach to sell: like dead fish do in a stagnant pond. "We were going to fire him anyway. He didn't have the right attitude."

Suddenly Jack Schtipting strode out of his office and went to the front of the room. You could hear a pin drop instantly. Everyone shut up.

"Really nice to see all you guys here. You are part of the *Collier's* family. You are all like family to me, and you better know it. Speaking of family, you all know my brother Robert, head of the Sacramento office?"

A man who looked like a thinner and older version of Schtipting walked up to the front and raised his hand.

"All my guys from Sacramento, let's see who you are?"

Several guys raised their hands and started shouting:

"SACRAMENTO! SACRAMENTO! SACRAMENTO!"

Robert Schtipting smiled exactly as his brother did—in that same frozen-eyed shark kind of way.

"We're gonna cream you San Francisco sissies in the next month. Know that? We are setting such quotas for ourselves that you're either gonna go belly-up or work your tails off. No rest, get it?"

"OK, OK," Jack Schtipting said. "Down boy. We'll do all that at the sales meeting. The truth is, I love all of you! Every one of you! You're my family. But like any family you need to know what is good for you, and what is not. Some of you are starting to feel about *Collier's* like it's just another job, and not your whole life. I get it. You got families, wives, kids. But they ain't payin' the bills. *You* are. And in sales, everything is your attitude about yourself. You either got to love it or leave it. I see some sharp suits in here, and I'm glad. I wanna see Cadillacs in the parking lot today. I want to see that you are putting your own wallets where your mouth is—you are showing us you *are* successful. Like Alex here. Alex stand up!"

Alex Tournier stood up beaming 150 percent. He was wearing another expensive suit, and his hair looked like it had just come from the stylist thirty seconds earlier. He did a sharp one-eighty-degree turn around, so that everyone could take a look at him.

"Alex is what I want you guys to look like, and drive like. You gotta believe in yourself. 'Cause if you *won't* believe in yourself, I won't either, and you're gonna be outta here. Just remember that."

I rode in the back of Jim's car to the sales meeting. It was filled with other young men, some of them who'd come in from Sacramento. Everyone was extremely friendly, yet guarded at the same time, like the friendliness was ironed on to their faces, and they knew just when to take it off. Sometimes I looked at Jim in the rearview mirror and our eyes met. I wondered if he had any idea what I was thinking: that this was a hustle that was only another brand of what happened on Market Street, except that the hustlers there were hounded by the cops and despised by so-called normal people.

The meeting was in a banquet room of a second-class motel. About a hundred men were there, from all parts of Northern California and some neighboring areas, as far as Oregon. Both Schtipting brothers got up and made speeches, and then a few words—very few—were said by Alex and some of the other district managers. Then, as Jim told me, "the good part" started.

The district managers and regional managers started betting on who would bring in the most sales. Everyone had to put in some money, except for the newbies and people like me who hadn't cracked. The money was considerable, sometimes several thousand dollars. Like Jack Schtipting telling us that we should all buy Cadillacs and look sharp, the idea was to go out on a limb and risk or invest as much of yourself as possible, deeply, on a gut and wallet level.

"Who believes in himself?!" Jack roared.

"I DO!" the whole room roared back.

"Who is gonna break every sales record this month?!"

"WE ARE!"

Suddenly I felt like the air had been knocked out of me. How could I ever come up to this level of commitment, for something I didn't believe in at all? Then I realized the only thing I did believe in was my own survival, and that would get me through this.

You could feel the tension and excitement in Jim's car, as he drove us out to the evening's territory. The food at the sales meeting again had been hamburgers and french fries, so at least I wasn't too hungry. After he had parked and the other guys had left, he said to me, "Perry. This is your night. You're going to crack tonight. I can feel it. Now just believe in yourself enough, and go out there and make appointments."

I did. I felt like a new person was taking over. I just wasn't convinced that this new person was strong enough and as completely dominant over the old one—the Jewish kid who had grown up in a public housing project knowing he was secretly queer—as he needed to be. But this new person was aggressive enough to get me two appointments.

I told Jim about it, and gave him the addresses.

"I'm not going to go with you on these," he said, confidently. "They're for you alone. But I might pop in later, just to see you close."

The first appointment was with a Hispanic couple, the Gonzálezes, who lived in a nice but definitely "lived-in" house with their three kids. I noticed broken-looking kids' bicycles and other toys in the front yard, and the furniture looked forlornly secondhand. Mr. González worked in a factory as a foreman, and Mrs. González stayed home, but I could tell she wanted more.

"I want my children to know about things," she said to me earnestly.

I nodded and smiled at her, then him, sitting next to her on the couch.

Now was the time to go into my own hustle, my own act. I'd thought about it—what kind of person was I going to play to sell people these "free" books.

"I can tell you do, Mrs. González. These books will bring the whole world to them. I'm a student in medical school and I have a full set of *Collier's* at home. It's what's getting me through college."

The word "college" lit both of them up. They smiled, and I brought out the sample volumes and dropped one on the floor, and asked Mr. González to pick it up. He did, and leafed through it. Then suddenly the light in his face went out.

"I don't think we can afford these," he said. "We don't have anything like this in the house."

"But don't you want your kids to have things that you didn't have?" I asked.

His wife nodded.

"We do."

"This will bring those things to them, Mrs. González. They will be able to have things you never had. I know that. I'm the first person in my family to go to college, too."

That was the truth. I had been, before I dropped out after one year at the University of Georgia, a place I loathed.

The both of them just looked at me, and for a moment I felt completely lost. I kept thinking about what Jim had said, about this being the only job I would have in the world. Suddenly I felt terrible. My only job would be to lie to these people.

I took the volume from Mr. González's calloused hand, and handed it to his wife, but she put it down without even looking at it. A moment later there was a knock at the door, and Jim Hodges came in. I introduced him as my manager. He smiled at them and the words just flowed out of him.

"I know you have a lot of questions about *Collier's Encyclopedias* and why we'd want to have them in your house—you see, Mr. and Mrs. González, we want other hard-working people like yourself to see what these books can do for their kids. That's why we'd be honored to have them in your house. We can see you are truly *serious* people who are serious about your kids. What are their names, and ages?"

They started talking about their kids, and Jim knew exactly what questions to ask about them. How they got along in school; who were their playmates; what kind of future did this couple see for them?

He brought out the application, and started filling it out for them. I felt terrible. Like shit. He was pushing it on them—and this innocent couple had no idea what kind of debt they were getting themselves into. Then Jim asked me to wait outside.

"There are some things I want to talk alone to the Gonzálezes about."

I waited in their front yard, sitting on a rusted lawn chair. It was a beautiful night, and there were lots of stars in the sky. About fifteen minutes later Jim came out.

He shrugged his shoulders to me.

"We couldn't sign 'em," he said. "No fault of yours, Perry. I don't think they were great credit risks, but—"

I got up.

"What?"

"I could tell you just weren't putting out enough energy for them. You got to get them so excited about this that all they want to do is rip out their wallets and sign up. They'd sign up for anything. That's what a good salesman can do."

I nodded to him. I felt pretty enervated suddenly, but as I walked over to the next appointment in the night's territory, I told myself I could do it. I had to. At that moment what else did I have going for me?

The next appointment was at a much better-looking house, but the people in it were not as welcoming at the Gonzálezes. They were a well-off Anglo couple. A blond, hip-looking attractive young wife, one you could imagine in a yoga class in a leotard, with a middle-aged, quiet, very serious husband. Almost as soon as I walked in, he tried to throw me out.

"I don't know what my wife said to you, but we're not interested in whatever you're selling."

I told him I wasn't selling anything, but I was trying to work my way through medical school, and I believed in the educational effect of having *Collier's* in the home.

His face lit up. "I'm a doctor myself," he said as he led me into their den.

"I understand what you're going through. Where are you studying? Do you have a specialty yet? You should think about dermatology. That's what I'm in. If you need any references for a fellowship in dermatology, I'd be happy to work with you."

Now I felt like I was on the thinnest ledge I'd been on in years. I told him that I was going to school in North Carolina and taking a semester off—"so I can afford the next one," I said seriously. "See, there's no money at home. My father's dead (the truth), and my mother's—well, she has psychiatric problems."

He looked at me very thoughtfully, and put his hand on my shoulder.

"I really do feel for you, young man. Tell us all about these *Collier's* books."

I did, I went through the whole *schmear* with the books, then I realized something. Even if you did get them to buy who you are, it doesn't mean that they will buy the craziness of what you're selling—at least not from me.

After I had said what I needed to, I knew it: it was as plain as their own faces. *I didn't crack again.* Jim didn't come up to the house this time, but I left with Dr. Woodman's card in my pocket.

"Like I said, young man, if you need me as a reference for dermatology, let me know. You should come around to my office, and see what it's like. I think you'll like working with skin. It's a great field."

On the drive back into town, Jim didn't say much to me—just that he'd see me the next day at the office. But as I got out of the car, he said to me, "Don't give up, Perry. I like you. You know that."

I had a hard time sleeping that night. I kept thinking: How many lies am I supposed to tell in order to do this? There were so many lies I had to tell being gay. It was like your whole life was a lie; but I had learned that already, growing up in the South where my very existence was constantly questioned and threatened.

I got into the office, had some coffee and a doughnut, and said hello to some of the other salesmen. Jack Schtipting came out of his office and asked me to come in.

I did, and he shut the door. For a moment he looked around, like he wasn't exactly sure what to do with me.

"How ya doing, Perry?" he asked gruffly.

"OK," I said.

"Then how come ya ain't cracked yet? What's wrong with ya? Most guys crack in half the time."

I knew this wasn't exactly true. I had spoken to some salesmen who told me that it had taken them weeks to crack—but I also realized they were different. They were married, looked more solid, manly. They had families. You could see it all over them: that wary look in their eyes, the seriousness of them, also a kind of feeling of always being inside the club. They were playing ball for the home team, and they knew it.

I looked into Schtipting's square, very fleshy face. There was nothing noticeably interesting about it. Except for his eyes. They were always filled either with anger or hunger.

"I'm trying hard," I said.

"Let me ask you something, Perry, straight off. *Are you normal?*"

I looked at him and smiled. This I could do. I hated him.

"Sure," I said. "I'm as normal as you are."

"Then prove it. I want you to crack tonight. I don't care what you do to do it, but I want you to do it."

I got up and shook his hand and told him I would. He looked at me completely convinced, or at least not letting me know that he wasn't. He gave me his bone-crushing handshake, and after I extracted my hand, I looked at him for a second.

Suddenly I realized exactly what Jack Schtipting was: he was about 275 pounds of bullshit upholstered into an $800 suit.

I really started smiling at him, and walked out his office.

That afternoon making appointments I hardly cared what I did. But an interesting thing happened. I knocked on a door in an old apartment complex and a middle-aged, dumpy-looking man with several days' growth of beard answered.

When I told him what I was doing, he smiled.

"Which Schtipting do you work for, Jack or Robert?"

I told him Jack.

"What do you think of him?"

I told him "not much," but said that I liked a lot of the other guys, especially Jim Hodges, my manager.

"I don't know him. I know some of the older salesmen. I used to work for him. He'd eat his own mother for a dollar, but most people know that. You know he was thrown out of South Africa? That's where their whole scam started, in Cape Town. He led the Cape Town office, until the government threw them out. The whole thing's a fraud, and the South Africans knew it. They only sold their 'free' encyclopedias to white people, of course. That was their problem. You can't fuck with the whites there."

"What do you do now?"

"I still sell books. I just don't do *Collier's*. I sell *World Book*—we don't have to resort to the lies and tricks the Schtipting brothers peddle. One day they're going to be closed down here. Maybe the cops themselves will do it, like they did in South Africa. Ask Jack Schtipting one day about South Africa. If you can stomach him enough to do it."

This really changed my feeling. Now I had to go through the whole charade that night. I managed to make a couple of appointments, but nothing came of them. And when I got out of the car later on, I knew I'd never see Jim Hodges again.

I called him the next day and told him I wasn't coming back.

"Belly-up?" he asked. "I knew you didn't have the nerve to do this."

"I'm sorry," I said. "I can't lie anymore." Then I hung up.

Chapter

16

Now I really had to figure out a way to stay alive. I had barely enough money to eat on; my rent was soon due at the Waterton, and even at eighteen, I knew I wasn't getting a whole lot younger. I called Al Dimitre, my friend at Snelling and Snelling who liked to be whipped and beaten up. He told me that he had nothing for me.

"I heard you just skipped out of the job I got you at the *Journal*. That wasn't a good move, Perry."

"Al, I thought I had something better going. I didn't."

"Wanna have dinner with me?"

I hesitated for a second.

"Sure."

Al picked me up at the Waterton. I had to sneak past Mrs. Cook; I was already a few days late on my rent. But I ran into Ray, her son, who looked at me with a concern on his face that I could see even behind the dark glasses he always wore.

"You OK, Perry?" he asked.

I shrugged, and told him, "Sure. I'm just having some money problems. Everybody gets those, right?"

He looked straight at me.

"Money problems? Sure. Just don't bring 'em here. My mom gets upset by that."

He smiled at me, and suddenly gave me this pat on the back that got very close to my ass. I sped out onto the street, where Al was already parked.

"I'm glad you could have dinner with me," he said, after I got into his small stick-driven Datsun. "There are some things I've been wanting to talk to you about."

We went to a small Italian place in North Beach, which was then still filled with Italians—it was very unpretentious, with the necessary dripping candle nubs stuck in straw-wrapped Chianti bottles, red-checked tables, and lots of red sauce on the menu. Al, who looked like a regular-Joe, beaten-down suburban husband, fit in beautifully.

He ordered some Chianti, and the waitress, a big heavy-set senora named Patsy who knew Al by name, smiled at us and took our order. Everything seemed to have parmesan cheese on it. I ordered chicken, and Al ordered spaghetti with meatballs.

"The meatballs here are great," he said in front of Patsy.

"It's Mama's recipe," she explained. "She used to be in the kitchen making them until her legs got the best of her."

I had some of the Chianti and waited until Al started talking.

"I'm getting fidgety," he said, his voice low almost at a whisper beneath Dean Martin on the jukebox.

I had to lean in to hear him.

"It's been a long time since I had good sex. You know what I mean by 'good sex'?"

I didn't. To me all sex was good, except when it was so bad you couldn't or even *shouldn't* tolerate it. Bad sex was like what happened to me in LA. Being raped was bad sex. Being raped was a nightmare—and that was *definitely* bad sex.

"Tell me," I said.

"I want some guy to overpower me. To make me feel small, like a kid. I'll pay him. I'll pay him twenty-five—OK, thirty dollars—to do it."

I immediately thought of Raymond. Maybe I should pass this on to him. He'd do it.

I had some more of the Chianti. I was lucky: I could get drunk off almost anything. I looked at Al. He couldn't get me a real job—in his book I had fucked up by leaving the *Journal* too soon. But this was no worse than selling encyclopedias door-to-door. If I could do that, even as badly as I did—

Dean was going into his third song, "That's Amore." "What would you want me to do?" I asked. "Be specific."

Al started trembling. I felt bad for him. He was really a nice guy, nobody's image of a beauty, but a nice, by most standards, "regular" guy. If this is what he really wanted, I felt like I was doing some special kind of social service simply giving it to him. After all, I was in fact keeping him away from someone like Ray, Mrs. Cook's son, who'd might have robbed him, and maybe even really abused him . . . like, badly.

I mean not *nice* at all, not even for a masochist.

"You're a nice guy," he said. "Maybe even too nice for me. I like 'em to be a bit more rough. More commanding, say?"

Patsy brought our food, and I dove into my chicken parmesan. Al began playing with his spaghetti, drank some more Chianti, then looked at me.

"You know what I'm saying, don't you, Perry?"

"Yeah. You don't want me to be nice?"

"Exactly."

Al paid me the money at the end—I trusted him. After all, I did know him. I did things I never thought I'd do, like really hit a guy who was naked with his hands tied behind him, and curse at him, calling him "scumbag" and a "low piece of shit."

Actually, I wasn't sure what to call him, or how to do it, but I remembered some things that Joey, my hustler friend with the overbite, had told me.

"The important thing is that they believe what you are, because— gee!— sex is all about that. See, for the most part pussy is just pussy. Dick is just dick. It's that 'act' that they really want."

So I gave Al the act. At the end he was beside himself, jerking off and crying, whimpering, begging for me to give him more. I did. The more I hit him, the more he liked it. Finally, I felt like somebody else was doing it. I could just stand back and watch me doing it. I was that removed from it; for a moment, I wished I had been able to do that with the damned *Collier's Encyclopedias*.

But the money was good. Al gave me thirty. That was two weeks' rent, if I didn't eat anything. After he handed me three $10 bills, Al asked me if I wanted another date with him. I told him I'd think about it. I was still scared of the cops—and I could see this getting into something I didn't want to get into: like friends of Al's calling me for services now.

I paid Mrs. Cook her rent money, and she smiled at me. So did Ray when I saw him later alone in the hallway. He was in his usual outfit: tight white T-shirt, very tight jeans showing full crotch.

"I see you got your money problem solved for a while. Right?"

I nodded.

He grabbed me by the arm, and put his other hand on my ass.

I jumped away from him.

He just grinned. "Wouldja ever think about workin' with me?" he asked. "You're cute, Perry. But you must know that?"

"No," I said. "I wouldn't think about it. But thanks."

I now had a small amount of breathing room around me, between me and either starvation or living on the streets—neither of which alternative appealed to me. I decided that if I knocked on enough doors, I could get a job—a real one, and not something involving either lying and selling something door-to-door or hustling, which could easily get me locked up again. I printed up some cards with my name on it, and the phone number at the Waterton, and began fanning out through the Central Business District near Market Street downtown. I asked everyone if they knew of any jobs available for a guy eighteen.

During my third day doing this, I was taking a break, sitting down over coffee in the cafeteria of a department store—department stores had them in those days—at a large table. Suddenly three very obviously gay young men sat down with me.

"It's not my fault!" one of them said, out of patience, his voice shrill enough to be heard three tables away. "Mrs. T just doesn't know what she's talking about. That window should be that color, and not the awful throw-up pink she wants."

"She knows what she wants," another young man said. "It's just that it's not what *you* want, Stewart. And she's the boss. It's her money that runs the place."

"That old Jap—" Stewart said.

"Careful," the third man interjected. "You don't know who's sitting around you."

I guessed they meant me. I smiled. "I won't tell anyone," I promised. "Who is Mrs. T?"

"Mrs. Takahita," Stewart said. "She and her husband run Takahita's, the Japanese design place that sells all that crap from Japan in all those colors. We work for her. She's a dragon, but she just loves us boys, if you know what I mean?"

"Yeah, I do," I said. "I'm looking for a job."

"You should try her," the second guy, whose name was Bob, said. "She's always looking for new talent. Can you draw? She loves guys who can draw a window or a store display. Just come back with us to the store, look around, and see what you can do."

I was excited. I could draw. I could draw very well—I'd had a year of training at the University of Georgia in drawing. I thanked them sincerely. They told me not to arrive at the store with them, but just to come in casually, and they'd show me around. One of the young guys, the third, was not much older than I. He smiled at me and shook my hand.

"Roger," he said. "Just come by and see me."

I waited about an hour, then with some nervousness walked into Takahita's on a street close to Union Square. It was filled floor-to-ceiling with displays of table and housewares, novelty bric-a-brac—lamps, ashtrays, umbrellas, and stuff—all in bright trendy, sparkling colors, with an immediate "Pow!" pop-art flash to them, meant to attract young people, or those who wanted their friends to think they were hip and on top of the world. Nothing was cheap, but it wasn't priced prohibitively either. The whole aura of the large store was artsy and laid back, with friendly salespeople, some of them young blacks or Asians—unusual for most of America then.

I asked one if I could speak to Roger. She said, "He's on the fourth floor, in the design studio."

I took an elevator up. My heart was really fluttering. A design studio! Wow, after being used to the dusty mailroom of the *Wall Street Journal* and the other schleppy jobs I had had, "design studio" seemed like a dream. I walked through a hallway punctuated with doors assigned to tasks, then at the end saw: DESIGN STUDIO.

I knocked on the door.

Roger opened it. "Come in!" he said.

It was a large room filled with drawing tables and areas for signs and displays to be crafted. Bob, the other guy, was there, busily working on a sign.

"We don't do much regular design here," Roger explained. "Mostly we work on signage or displays. We talk to Mrs. T. about it, and she tells us what she wants. If we get it right, she's happy, and if we don't—then we just do it until we do."

Bob looked up.

"Sometimes we blow a little dope!"

"Shut up!" Roger said, joking. "We don't want this kid to get the wrong idea."

"Maybe I already have that," I said. "When should I meet her?"

Bob walked over.

"The Great Ozzett doesn't get met that easily . . ." He put his fingers together thoughtfully. "These things have to be done," he lowered his eyes, like a geisha, "*carefully*."

"He means," Roger said, "You need to plan it. Don't just go into the meeting with nothing. Have some drawings you can show her—she likes that. She likes people who can think visually. Even if it's just stuff you cut out from magazines. It shows you are thinking about where the store can go."

"Yeah," said Bob. "Go downstairs again, and look at the stuff. Think about things that might improve the displays, or some kind of cup, say, that Takahita's should sell. Then sketch it up, and bring it in. But first call her secretary."

He wrote down a phone number and handed it to me. I put it in my pocket and beamed. I couldn't believe these guys were helping me, and they were gay like I was. But they were *regular*; they weren't hanging out on the street or hustlers. Roger had some work to do, so Bob walked me back to the elevator.

"Don't be scared," he said. "I think Mrs. T will like you. She likes young creative guys like us. But you need to get on her good side, and I have to tell you, there's a bad side too."

"What is that? Is that when she fires you?"

"Sometimes. But first she'll make your life hell—even if she doesn't fire you."

"OK," I said, gratefully. "I'm glad to know that."

I went downstairs to look at everything, then returned to the Waterton, and took out my sketchbook. I did several sketches of the store from memory, and with watercolors indicated ideas I had for new displays, or arrangements of stock. The sketches looked pretty amateurish, I knew that, but I tried to make up for it with overlapping washes of vivid color and some interesting patterns I copied out of old-style magazines. I had found the magazines on the streets months ago; now I had a use for them.

I spent two days doing this, then called Trish, her secretary. I told her that I was a young artist, and I had spoken to Roger and—

"Oh, I see!" Trish interrupted. "You want an appointment about a job?"

I told her I did.

She sighed dramatically.

"We don't have a single opening now. But sometimes Mrs. T just likes to meet new people she can file away in case we do."

I smiled. I'd do this—I knew it. No matter what, I was going to get a job there, working with young men like Roger and Bob, designing things, using my talent. I was in heaven before I even got off the phone.

The next day I took the same elevator up to the fourth floor where Mrs. Takahita had her office. It was at the other end, opposite the design studio, and had her name on the door. I knocked, and a young lady opened it.

"You're Perry? I'm Trish."

She was only about four years older than I was and perfectly groomed and extremely smartly dressed, like she had been clipped right out of a fashion magazine herself and didn't actually need a job the way I did. She smiled brightly and escorted me to the end of a large, well-furnished office, filled with boxes of merchandise, and masses of porcelain samples out on tables. There, in the middle of four other stylish young women, was Mrs. T, the star. She was at least a hundred years old—OK, maybe sixty—dressed in a beautiful Chinese-inspired gray silk suit with a mandarin collar, lots of jewelry, and her face heavily made up like a mask.

"This is Mr. Brass," Trish said. "He called yesterday. He's interested in working for us."

"Is he?" Mrs. Takahita asked. "Do you have something to show us?"

"Yes." I brought out the sketches and showed them to her.

She looked at them thoughtfully, and asked me questions: "Where do you see this in the store? What kind of merchandise is this? Who would buy it? That is always the most important question in retailing: Who will buy what you have to sell? It may look wonderful to us, the sellers, but it has to look even *more* wonderful to the buyers."

"People interested in really wonderful things," I answered, "that are fascinating and unique."

"I'm afraid that is not going to be enough, Perry." She narrowed her eyes at me. "San Francisco is filled with people who are interested in wonderful things. *They* are fascinating. *They* are unique. But you have to have something they want. I am always on the lookout for young people because you have your fingers on the pulse of the times. I can tell you are multitalented, and very smart. Tell me, how long have you been in San Francisco?"

"Seven months," I told her.

"Ah, then you understand by now that this city is filled with all the vices of the world. It can be an evil place, but also very beautiful. What do you like to eat? Do you like Chinese food?"

Now I felt lost. I wasn't sure what I could say about Chinese food. But I noticed that Trish was now behind Mrs. T and she was nodding to me, and smiling.

"Yes!" I said enthusiastically. "I *love* Chinese food."

"Do you cook it at home?"

I had to be honest. "No."

"It is really very easy. The Chinese produce very natural food. They take everything the earth gives them, and pay it the compliment of cooking it beautifully. When Mr. Takahita and I first came to this country, we were very poor. I had to learn how to cook Chinese instead of Japanese, which requires more expensive food. We lived off of egg foo yong for weeks. It is very easy to make. It is like an omelet but it has all sorts of things in it. But you must be careful. Don't put asparagus or spinach in it. If you do, it's like cooking dollar bills, and we all know how expensive they are to cook."

Suddenly every young woman in the room started giggling, as if all of this had been said before, maybe to other job seekers.

I left shortly after. I made sure that Trish had the phone number at the hotel and thanked Mrs. T several times.

She allowed a slight grin to soften her face.

"When we have an opening, I will call you. I would recommend that you don't take another job too fast—I think something may happen sooner than we think."

On the elevator down, I gripped my sketches so tightly that I thought the blood in my fingers might pop. I realized I had been sweating terribly. How was I going to deal with all of this: I was a broke kid living in a Tenderloin hotel, trying to appear normal, but "artsy."

Then I realized, this old lady must have seen right through that, and I didn't feel so bad.

I called Al Dimitre once more, and as expected he invited me to dinner. This time it was in a diner out on the Peninsula. In this kind of glum setting, surrounded by truck drivers and several anxious-looking couples and families on the road, he looked even more forlorn. We sat in the back, where we could have some privacy.

"You been really good for me, Perry. I feel so much better after our"—he hesitated, then said, "session."

"You don't look happy," I noticed.

"They're giving me shit at work. I work my tail off for Snelling and Snelling, and they treat me like I'm some sort of circus freak."

"They all know you're," I lowered my voice until it was just a mere fraction above a whisper, "gay?"

"Hell, half of them are queer," he hissed. "The women aren't, and they aren't very happy about it, lemme tell you. No, it's that they want me to produce more. Make more placements, bring in more commissions—but they don't give me any high-class jobs. I'm still finding work for kids like you, and they want me to shake the gold off the trees with your kind of jobs."

I thought about Jeremiah Leopold. True, he was in another world—the really fancy-schmancy jobs in the nascent computer/tech world. But he had done nothing for me except to get me high and try to fuck me. I realized then that the only real job I had had in San Francisco, Al had gotten for me. I felt sorry for him. But I still wanted him to pay me for what I was going to do.

"Maybe you'll feel better," I said, "if we do what we did again."

Al paused and looked at me.

"Maybe. But I can't pay you what I did. I can only pay you twenty."

I had to hold my cards close to my vest.

"Maybe I don't want to do it for twenty."

"Come on, Perry. I'm taking you out for dinner here. You know I'm your friend."

"Yeah," I said. "Twenty-five."

Al hesitated, then said, "OK."

The truth is, I really didn't like doing it. There was something about hitting a guy like Al and saying those things that really got to me. It wasn't the kind of person I knew I was; and if I hadn't been so close to scraping bottom, I wouldn't have. We went back to his apartment, and he had me try on some clothes that he felt fit the role: ripped jeans, an old leather jacket, and a T-shirt that was grimy with dirt and hadn't been washed in decades. As soon as I put them on, he smiled. He lowered the lights, and we began.

Three days later, I got a call from Trish. There was an opening at Takahita's.

"Mrs. T is opening a new branch in Ghirardelli Square, and she wants you to work in it. It's pure sales work. You won't be doing any design or stuff like that, and you'll be working for Norma Taylor, she's the head of the branch. I think you'll like her. She's very smart and really understands retailing."

I was so excited I could barely hold the phone in the hallway at the Waterton.

"When do I start?"

"That's the bad part—well, one of them. In two weeks. I hope that's OK with you? You'll be paid after your first two weeks, so you don't have to go very long without a paycheck. Oh, and I have to tell you: you *will* be on probation. If we feel that we can't use you, then we won't keep you after your first paycheck."

"Fine," I said. "You won't regret it."

I put down the phone and went back to my room. I was very happy. I was going to have a real job again, not some craziness like selling phony encyclopedias door-to-door, or hustling old men, or any of the other things I was qualified or, even worse, not qualified, to do. Now I had to figure out a way to live for the next month, before I got paid by Takahita's. I went back to the "starving artist" gallery in North Beach that had sold my painting, and offered him some more work. The man was reluctant to take it.

"We have more stuff here than we can show," he said sadly. "The art world just ain't doin' it." I reminded him that one of my paintings had sold.

"That was months ago, and it was to this older guy who came in looking for it. He must have been a friend of yours—so it doesn't really count."

I put on as much charm as I could, and left him some small acrylic paintings. On the way out, back down to my hotel, I thought about calling Ryan Fitzgerald again, who would pick me up in his Lincoln, then realized I couldn't do it. This part of me just rebelled—it was a part that couldn't face my own past, and he was a part of that, too. Just like my mother was, and her wrenching mental health problems, or the fact that I had grown up in a poverty that was bludgeoning, like being hit by a hammer—something Southern Jews weren't supposed to be a part of—but I had become good at dissembling that, too.

Hiding it. Never letting people know exactly how I had grown up and what I had come from.

No, I was not going to call Ryan Fitzgerald. He was now folded back into my past, exactly like my problems with the law in Los Angeles.

I made sure my rent at the Waterton was paid up for the next two weeks, then I started going back out again at night to Market Street and the areas off Union Square and parts of Polk Street. I felt very self-conscious, because with a juvenile court record, I knew I couldn't be picked up again by the cops—I did not want to end up back in the system.

This was the famous City of Night of San Francisco, where the queens, leather-jacketed *machos*, furtive husbands and other moneyed closet cases, and boys like myself—the ones too impoverished to pass through the gates of the middle class (or to "pass" as anything, frankly)—met each other. Sometimes I'd see friends like Joey, my hustler buddy with the overbite, or Raymond (aka Ramón), David Pitts's hustler boyfriend. Mostly what I was trying to do was just get fed, make a little money, and escape my own loneliness and boredom.

I hated going back to the Waterton by myself. So sometimes I'd just pick up a man, a real adult man, and bring him back with me. In the morning I'd tell him how broke I was, and he'd see the hotel room, with its roaches and blotchy tattered wallpaper, and give me something. I was living off eggs and fried salami, and waiting for the days to change, like you do when you're very young.

One night near Polk Street I was very shyly approached by a youngish, trim, good-looking guy, maybe in his late twenties, wearing a trench coat and hat, resembling something out of a Raymond Chandler novel. He didn't say anything to me for a few minutes, but just looked at me with soft brown eyes. Under the dim streetlights and his hat, I could tell he had a nice-looking face with a very pleasing nose and mouth.

I smiled at him.

"Can I talk to you?" he asked.

"Sure. What do you want to talk about?"

He hesitated, then said: "Are you a hustler?"

"No," I shot back. He could be a cop. I started to get away from him, but he followed me, picking up his pace to match mine, certainly giving up his initial shyness.

"I'm not a cop, believe me. I work for the Archdiocese of San Francisco. We're doing outreach with men and boys on the street here. I want to help you."

I stopped. Wow! No one had ever said to me, "I want to help you." I asked him if he was a social worker, and he said yes. He was finishing his studies in social work at Berkeley, and he was doing fieldwork with us boys. We went into a late-night café, and he bought me a mug of coffee and a piece of apple pie.

I asked him his name. He told me it was Ronnie. "Ronnie LaCoutier, I know—it sounds pretty queer, doesn't it. A French name. My parents are French Canadians. They live in Hartford, Connecticut. Whenever I tell people out here my name, they think I'm making it up."

He started asking me questions, bringing out a notebook from a small bag, and taking notes. How long had I been out on the streets? Where did I come from? How much education did I have? He was impressed that I'd had a year of college; he was impressed actually by me. I could understand that. Most of the guys you met on the streets were not like me, a fact I knew.

I told him a lot about myself. It just poured out of me, as I realized how alone I felt. Here was this man who worked for a religious organization who did not want either to use or exploit me. At the end of our conversation, he asked me if I needed some money. I told him sure, and he handed me a $5 bill.

"Don't worry," he said, smiling. "I'll be reimbursed for it."

I wasn't worried about it at all. All I knew was that I wanted to see Ronnie LaCoutier again. He handed me his card. It had his name and a phone number on it, but nothing else. I asked him why it didn't mention the Archdiocese. He explained that this project was still kept under wraps. "The Catholic Church in San Francisco doesn't want the public to know that they are welcoming hustlers. Actually they are not, but they *do* want you to know that they care about you."

We agreed to meet in a couple of days, back on the same corner where we had met before. I went back to my hotel feeling a lot better, just knowing that Ronnie LaCoutier was on my side.

Around that time I went back to see Jody and Karen. They had moved to a larger, really beautiful apartment near Pacific Heights, and Jody was with a new boyfriend named Tom, who was also from the Midwest. He was tall, broad-shouldered, and extremely good-looking, with the most exquisite skin imaginable: it had a golden glow to it. He didn't say much, and I quickly realized that he was rather dull, but . . . certainly beautiful. He also had some money, and he had been able to get the apartment that the three of them now shared. After I spent an evening with them, I felt dejected on the way back to the Waterton—like I had lost something; like Jody and Karen were now inside this fantasy of a life I could not have, with a beautiful, warm apartment, and Tom, this exceedingly handsome man.

I saw Ronnie several times before my job with Takahita's started. We would meet on the streets and walk around a bit, and then have coffee together. It was always coffee and never dinner. And I never got to see where he lived, or what he really did. But he told me a lot about himself, that he had come from a very conservative French-Canadian family who were now in New England, and that he had been gay most of life, and that coming to grips with it had been the most difficult thing in his life.

"I thought about killing myself many times," he told me. "If there were some way of just closing my eyes and coming to the end of this, I'd do it. For a Catholic, that is a worse sin than homosexuality, but I did think about it. That's why I want to help other people—especially young guys like you."

I was really taken with him. He was never judgmental or threatening, like

Ryan Fitzgerald had been; he was never manipulative, trying to get me into bed with him, like other men I had met who were "interested" in me. One of them in Savannah had been an Episcopal priest who had befriended my mother. His name was Father Joseph, and he had told her that his specialty was "working with boys." My mother, who was always on the lookout for men who could be a "role model" for me, and whom she could use to punish me—the "models" always seemed to be either physically rough, or verbally threatening, as in "Boy, you better change your behavior"—had jumped at the chance to have Father Joseph "work" with me.

He'd started following me, popping up in places where Mother had told him I would be. He was a short, ugly man but he drove a very sporty red Mustang convertible that attracted boys to him. Finally he'd invited me to go away with him to Augusta, Georgia, for an overnight conference.

We were to be in a hotel with a room with two beds. We'd had dinner at the hotel, then he'd told me to go back to the room and get into bed while he had a drink at the bar. About an hour later, he'd returned to the dark room, taken his clothes off, and tried to get into bed with me. He'd stroked my back and legs.

"What a good friend you are, Perry," he'd said softly. "A really good friend."

I'd pretended to be completely asleep, with my head turned from him. I froze; I didn't move.

He'd gotten into his own bed, and the next day at breakfast mentioned nothing. On the drive back to Savannah, we'd had a talk about sex. He'd asked me, "Do you believe in the free expression of sex?"

I was sixteen, but had not come out yet—sexually. I knew what he was talking about though. I could just smell it.

"I never thought about it," I'd said.

Then he'd mentioned homosexuals. He'd said he had "several homosexual friends. They're very good people, but most people don't understand them."

I'd pretended to look out the window, ignoring him. When he'd dropped me off at the housing project where we lived, I knew I'd never see him again. It wasn't so much that I resented that he had tried to get into bed with me—although I wasn't ready for it and thought he was repulsive—it was that I felt that he was really working for my mother. She had put him up to it, to

145

"set me straight," as she put it. I was too rebellious for her; she felt Father Joseph would inculcate some "morals" into me, foremost being that I would honor and obey her. She also knew that I would go off to college and leave Savannah at the end of that summer, so she wanted one more chance at me.

Ronnie was not like Father Joseph at all. There was something simply genuine about him, like I could believe every word he said.

Finally, just before I started my job at Takahita's, we met one last time.

"I've been offered a great job," he said. "It's back in Hartford. I'm going to take it. I'll miss you, Perry, but I'll write to you when I get settled. Maybe you can come visit, if you're ever in the area."

I felt very bad that he was leaving, like one of the few adults I could ever think about trusting was going. But it was mitigated by something: I had made contact with Rodney, the beautiful hustler I had fallen in love with in LA at Pershing Square.

It happened in a crazy way. I was looking in the back pages of the San Francisco newspaper and saw a small ad for a detective agency. It said, "Lost Love? Lost Relatives? We can trace any address or phone number for you, all over the country or world."

I wrote to the agency and told them about Rodney, that he was my age, 18, and lived in Nashville, Tennessee. A few days later I was written back: they had Rodney's address and phone number, and would send it to me for eighteen dollars. I sent them back the money in cash, and a few days later got it.

I immediately wrote him, telling him that I was living in San Francisco, but that I wanted more than anything in the world to see him.

He wrote me back that the next summer he was going to Fire Island in New York, and that he would stay at the Cherry Grove Hotel, where "we could walk on the beach free, proclaiming our love. I will be registered under the name Adrian Baroque. You will be able to find me. I can't wait, Perry."

Now I felt as if I were walking on air, with fresh oxygen pumped into me, singing his name. A movie with James Garner and Julie Andrews had just appeared called *The Americanization of Emily,* and the theme song, by Johnny Mandel with lyrics by Johnny Mercer—another Savannah guy—repeated the name "Emily" over and over, in this searching, utterly romantic way. I had seen the movie, and substituted "Rodney" for "Emily," singing "Rodney . . . Rodney . . . Rodney."

I could see Rodney's clear, bewitching green eyes floating in the sky above me, but I knew I had to be patient. The next summer seemed like years and years away from me.

Chapter

17

I was nervous my first day on the job at Takahita's at Ghirardelli Square. I made sure I got there on time, although now, with almost no money, my breakfast consisted of a cup of coffee.

The store had not officially opened up yet, and Norma Taylor met me at the door. She was a posh-looking woman, very fashionably married with kids. Her husband was wealthy, she could afford help, and, as she told me, she "didn't want to be, well, just stuck in the house. Know what I mean?"

I nodded enthusiastically. Of course I did. I didn't have enough money to eat, but I certainly didn't want to be stuck in the house. She showed me around the small store. It was very chic and fashionable with shelves of brightly glazed crockery and colorful knickknacks and eye-catching, cute tchotchkes for tourists. My job was to make sure that everything was kept spotless.

"This store sells on its color and it's cleanliness," she said. "We want people to feel that they are at home here and not out on the street, which can get kind of grungy, right?"

I nodded again and just listened to her. I was hungry and spotted a candy section, with old-fashioned, brightly colored candies, like peppermint sticks in about twenty flavors, and I knew at some point I'd be sucking on them for pure calories. She asked me if I'd like a cup of coffee and a roll, there was an expensive coffee shop one level down and she was going there.

"It's on me," she offered, and I took her up on it.

I was now alone in the shop and I could really look at it. There were things I would have changed, items I would have moved to look better in another location. I decided not to say anything for a few days, and just keep everything spotless and wait on customers when I could.

She returned and I was very happy to eat the roll and drink the coffee. There was a ladder in the back, and I had no problems getting up on it, to clean things next to the ceiling. Norma was often on the store phone talking with her husband or her kids, and then I waited on customers. They could tell immediately that I was from the South, and soon they told me how much they loved Savannah. It was a beautiful city, and at some moments I felt homesick for the place: just the sheer physical beauty of it. But I realized I couldn't go back; there was no way I could go back.

In the afternoon, a dark-haired, very pretty college student named Pauline came in as part-time staff. She was about nineteen or twenty, a transplanted New Yorker, whose father, an electronics engineer, now had a job in San Francisco. She was friendly, and we talked easily. She had lived in New York on Central Park West and had been a child ballet dancer. She had danced with Jerome Robbins and George Balanchine, and had attended the Professional Children's School. She was very sophisticated and looked down on San Francisco, which she felt was a backwater. After ballet, she had wanted to work in fashion, but there was no possibility of that in San Francisco.

She was extremely knowledgeable about clothes, and in the next several days told me all about Yves Saint Laurent, Pierre Cardin, and André Courrèges.

"People think that Courrèges is so wonderful, you know with his space look, but Saint Laurent is really the greatest. He really knows what's going on and uses everything. Nobody in San Francisco wears real fashion. They're all stuck about thirty years in the past." When Norma was out of sight, she said, "Norma thinks she's so fashionable. She's a frump. She just got this job because her husband is a friend of Mrs. T's. She knows nothing about style or what looks good in this shop. Some of the stuff here looks terrible. The colors clash, and the way she has it arranged is"—she stopped for a second, then lowered her voice. "Awful."

As soon as Norma came back within earshot, Pauline clammed up and just smiled at her. I admired Pauline. She still carried herself and looked like a dancer. She was part of this glittering New York world that I had never experienced but in Savannah dreamed about. One of ballet, fashion, smart people, and art.

What young gay boy would not dream of that?

I got off work at 5 o'clock, and Pauline stayed until closing. There were other part-time workers who came in for the evening shift, since the store stayed open until 8. Sometimes I had to stay late, if one of them could not come in. Norma told me that my staying late was not voluntary.

"It's part of the job. If we need you, you'll have to stay. But we won't ask you often. And if you have real plans, just let me know."

I told her I'd make sure in the next few weeks that I had none of them. There was a lot resting on my probation period, and I knew it.

I was just kind of treading water until my first paycheck. Often I was extremely hungry. I discovered that a posh bakery in the Square threw out its old rolls and muffins in a back alley. There were big bags of them with the trash, and I snuck handfuls of them back to my hotel room. There was a lot of life around Ghirardelli Square; it was a magnet both for well-heeled tourists and for hipsters trying to make money off them. In the afternoons, further down toward the water, a black dance troop and a group of bongo players set up shop. You could hear the drumming a long way off, and young people of all colors started dancing to it. Often I stopped by there after work, just to relax and unwind before getting a bus back to the Tenderloin.

One day I was sitting on one of the risers that led down to the street level of markets when a young black man in a very colorful dashiki came up to me. He asked me my name and where I was from. When I told him, he frowned.

"I'm surprised you are listening to this kind of music, Perry. It's not the kind of music you people in the South like. In fact, you shouldn't be listening to it."

"Maybe I am not your regular kind of person from the South," I said.

He extended his hand to me.

"In that case, we can be friends."

He told me his name was Jimmy Abeke. His father had been African and his mother "an American Negro from the South—where they hate us."

His eyes searched at me, like they were staring through me; I wondered why he was sizing me up so much. He knew all the drummers and the dancers and he went off to the dance with them. I watched, and sometimes he would give me this cold look that seemed to say, "What are you doing here?"

I didn't think much of it, until the next day when I returned after work. I was standing up next to the drummers, a flute player had joined them, and they were really cooking, doing riffs on popular tunes and coming up with new ones.

Jimmy appeared and approached me.

"You can't leave these people alone," he said, smirking. "Why can't you just leave them alone?"

I had no answer for him; the truth was I couldn't even understand the question. Then from the group of people dancing two very attractive white girls, about a year or two older than I was, appeared. One walked up to me.

"Do you want to dance?" I told her sure, and we started dancing together like we already knew each other.

"You're Jewish?" she asked.

I told her yes; she looked at me beguilingly.

"I love blue-eyed Jews. My name's Fern. I'm here with my girlfriend. We're from Philly—we're both go-go dancers."

She smiled at me like we were coconspirators now. "She's my real girl-friend. Know what I mean?"

I told her I did. She looked at me with an expression of complete openness, like she had finally found a guy she could talk to. Her girlfriend's name was Alice. She had bleached blonde hair that on anyone else would have looked garish, but on her looked kind of funky and striking. They asked me if I wanted to go get something to eat, and I told them I was really broke.

They knew a very cheap place in Chinatown, and Fern told me that they could pay for me. The place, downstairs below street level, was fabulously mysterious in an old Sydney Greenstreet sort of way with all the booths separated by dark beaded curtains. They talked nonstop, and I loved listening to them. They had hitchhiked to San Francisco, stopping at various towns to work in bars as dancers.

"All the guys want to fuck us, but we're not interested in them," Alice explained. "We're gay but not dykey-gay like so many lesbians in San Francisco are. You're gay, too, Perry, aren't you? I could tell immediately, so could Fern. That's why she went up to you."

I asked her how could they tell?

Fern smiled. "You have this thing—you're not queer-sissy gay, but you have it. It's like you just stepped off a cloud. You're so good-looking, too."

I thanked her. I never thought that women found me attractive. I knew men did, gay men, that is. We exchanged phone numbers, and they told me that they liked hanging out in Ghirardelli Square, so I'd see them again.

They were working in a bar in North Beach that night, so had to leave. I walked back to the Tenderloin, and thought about them, especially Fern. There was something about her that I was almost crazy about, just the way she looked at me.

At the end of my first week at Takahita's I thought things were going very well. I worked hard, was always on time, and managed to get along with Norma, who almost worked at alienating people. At times she could be very open, confiding in me about her problems at home with her husband or kids; then other times she would come down on me like a ton of bricks—I had missed cleaning something, there was dust someplace, or I wasn't watching the store enough.

"You have to be really careful," she warned. "Shoplifters come in all shapes, and sometimes they look like they could buy out the store, while all the time they're stealing from you."

I did not want to just follow people in the shop and stare at them, but if Norma was around, she'd order me to tail customers, especially if they were young or of minority origins.

"I'm not prejudiced," she said, "but these people! They can't afford the stuff in here, so they will steal it."

I made a date to see Fern during the weekend. I was not sure what her relationship was with Alice—maybe it was just that we were all so young and relationships were in flux anyway. We met on Saturday afternoon in Union Square, and just strolled up to North Beach and then Ghirardelli. It was a beautiful bright day, like San Francisco could have in early March. The earlier weeks had been cold, but now it felt warm and inviting again. I took her hand. It felt wonderful to do that, then, at some stop along the way, I kissed her.

She kissed me back, her eyes closed, like she really enjoyed it.

After a few minutes, we came back to earth again.

"You're gay, Perry," she said, her voice low.

"So are you, aren't you?" I asked.

"Yeah, but not the way you are. Women are different. I know that. It's like, I don't know if I'll always be with Alice. I like it right now. Being gay is a lot easier than being straight."

"You think so?" I asked. "It hasn't been easy for me. I've been close to being killed a couple of times."

"I meant," she explained, "being straight, you're with a strange sex. Men are still kind of strange to me, but girls—well, I know girls."

She smiled at me again, in that coconspiratorial kind of way.

"Would you marry me?" I asked. It just came right out of me. But that moment it felt right. I could marry Fern, and we could settle down someplace and just do what we needed to do to stay alive and be happy.

"Perry, you don't have any money at all. You're dead broke. How can you marry me?"

We'd been walking, and suddenly I stopped for a second. She was right: I was dead *broke*. Always. I felt like a pail of ice water had been thrown on me. I didn't say anything for a while, until we got back to Ghirardelli Square. There were more musicians besides drummers there, most were black, but they were playing pop songs, even some Beatles stuff.

I started dancing with Fern and held her, then the music got louder and faster, and Fern went off for a moment, dancing by herself. Suddenly Jimmy Abeke materialized.

"I told you, you can't leave these people alone!" he said triumphantly. "Why can't you, Perry?"

Now, instantly, I understood what he was saying: I was just a white faggot, poaching on his culture. That was all I was—he could look down on me, no matter what he was.

He gave me this grin that infuriated me.

"That girl?" he asked, referring to Fern who was now out of earshot. "Are you giggin' her?"

"That's my business," I said, furious. "Why don't you drop in a hole, Jimmy? OK? Find yourself a good hole."

His face collapsed.

"I didn't mean for you to take it so personally, friend. I'm sorry if I offended you."

I didn't say another word. I walked over to Fern and took her by the arm. I told her I had had enough of this place. She kissed me on the cheek, and told me she hoped she'd see me again. I walked away and then for a moment looked back and saw her in the middle of a motley group of kids, dancing. She looked so natural doing it. I just wanted to look at her for a few seconds more.

The next week at Takahita's in the Square, things did not go well. Pauline and Norma seemed to be barely speaking to each other, though Norma always had good things to say about her. One afternoon when Norma was away picking up her kids, Pauline approached me about a display in the store.

"Do you like this?" she asked.

Crockery and knickknacks were piled up in a casual way that didn't mean anything or sell well. I told her no.

"Good. Why don't we rearrange it? You must have some ideas what to do with it."

I told her I'd think about it, and I did. I did some small sketches of what I thought might work, and handed them to her. She smiled.

"These are really good. Why don't we do it and surprise Norma when she gets back?"

I was nervous about this, but Pauline assured me that she'd vouch for it, and before I knew it, she had dismantled the old display and was following my sketch for a new one.

We were both right. It looked a lot better. But when Norma came in, she was furious. Her eyes immediately went up to it, and then she stormed up to me.

"Why did you do this, Perry? I told you I'm in charge of displays at this store. You weren't hired to do that."

Pauline came forward and admitted that she was part of it, too. But that did nothing for Norma. She just waved Pauline off.

"Perry's full-time here and he should know better."

She put the display back together exactly as it was.

"Color is what sells the store," she fumed while she did it. "And these colors work. I may not have the talent you have, Perry, but I know retailing. I've been doing it most of my life."

I felt terrible. I apologized again, and offered to work later. Norma smiled.

"It's OK," she said. "We won't be needing you in the evenings this week."

I went back to the Waterton that evening feeling deflated and anxious. I was behind in my rent for the first time, but hoped that Mrs. Cook would overlook it. After I had walked up the back stairs on the familiar threadbare mildewed carpets to my door, I was greeted with a padlock on it. I froze. What was I going to do now?

I went down to Mrs. Cook's apartment and saw her.

"You're almost two weeks behind, Perry. You gotta do something about that."

I told her that I had a new job and I'd be paid at the end of the week. I promised I'd pay her as soon as I got the money. Ray, her son, came out and looked at me with a mixture of anger and disappointment. Mrs. Cook handed him the key, and he went up with me.

"If you need money," he offered. "I can introduce you t' some customers, Perry. You still got what some of 'em want." He gave me a very eager smile as he unlocked my door. I suddenly figured out what he wanted, too. But I didn't ask him to come in.

At the end of the day on Friday, Norma handed me my pay envelope.

"I'm afraid we're not going to keep you, Perry," she announced. "You did not pass your probation."

I was more stunned than surprised. I thought I had done everything I could to smooth anything over. I told her that I'd work a lot harder, and do anything to keep the job.

"You're just not the right person for this place," she explained. "You have too much of a mind of your own. You're talented. Mrs. T. could see that— that's why she insisted that I hire you. I would rather have hired some girl who would do what I wanted. If something else happens in the main store, in the art department or—whatever—she'll let you know."

I knew that was not going to happen and I couldn't survive it anyway. I didn't have a home or parents supporting me. I was basically out on the streets supporting myself. I put the check in my pocket, and went straight to a check-cashing place I had established some trust with. They cashed it, and then I went to a Woolworth's on Market Street and sat down at the counter. They had a fried chicken special that came with french fries and a Coke. I dove into it, I was that hungry.

Then I returned to the Waterton and gave Mrs. Cook the money I owed her. She took it very dryly without commenting. Then she told me, "You have a letter," and handed it to me. It was from Ronnie LaCoutier. I was so excited. How did he know that I wanted to hear from him so much? It seemed impossible . . . until I read it in my room.

My hands started trembling as I read:

"How are you, Perry? You must still be enjoying San Francisco. Life here in Hartford is OK. I got a great job and a new apartment so I'm no longer living with my parents. The war in Viet Nam is going full blast here with all the factories and stuff, and there are jobs all over the place. If you are ever in this area, please come and visit. I'd love to see you."

It did not take a lot to put one and one together: there was nothing for me in San Francisco except more dead ends, more fake situations, more Norma Taylors and Mrs. Ts, and Al Dimitres. I was sick of living in the Waterton with mice in my room and cockroaches in the bathtub. Ronnie had given me a phone number. I got all the change I had and went down to a pay phone outside. I knew it was late in Hartford, but I needed to talk to him. He was surprised when I called, but happy to hear from me.

After a minute, I asked him: "Would it be all right if I came to see you?"

He hesitated, then asked, "You mean, like, stay here and get a job?"

I told him yes.

"Sure, Perry. It's crazy here. There are jobs all over the place. The newspapers are filled with jobs. It's not like San Francisco—I mean in *every* way."

"Fine," I said. "I'll get there in about a week."

Chapter
18

I started putting up signs in student hangouts and hippie coffee shops and bookstores, in any place that I thought they'd get read: "Young man needs ride to East Coast, New York or New England. Will split expenses. Cannot drive, but excellent conversationalist." I included the number of the Waterton.

It was the first week of April, and I figured that a lot of people must be making the trip. I was right. Two days later, a man called me.

"So you're an excellent conversationalist?" he asked jokingly.

I told him I was. He immediately heard my Southern accent and joked about it. I liked the way he sounded; he had a kind of sharp, preppyish East Coast accent. He told me he had been working in banking and hated it but had been offered another job in New York, where he'd be staying with a girlfriend. He could take me that far. We'd split gas and sleep in the car or at motels—"Cheap ones," he said. "I don't have a lot of money for this trip."

I told him that was fine, and expected that he'd want to meet before we took off, but he didn't. Instead he said he'd pick me up at the Waterton in three days and we'd head out. His name was Richard Myer. I felt good about the conversation. It occurred to me that some men might have just called me just to set up a date—obviously, he wasn't doing that; after all, he was "staying with a girlfriend" in New York.

Packing was easy; I knew that. I hardly had anything, except for my drawings and a few watercolors and acrylic paintings. I told Mrs. Cook what I was doing, and she gave me a large suitcase that had been left in her rooms years ago. "I know a boy like you can use it," she said. I put the art and most of my clothes in it. Even with as little as I had, it was so heavy I could barely lift it, but I'd have to. I had a smaller bag to put overnight things in, and I'd use that on the trip.

I wanted to say goodbye to people. I met Fern and Alice, and told them I was going to New York—not Hartford. Fern was very sorry to see me go, but she understood. "There's really not a lot here," she said. "You'll be a lot happier in New York. It's close to Philly. Let's keep in touch. I know Alice and I are going to end up back there. You never really leave Philly. It stays in your blood, like all those cheesesteaks and Italian calzones and stuff."

I kissed her, and now it just seemed like kissing another person, not someone I had proposed to.

Shortly after, I said goodbye to Karen and Jody, and of course Tom, Jody's handsome boyfriend. Jody was really sorry to see me. "You're such a nice guy, Perry," he said. "You don't meet nice guys so often in San Francisco."

"That's why I want to move back to Michigan," Tom butted in. "I'm tired of this place. I hate the weather. It's dreary. Not warm, not cold, just dreary. People kill themselves here. They're always jumping off the Golden Gate Bridge."

Jody put his arms around him.

"We'll go. We're not going to stay here forever. But you know, Michigan is not the easiest place for guys like us. It's easy to end up in the wrong place there."

Tom who was all muscle looked seriously at him.

"And not here? All these straights want to kill us here. They drive into San Francisco looking for us—I know that."

I left soon afterwards. Tom was right: the weather was dreary. It was a rainy, fog-and-mist-soaked night, like so many in San Francisco. I decided to walk up to Fisherman's Wharf, just to stroll by the water once more. I got as far as the Buena Vista Café and ordered a coffee there. It was not crowded, and I sat by a window and looked out. I'd had some wonderful times in San Francisco, but I still had not figured out anything about myself. What was I doing, really?

I finished the coffee and went outside. I was close to Ghirardelli Square and the area where I had met Fern. Suddenly I started crying. I felt very empty and lost—a feeling I had worked so hard not to have. Then I thought about Rodney. I'd see him again; no matter what, I'd meet him again. I was still in love with him—just crazy about him. I kept hearing his name in my head, all the way down to the Waterton and in my room.

"God!" Richard Myer said. "What the hell do you have in here, your whole life?"

We were having a hard time stuffing Mrs. Cook's suitcase into his trunk, but it did fit. He had several smaller pieces of luggage, matched Samsonite, and he looked almost like his voice, thirty-two or so, except huskier, with a definite preppy, button-down look to him. We had almost no time to get to know each other, then we were off.

The trip would take four days, *or so*—Richard had plans for stopping in places. He was not crazy about driving, and since I didn't, we stopped often for coffee or just to look at scenery. Richard talked a lot about his life: he did hate banking because he was not a banker; he'd been a theater major.

"Not an actor. I wanted to be either a stage manager or director. The problem is you can't make a real living at it, but the job offered to me in New York is in theater. It's working for a small company. I'll starve, but I'll be happy."

I got over any reticence about telling him I was gay, and he smiled.

"I knew it pretty fast," he said. "You have this kind of twinkle to you. It's not, like, queer, but different. A lot of people are sure I'm gay because I work in theater, but the truth is I've always liked girls—I get along well with them. I don't even understand being gay. Like how do you lead your life as a gay guy? I know you have that kind of 'coming out' thing. Like you go to bars for the first time, and everybody applauds. But I still don't understand it."

"There's nothing to understand," I said. "It's just something you feel that makes sense to you. I knew I couldn't be that way back in Georgia. I'd get murdered."

He glanced over at me.

"That's sad, really terrible. When you work in theater, you get used to accepting people. My parents accepted everyone—they got out of Germany just before the ax fell, so they understood what it was like to have people hate you because of who or what you are."

Suddenly I really liked him. I had so little money we squabbled about things—like who was going to pay for what. We also stopped in Salt Lake City, where Richard had an old professor from his college theater days who was married to a Mormon woman; they had several kids. His prof, Allen, took us to a "key club," that is, a Salt Lake City bar where you kept your own alcohol in a locker and paid a yearly fee for a "key" to lock it up.

"The Mormons," Allen explained, "don't allow any alcohol to be sold over a bar. It's crazy—you have to bring your own booze, buy it at state liquor store, and then pay them to pour it in a glass. I like Salt Lake, it's a beautiful place, but there are times when I think that I fell in from outer space here." Richard and I had told him that I was gay. He looked at me. "Being gay here, you might as well just die. The Mormons can't believe it—I don't think it's in their vocabulary, although I think that somewhere in Salt Lake they have drag shows. Every town in the West has them."

Allen, his wife, and even the kids were very nice. His youngest daughter, who was four, took a great shining to me. She cried when she knew we would leave the next day. The scenery around Salt Lake was gorgeous, but soon we were in the flatlands of the Midwest. There we stopped in Omaha, Nebraska for a night. Richard had an old friend from his banking days in San Francisco—a middle-aged woman who had returned to Omaha to run the family bank. She lived with her husband and their kids in a beautiful area of the city. She and Richard talked about banking—it was like he put on another face and head. He did not tell them that I was gay, and I got the feeling that these people were a lot more square than his friends in Salt Lake. I also learned things about small banks in small towns; how the bankers get to know everything about the town, and its people—every scandal and problem. I was fascinated.

After driving about twelve hours from Omaha, Richard said he was tired and we needed to check into a motel. I couldn't afford a room of my own, and offered to sleep in the car. He said no, we'd sleep in the same room. We found a motel that, again, looked like it should have been managed by the Bates family, and unloaded some of our things in it.

There was one bed. I went into the bathroom and decided to shower. When I came out, Richard appeared to be asleep. I got into bed with him, and suddenly he turned to me.

"I'm really glad you're here, Perry," he said.

I told him thank you. Then suddenly he kissed me, lightly on the lips.

"I don't know why I did that," he said.

I told him it was OK. My heart was pounding. I didn't expect it.

"I mean, I'm not gay," he explained. "But there's something about you.

Maybe it's because you're from the South and you talk the way you do. And you're good-looking. I didn't expect that. I should just go to sleep."

I said "OK," and then turned from him. He was wearing boxer underwear, and I was in briefs. I was still too young to want things to go further—after all, I had just proposed to a girl, Fern. Everything seemed very complicated.

Years later, I met Richard again in New York, at the Metropolitan Museum. I had not seen in him in several decades. He told me that he had come out—"Finally! It took me long enough. Now I wish we had done something in bed." He had made a whole career out of stage-managing shows, and had never returned to banking. He was a handsome guy, kind of bulky, with a deep voice.

The last thing he said to me was, "What happened to your Southern accent? God, it was so thick I could barely understand you sometime. You sounded like a pickaninny!" I didn't realize when he said that that it was an offensive term. But no one had ever said it about me.

About a decade or so later, I was looking through the obituaries in the *Times* and saw his name. My heart jumped. He had died of AIDS.

We drove through the Holland Tunnel into Downtown Manhattan early the next evening. Richard's girlfriend lived in a walk-up apartment on Waverly Place, in the West Village. We parked the car outside the building, and she buzzed us in. It was on the fifth floor, and I realized that I just could not schlep that big suitcase up all those stairs. Richard said I could leave it down in the car overnight, until I went to Hartford the next day. His girlfriend, Carol, offered me the living room couch for the night. She also said there were several bars in the neighborhood and I should check them out.

"Just don't come back too late," she said.

I promised not to, and then headed down the stairs. I'd never been to New York, and it excited and scared me at the same time. I easily found Washington Square Park, which was quite dark, and then walked around the famous Greenwich Village. Before I knew it, I was in Julius's, an equally famous bar that had been a speakeasy in the 1920s and still had a secret quality to it. Ostensibly, it was an old-fashioned sports bar; the front of the bar served a lot of single men, or men in small groups. The back of the bar was cordoned off. You had to have a "date," that is, a girl or woman with you, to sit there at the tables. Unlike other specifically gay bars, it was very brightly lit, with plate-glass, café-curtained windows looking out onto the street.

As soon as I walked in, I realized I was the youngest person there, and I got a lot of attention. Like all sorts of heads swiveled toward me. In New York then you could drink legally at eighteen, so at least I was "legal" that way. I was still somewhat jailbait as far as sex was concerned, but that did not seem to hinder all those eyes and heads. Immediately, a balding, not terribly good-looking guy in his late thirties trotted toward me, introduced himself, and invited me back to his nearby apartment.

I did not expect this to happen so fast—I had heard that New York was much colder than San Francisco or LA—but anyway his apartment did seem like a nicer place to sleep than Carol's couch. Jim, it turned out, also worked in theater, as a theatrical designer, and had just accepted a job upstate in Rochester with a regional company.

"It really scares me, the idea of leaving New York," he said.

I asked him why.

"Well, you just got here, so you don't really know what the city's like. But it really provides a lot for you, if you know where to look."

He was very warm and friendly; I liked him and realized I'd never see him again. Since I had no idea exactly where I was, he walked me back to Carol's building the next morning. She rang me in, and met me at the door. Richard was up, looking very bad.

"What's wrong?" I asked.

"The car was broken into last night. That big suitcase of yours is gone, and so is a lot of stuff I had left in it, like my briefcase. It was empty, but still I liked it. And a portable typewriter I've had for years. Shit! What an introduction to New York."

Carol put her hand on his shoulder, and turned to me.

"We get used to it here, Perry. There are junkies all over the city. A lot of them live Uptown, but the West Village is a favorite of theirs. You know, everything is a little bit looser here. Do you have enough clothes to keep you going?"

I didn't, but the worst thing was that the suitcase was also filled with drawings, watercolors, and some acrylic paintings. I hated losing those. Now I knew I had to leave New York and get to Hartford and Ronnie LaCoutier as soon as possible.

Carol told me that I needed to get to Penn Station, where I could get a train to Hartford. I had no idea how to use the subway. She suggested I get a cab—"They're pretty cheap. You can get to Penn Station for less than two dollars."

I looked in my wallet. I had about $12 left. I decided to do it, though. I said goodbye to Richard and Carol. Richard was so upset about the break-in that he hardly paid any attention to me. I realized on the long way down the stairs to the street that I didn't even know Carol's address. But in a way, it didn't make a difference. Not in this new, strange chapter of my life.

Chapter

19

About six hours later, I arrived in Hartford. Between the cab ride to Penn Station—the driver overcharged me by more than a dollar—the train fare, and a hot dog at Nedick's at the station, I had exactly fifty cents when I arrived. I managed to get directions for a city bus, and was dropped off within several blocks of Ronnie's apartment, which was in a very pleasant residential area of well-kept lawns and small parks. It wasn't until I rang his bell that I realized I had not even called him when I got to New York.

I rang several times with no answer. I decided just to sit on the stairs in front of his door.

Several people walking in asked me whom I was looking for. When I told them, they said, "Oh, I think he's out."

I was starting to get anxious when Ronnie came up.

He looked different than he had in San Francisco, like he had aged several years. It took him a moment even to smile at me. He unlocked the door, and we went up the elevator to his apartment on the third floor of a four-story building. The apartment was very pleasant with new furniture and wall-to-wall carpeting. We sat on his new couch for a moment; it was gray with a slightly raised check pattern.

"I just got this," he said, gesturing to everything. "I was living with my parents and had to get out, so they helped me with the furniture. My parents are really good people, but they know I'm gay, and it's something we can never talk about. You'll meet them. They want to know everything I do and who I'm with."

"Why do you tell them?" I asked.

"I'm just used to it—telling them everything. I'd really like to kiss you. I never kissed you when I was in San Francisco. I didn't think it was right then."

I got closer to him, and we kissed. He was trembling all over.

"There's so much I need to tell you, Perry. I hope you'll understand it, and not judge me badly."

"I won't judge you at all," I promised. "How can I?"

"That's good." He kissed me again. "God, you're wonderful to kiss. I wanted to kiss you in San Francisco, but I knew you weren't that kind of boy."

I didn't understand what he was talking about—"that kind of boy." What did he mean? Then he explained it, trying very hard to hold on to his composure and not break into tears.

"Most of what I told you was a lie, Perry. I am not a social worker, and I was not working for the Archdiocese of San Francisco with boys on the street. I am Catholic, but believe me the Archdiocese is still not going to stick its neck out for kid hustlers. I did what I did to get closer to them, and to go to bed with them when I could. I figured that if I got to know them, it would be less dangerous and I could get what I wanted. I have never felt good about being gay. My parents will never, ever condone it. So hustlers, especially the real hard-core ones, I feel like I'm not really being queer when I'm with one."

"Why'd you get so close to me?" I asked.

"Because you weren't one of them. I knew that. I wanted you as a friend—although, what can I say? You're really pretty, and, God, you're only eighteen!"

"What about your job?"

"It's not as a social worker. I'm working as an administrative assistant at Pratt & Whitney Aircraft. It's like I wrote you, they'll hire anybody. I can get you a job there. I know people in Personnel. I'll put you in one of my suits, we'll write you a résumé saying you are studying engineering in California, and want some experience before you go back to school. We'll say you're twenty-two. Not eighteen. At eighteen you're too young for them to hire. We'll say that you are interested in becoming a sheet metal apprentice—that's one of their big programs. They have a whole school set up for it. Sheet metal apprentices become foremen and then managers. I bet in a suit you'll really look like an engineer."

Two days later, I had an appointment with Personnel at Pratt & Whitney

Aircraft. The Personnel office was in a building by itself on the vast grounds of the plant, which took up many acres, like the size of maybe three or four large airports. I was wearing Ronnie's wool navy blue suit, which itched and was a bit too long for me (he was about two inches taller than I was), but when I stood up really straight I could pull it off. I was wearing a freshly ironed white shirt and a nice tie.

Kate, the young, collegiate-looking woman interviewing me, asked, "Why do you want to work in an aircraft factory after having so much college? You're in a master's program—won't this hold you back?"

I told her I wanted real experience in the working world, and turning on my charm a hundred percent, said, "I've long admired Pratt & Whitney as a leader in engineering and science. It would be an honor to work here."

She glowed.

"You're the kind of young man we wish we had more of here. But what about your draft deferment? Won't you lose that?"

"I'll tell them this is part of my college work, and I will be in your sheet metal apprenticeship program. By the time they draft me, the war could be over."

"I don't know," she said, tossing her head. "This war's given us huge business. We're working twenty-four hours a day making fighter jet engines for Viet Nam and other parts of Indo-China. Let's just hope that it keeps Pratt & Whitney humming for a while!"

She took out several papers and had me sign them, then handed me a small packet of information that also included a pair of safety glasses.

"You'll need them when you work on the floor, for sparks. If you wear prescription glasses all the time, we can have them remade as safety glasses."

I was given a start time in six days, but told to report again on Monday to meet my floor foreman; he would have to sign off on my employment. I felt very good on the bus back to Ronnie's apartment. He came in later from work; the weekend was up ahead. I felt bad that I had no money at all. I decided to do something that I had never done since I had left home: call my mother and ask her if she could send me something. I did. She was happy that I was no longer on the West Coast.

"At least we're on the same coast."

When I told her that I was completely broke, she said, "You know I have no money. I can barely make the rent."

She agreed to sent me $20 in the mail to Ronnie's apartment. I felt better now. I could borrow a little from Ronnie and then pay him back. The weekend with Ronnie was very interesting and strange. There were times when he seemed to float away from me, like he was no longer there or in real consciousness. He said it was because of some tranquilizers he was taking.

I asked him why he needed to take them.

"I'm a lot sicker than you know, Perry."

He explained to me that he'd had several major breakdowns when he was younger, starting in high school. A raft of therapists had given him several diagnoses: adolescent depression, schizophrenia, sociopathic psychosis. A lot of it had to do with his being gay. He had never succeeded in hiding it, and his parents, observant Catholics, had thought that if the priests couldn't do it, modern psychiatry would efficiently "cure" him of it.

We went out shopping on Saturday; he seemed ebullient, almost giddy. He was very happy I was there. I had this huge need to create something—I had not done anything in weeks like that—so I bought a drawing pad and started drawing when we got back. He was very taken with that.

"You're an artist," he said. "Like Andy Warhol!"

I noticed he was drinking a lot. Suddenly he had an idea to invite some other gay men over.

"Hartford is a lot gayer than people know," he said, dialing the phone. "We have a couple of bars here, and some restaurants. A lot of the guys work in the insurance companies, but some work at Pratt & Whitney, too."

It was easy to get them over—I guess there wasn't that much to do in Hartford. Three of his friends came over, and they all drank more. He showed them my drawings. They said nothing about them.

"Perry's a real artist," Ronnie said. "He's the first real artist I've ever met. I'm glad he's here, even though he's living off me."

I felt embarrassed that he had said that, then realized he was drunk, and the others were pretty polluted as well. A few minutes later, he turned the lights down and started taking his clothes off. Two of the three left, but one remained, and Ronnie had sex with him in the living room. I was tired and soon fell asleep in Ronnie's bed.

The next morning Ronnie woke up on the couch, hung over. The apartment was a mess.

"I'm sorry I did that," he said. "I hope those guys weren't grossed out by me—when I drink I can't control what I do sometimes. I'm supposed to go over to my parents for Sunday lunch later. I told them about you, and they want to meet you."

I was not crazy about meeting his parents, but knew that I should. They lived on the second floor of a group of tenement apartments in a very hard-scrabble, working-class area of town. It was a dull, overcast day, which did not make the neighborhood, stocked with low-rise, broken-down-looking frame buildings, look any better. We walked up the stairs to their apartment.

His father, a short, bald man who did not look like his more handsome son at all, met us at the door. He shook hands with Ronnie and then with me.

"So you're Ronnie's friend from the West Coast? How you like Hartford, not much is it?"

"It's fine," I said. "I've never been here. I've never been up North at all, really."

His mother, a heavyset but still attractive-looking woman, wearing make-up and an apron, emerged from the kitchen. She looked like she might have been at some point earlier in her life taller than his father.

She walked up to me and hugged me.

"You're from the South! I like Southerners. They're friendlier than people here. Hartford's about as friendly as a refrigerator!"

"They're plenty friendly, Ruth," his father said. "You just got to make an effort to meet 'em. You never do that."

"That's 'cause I know better," she said and offered me a drink.

We sat around the small living room that was filled with pictures of Ronnie. He was their only child, and I could tell how puzzled they were about him, and not at all happy to let go of him. Ruth went to church religiously, but still did not get close to people. Her husband, Pete, who might have originally been Pierre, was actually more outgoing when you got past his own frostiness. He talked about his friends and family. Several of his brothers and sisters lived in Hartford with all their kids. His eyes sparkled when he talked about his nieces and nephews; there was this obvious, terrible yearning in

Chapter Nineteen

him—he would never have grandkids.

He asked Ronnie how he'd been sleeping. I didn't know that Ronnie had chronic insomnia.

"It's been OK," Ronnie said, not wanting to dwell on it.

Pete turned to me. "He's been that way since he was a kid. Must be hard with someone else sleeping in the same bed. Right, Ronnie?"

"It's fine," Ronnie answered, his face down. "Perry doesn't squirm at all."

"Ronnie's got quite a pad there," Pete said, now glowing. "He's furnished it nicely."

"Not like this place," Ruth broke in. "We haven't bought a stick of furniture in forty years."

"If you didn't spend so much money on yourself, Ruth—"

I was glad when Ruth said it was time for the lunch. The food was very heavy. Pot roast, potatoes, canned beans. There was no dining room, but a small nook off the living room to eat in. I kept looking out the window at the gray sky. It seemed like Hartford was never sunny at this time of the year, in early April. I hardly said anything else while Pete and Ruth went after each other, and Ronnie simply nodded or said something inconsequential just to keep up the appearance that he cared about the conversation.

Just before we left, Pete offered him some money.

"Just in case you ever need it," he said to Ronnie. Ronnie refused it, and then shook his father's hand and then hugged his mother.

"You come back," Ruth said. "We're glad Ronnie has a real friend here."

Ronnie had bought an old used Chevy when he had returned to Hartford, and he drove it back to his apartment.

"What do you think of my parents?" he asked.

"They seem nice. They love you."

"They're better now. When I was a kid, they put me in a hospital." He sighed, then added, "several times. I had shock treatments; I'll never forget what they were like. It was awful. I couldn't tell if it was because I was gay or something else."

Suddenly I felt very angry. How could they do that to this beautiful man? They seemed nice enough; maybe that was the problem. They were *only* nice enough. I remembered that my parents had wanted me to go see a "child

169

doctor" when I was eight or nine. They'd been alarmed that I didn't seem like a "regular" boy. I'd had no interest in sports of any sort. It was like this heavy curtain had come down between me and the normal boy's world of competition and "snips and snails and puppy-dog tails."

I learned that the child doctor was a child psychologist, and it had been my mother's idea that I see him. My father was more tolerant, encouraging actually. I was enchanted with puppetry. I wanted to make puppets. He brought me books from the library on making them, and built a puppet stage for me.

Helen was furious.

"You're letting him play with *dolls*!" she spat out.

When she called the puppets "dolls," she destroyed me. She would humiliate me in front of people, basically strangers, saying, "My son plays with dolls."

I didn't go to see the child doctor. My father refused to send me to him, and we bonded over the puppets. He was very pleased that I loved reading the way he did, and that I had an imagination.

I felt bad for Ronnie. There was no telling what his parents were really like—meaning how much pain they had put him through, or how much they had gone through themselves.

On Monday, I could tell that Ronnie did not want to go to work but forced himself to. He was in a fog of twisted thoughts and intentions. He couldn't find his belt or his shoes. I wondered if he was like this normally.

Later I got dressed and went into Pratt & Whitney for my appointment with the floor foreman. I was now for the first time on the work floor: it was huge and ear-splittingly noisy, organized into special areas for various parts of engine construction. I was working on pressing out metal parts of the fan blades that cooled the inner works. The presses were hydraulic machines exerting tons of pressure. There were signs all over that said:

KEEP YOUR EYES ON YOUR WORK
AND YOUR FINGERS ON YOUR HANDS!

I noticed quickly that a lot of men didn't do that, and were missing fingers. It was important to take off all rings and watches, which could become magnetized and pull you into the grasp of the presses. There were large clocks all over the floor, so I didn't need a watch, and I didn't wear a ring. I was glad for that.

"So you wanna work here?" Mr. Sanders, my foreman, a grizzled old man of about fifty asked. "Why? You look too smart. You're a college type. I can tell it."

I told him I needed a break from school, and I wanted the experience of working in the real world.

He laughed. "It's real enough here, kid. Just be careful. I don't want t' see you with your hand off or your arms broken or something. Know what I mean?"

I told him I did. He shook my hand and signed the papers I needed to start employment. On the bus back, I felt really good. The money Pratt & Whitney paid me was amazing: it was the kind of money I might have made selling encyclopedias if the promises they had made were real. This *was* real, although I had told every lie in the book to get employed, but that seemed to go with my life and my struggle to survive.

The sun was starting to set as I approached Ronnie's building. Suddenly a young woman came out of it and met me.

"You're Ronald LaCoutier's friend?" I told her I was. "He was just taken to the hospital. An ambulance came and got him."

Chapter

20

I realized suddenly that I didn't even have a key to get in. His neighbor called the super, who let me in. I was told that I couldn't stay there, but his parents would come to the apartment soon. They arrived shortly afterwards.

"We're really sorry about this," Pete LaCoutier said.

Ruth was in tears.

"It's our fault. He shouldn't have been living on his own. He wasn't ready to."

I asked what had happened.

"He left work," Pete said, "and then called us and said he was gonna kill himself. We called an ambulance. He's in Norwalk State Hospital now. That's the state mental hospital. He's been there before. I'm sorry a nice boy like you has to be in the middle of this. We're gonna have to do something with his apartment. Close it up and put the stuff in storage. Do you have a place to stay for the night?"

I told him I didn't, and Pete said I could spend one night there. Luckily, the money my mother had sent came that day. It was exactly one $20 bill. But at least it meant I wasn't out in the cold. I still had a week before I started at Pratt & Whitney. Now I had no place to stay at all. I had to figure out what to do.

The next day was bright, still sharply crisp, even a bit cold. I packed up the few clothes I had, and walked over to the large, comfortable YMCA located next to Bushnell Park. At the desk, I met a young man in his late twenties who turned out to be the director of the Y. He greeted me very warmly, and I told him I wanted a room for two nights.

Each night was less than $5, but I needed some money to eat on. I went up to the room. It was clean, warm, and had a view of the park. I felt happy. Even having a place for two nights made me feel secure. I went out to the park and drew scenery, then went back up and swam at the Y pool. The next day, when I went down, I met George, the young director again, and he asked me how I was doing.

I decided to be honest with him, as much as I could. I was a young man from Savannah, Georgia, and I had been staying with a friend who was suddenly taken ill, and soon I'd have no place to stay. But I did have a job coming up at Pratt & Whitney, and would be receiving a paycheck soon. He nodded.

"We can front you for two nights, Perry, that's all. When will you start work?"

When I told him it would be a week, he had an idea. He asked me my religious affiliation, and I said Jewish. A light went on; he pulled out a phone directory and found a number for Jewish Family Services. He called and made an appointment that day for me to see a social worker there.

The man I saw at Jewish Family Services, Mr. Cohen, was in a suit, middle-aged, portly, and stern-faced. He asked me a lot of personal questions, like why I had left home, and didn't I miss my mother, and what was I doing in Hartford, Connecticut, of all places?

I told him I had heard there were jobs there, and I was taking time off from school.

"We can give you a small emergency loan," he said. "And it's a loan, so we want it back."

He pulled out two $20 bills from a box in his desk, and put them in an envelope. He also told me that he could find me some brief employment before I started work at the factory. He made a phone call, and then wrote down a name and address for me.

"They are expecting you tomorrow at 9 AM. It's not that far from the Y."

The job was working in a foundry, mostly cleaning up and stacking lead and iron parts as they emerged, still extremely hot, out of the molds. I had to wear a large, rubberized apron, thick asbestos gloves, and goggles. The man I worked for was a very nice Jewish guy who owned the business. He told me that it had been in his family for two generations. They had originally come in from Russia.

"Hartford is a good place," he said. "But they don't like Jews very much here, unless you have a lot of money and live in West Hartford where all the nice insurance people live."

He asked me what it was like being Jewish in the South, and I realized I could barely describe it. All I could describe was growing up in poverty and knowing I was gay, and I couldn't talk about that at all.

I worked there for a couple of days, and he paid me on Friday in cash at the end of the week. I decided the first thing I'd do was go back and see Mr. Cohen and pay him back. When I arrived at the Jewish Family Services office and asked to speak with him, he came out of his office with the same stern look on his face.

When I told him I wanted to pay him back, he brightened.

"Most kids like you don't do that," he said. "You're an exception."

Working at Pratt & Whitney was actually fun. I got into it very quickly. I was on the afternoon-evening shift that began at 3 PM and ended at 11. At quitting time, I would take a bus into downtown Hartford and from there walk back to the Y. I discovered a late-night restaurant called the Rathskeller that sported an easily discernable gay shadow. There were tables of men who regularly ate together, and several of the waiters were unmistakable. I would have only a late snack, since dinner at the factory cafeteria was filling enough to keep me going.

The hard part about working at the aircraft factory was simply staying alert and not being bored, literally, to death, because the work was dangerous and it would be very easy to have an accident. I didn't have to worry about what I wore, except that you had to wear safety glasses and safety shoes with steel tips in them, in case something fell on your feet. No one bothered me. They hardly said anything to me, or asked any personal questions. I met some young men at the Rathskeller who worked there, and almost immediately we were out to each other. They were very careful on the work floor not to give anything away, but there was a definite "sparkle" to them that would set off anyone's gaydar.

Soon it became something for me to look forward to—talking to them on the bus, or saying hello at the cafeteria or at the Rathskeller. One was named Sheldon. He was slightly built and had a heavy, working-class New England accent. He had never been out of the state of Connecticut and was impressed that I had lived in San Francisco, which, among young gay men, had already achieved a mythical status of being the "gayest place on Earth."

He would introduce me to other guys as, "This is Perry. He's a real traveler. He's from Georgia, like 'Gone with the Wind,' y'know?"

Although Hartford was easily seen as a finicky, repressed bastion of New England Puritanism, it also had a palpable, often easily shaded-into-queer male underground. Many bars did not allow women to drink openly in them, out of an ingrained fear of prostitution. I noticed that some taverns and restaurants downtown actually had a "ladies entrance," so that women dining alone were seated in a special section. From a soft, leather easy chair in the lobby of the Y, I could see small bands of bankers and insurance men in crisp seersucker suits and straw boaters strolling together in Bushnell Park. Spring was approaching, and I noticed other men walking into the lobby of the Y, which I realized was a furtive but easily recognizable cruising area.

One night I came back really grimy after work, and with a towel wrapped around me entered the showers. All by myself, I turned on the hot water. Then a stocky, muscular young man a few years older than I came in. He turned away from me, got under the spray, and as steam started coming up, turned around and suddenly slipped on the wet floor right into my arms.

I backed away from him, but he held on to me and I quickly returned his hold that was more like a hug.

"Can we go to your room?" he asked.

I said sure, and we spent the night together making love nonstop. He was the most passionate guy I'd ever met. In the morning, I asked him his name.

"Larry," he answered. "But some people call me 'Amadeus,' because I love Mozart so much."

I asked him if I could see him again, and he said no. He was living with his parents in the suburbs, but sometimes he would sneak into the Y for this purpose.

"It's not diffcult late at night," he explained. "I think the guys who work here even know what's going on."

As soon as I got my first paycheck from Pratt & Whitney, I got on a bus to visit Ronnie at the Norwalk State Hospital. The day was cloudy, but penetrating shafts of cold New England sunlight would sometimes break through. The bus ride was slow, stopping at every small town, and took about two hours from Hartford. But it gave me a chance to look at Connecticut, especially on a gloomy day. I got to the hospital around 2 o'clock, and had to go through a security check for visitors. The place looked old enough to be medieval, with locked wards and gray, dirty-looking walls. Ronnie was in his room, in pajamas, propped up on his bed. He smiled at me.

"You're the first visitor I've had except for my parents. They come a lot; I wish they wouldn't."

When I asked him how he was, he said he was still depressed, but I thought anyone would be depressed there. He asked me how things were going at Pratt & Whitney, and I told him they were fine. I had no problems at all, just had to survive the boredom of it, doing the same thing over and over again.

"Yeah, you shouldn't be there. You're an artist, not a factory worker. But the money's good. I'm not gay anymore. I want you to know that."

"You're not?"

"No. I decided I really like some of the nurses here. I'm attracted to one of them. I want to ask her to marry me."

I thought about Fern and me, and just smiled.

"That doesn't mean you're not gay," I said. "Believe me. It doesn't."

"I want to make my parents happy. If I got married, they'd be really happy. I know that. It just kills me how much misery I have caused them."

I felt very sorry for him. His eyes looked like he had been drugged, and I knew he was getting shock treatments.

"Haven't they caused you a lot, too?" I asked.

He looked at me, and then his eyes closed.

"I'm tired," he said. "I wish I wasn't so tired. Thank you for coming to see me, Perry. After I get out, if I marry that nurse—her name is Barbara—I won't see you again. That's just the way it's gotta be."

(Ronnie did not marry the nurse. I did not hear from him for about eight or nine years, then I did. He was still gay, but finally happy—after both of his parents had died.)

After a few weeks, I got tired of living at the Y. I couldn't paint there for fear of making a mess, and I wanted to have a place of my own. I was making great money, for a kid, at Pratt & Whitney, taking home more than $200 a week. But with this much money running around from war profiteering, inflation had hit Hartford, and rents were going through the roof. I looked at several apartments that cost four and five hundred a month, and saw an ad in the Hartford Courant for a "large room. Private entrance. Quiet and clean. Off Wethersfield Avenue."

I made an appointment to see it before I went into work. The landlady, Mrs. Crawford, who lived upstairs in the building, was a cheerful but dignified New Englander who was pleased that a well-mannered Southerner wanted to rent it. She asked me what I did, and I told her that I worked at the factory, but was also an artist.

"I love art," she said. "I go to the Atheneum a lot. My only concern is that you don't have a lot of young women here, or rowdy parties. We can't have those."

I agreed with her: I would definitely not have a lot of young women, and no rowdy parties. I moved in the next day. The room was completely furnished, even the bed linens, and I loved it. It was bright, sunny, and reasonably quiet, although some of the neighbors who lived past the wooden fence in the back garden, where Mrs. Crawford had set up garden chairs and a table, could get noisy.

Once I noticed some of their kids destroying a small tree that grew on their side of the fence. Their mother came out, and I complained about it.

"What business is it of yours?" she snapped at me.

Suddenly I realized I was not in the South, where well-mannered people did not talk like that, and public infractions of behavior of any sort—at least the ones not buried in racial, family, or money secrets—were everybody's business.

Besides rent, I spent my first paychecks on art supplies, and began painting in earnest. The room was large enough for a big easel and a table for my paints. Even after getting to sleep at 2 in the morning, I could get up by 9 and start painting. I liked that I had a secret artistic life, certainly secret to the other people who worked at Pratt & Whitney, who figured that I was just this odd kid from the South working up North for the money. What I learned very quickly from factory work was that most workers were more interested in their paychecks than in safety or any form of organizing. I saw many situations around me that could have led to injury—big puddles of slippery lubricating grease left on the floor, areas where the lighting was too low for vision, machines that needed service but were still in operation—but no one cared. What floor workers cared about was the most amount of money for the least amount of work, getting what was called a "gravy job": one where you could sleepwalk through it and still be paid.

This was so different from my life as an artist, where you were awake and alive every moment doing work; in fact, time just roared past you—the opposite of time at Pratt & Whitney Aircraft, which seemed to crawl by. To make the time go faster, I started playing head games with myself: going through the plots of movies, singing Broadway show tunes to myself as I walked down the vast aisles of the factory floor from one work area to the next.

A lot of the women on the floor were black, and I got along very well with them; they thought I was kind of spunky and funky. The white women looked at me a little stranger—and questioned me. What was I doing in Hartford, and why didn't I have a family already? One attractive-looking young white woman looked at my hands.

"Those are definitely not man's hands," she said to me.

"No," I said. "They're mine."

On the weekends, I hung out at the Rathskeller or sometimes snuck into one of the gay bars in town. There were two. One was called the 1492, and it was kind of like the Rendezvous in San Francisco, filled with aging preppies in casual-chic clothes; the other was Last Call, and it was more working class, with drag queens or the Connecticut version of hair fairies, that is, guys who could be spotted half a mile away. I actually found the bar one night by noticing one such character and following him until he ducked into it on a dark side street. The bartender at first didn't want to serve me (I was eighteen, and a stranger to the bar), but I sweet-talked him into liking me. Sheldon, my gay friend from Pratt & Whitney, also frequented Last Call. We became good friends. He was fascinated with me being so far away from home. He had actually never really had a home—his parents had been divorced when he was a small kid, and he had been raised by a spinster aunt named Flossy.

He took me to meet her. She was fabulous: this busy old lady with bright copper-dyed hair and a raw New England accent that echoed Sheldon's.

"So you're the boy from Jaw-ja? Bet you ain't never been in no place like Hawtf'd before. My nephew Shelly's a nice kid, but he's always gettin' himself into trouble with guys who wanna do him f' something. I tell him, 'Shelly, whatever you do, watch ya money 'cause one day you is gonna be as old as me and ya friends ain't gonna take care o' ya.'"

The one thing you could not do in the gay bars in Hartford was dance, not with anyone of either sex. But Sheldon heard that there was a bar called Steve's in a town about fifteen miles away where on Sundays, after six, there was dancing.

He asked me if I wanted to go.

I said sure.

The problem was neither of us had wheels, and getting a bus on Sunday was out of the question. We would hitch.

We met at 5:30 just before sunset on the ramp to a highway that would go to the town. We had to wait a long time, then got a lift to within three miles of the bar. Back out on the street, another car stopped for us.

"Where you going?" the middle-aged, very nondescript white male driver said.

Sheldon told him the name of the street.

We got in, and the driver asked us what was on the street.

Sheldon swallowed hard, then said, "It's a bar called Steve's."

The driver let that sink it for a second, then said: "My son goes there."

"He does?" Sheldon asked.

"Yeah, I don't like it, but he does. I guess everyone has their problems. My son has his; I guess you have yours, too. Right?"

I smiled. Suddenly the man seemed like a human. He had a gay son. We were all in the same boat, just in different parts of it.

"We do," I said. "What is yours?"

"My son."

A moment later, he dropped us off in front of the bar. He didn't say another word, but just drove away.

The bar was a total letdown. There was almost no one in it, and there definitely was no dancing, although there was a large area in the back that could have accommodated a lot of physical activity of a dancing nature.

I asked one of the patrons what was going on, that we had come in from

Hartford to dance.

"Yeah, that's over," he said sadly. "They raided the place about two weeks ago. No more dancing. They didn't arrest anyone. They just said they didn't have a license for dancing, so they had to stop it. Really sad. You used to have about two hundred guys here on Sunday nights. Now it's just a couple of us who live close by."

We found out there actually was a bus going back to Hartford, and we soon took it. Sheldon was depressed.

"This happens a lot," he said. "I guess it's Connecticut. In the bigger cities the Mafia pays off the cops, but in smaller towns a bar appears and it's going good for a while—everybody feels free and happy—then someone finds out that 'perverts' are in it, and they get it closed down. I'd love to find out who did it. I'd want to kill him!"

"Maybe it was that guy," I said. "The one who picked us up and said his problem was his son."

Sheldon shook his head sadly.

"Now I feel bad about saying anything. You never can trust straight people. The only one I trust is Flossy. She's always been there for me. She loves me so much, but what am I gonna do when she dies?"

I had no idea. I knew I had no family now to call my own, except for my sister who was living with a foster family in Pennsylvania. She had left my mother and me several years earlier when she could no longer take Helen's vicious, often sadistic, paranoid behavior. They'd started fighting, slamming doors and screaming at each other. My mother divided all human beings into two categories: those who bought her story of the eternally wronged, victimized, helpless woman left with two impossible children—and who were willing, at least for a while, to get her through her bouts of sometimes violent schizophrenic episodes when she left reality completely—and those who didn't. My sister Nancy didn't, and had decided early on that she wouldn't. There was also the unspoken shadow of Helen's lesbianism; my mother had so deeply internalized Southern homophobia that she often said really cruel and vicious things about other gay people—I guess she wanted to throw folks off the scent—but still, even when we were small kids, we knew she was different.

Helen wore pants before most adult women in Savannah did; she even smoked small cigars. She was not interested in remarrying after my father died, and she had what became obvious to me as crushes on other women. They would appear suddenly. She would become intensely close to them, and then something would happen: they were gone. Often it was because they were more interested in men than in a relationship with her. Even if it was a relationship that no one could dare define as more than a "close" friendship.

By the time I went away to college, though, I did understand what it was—that she and I shared this extremely forbidden trait, and she was finally starting to have openly lesbian relationships, even a girlfriend—though we could still not talk about it, and no one in her family was ever supposed to admit it.

I wanted to be as far away from my mother's sprawling, successful mercantile family in Savannah as I could be. I didn't want to have to explain anything to them, or lie anymore. The lies were the worst part. For most gay men, their entire lives would be a lie. I felt vaguely envious of Sheldon and his Aunt Flossy, but I had a freedom I was not going to give up.

One night at the Rathskeller I overheard an older man talking to a young waiter about a new campaign of plainclothes men entrapping gay men every place they could.

"They'll come up to you on the street, or park their cars and try to get you in them. Once you do, they'll show you a badge and arrest you."

"What will they arrest you for?" I broke in.

"Sexual perversion, sodomy," he said.

"But you haven't done anything," I argued. "You just got in the car."

"That doesn't make a difference," the waiter, a handsome Mediterranean-looking guy named Theo said. "It's all on the books in Connecticut. It's worse here than in New York. You know, that old Puritanism."

Now I got really nerve-jangly walking home late at night from downtown Hartford on almost deserted Wethersfield Avenue. There was a small triangular park about a block or so from me, and I had to pass it to get home. Several nights after that conversation, I noticed a man in his late twenties parked by the triangle with his eyes riveted on me.

As I got closer, I noticed that he was really attractive, with a very athletic-looking face and body, his thinning hair cropped close, wearing very functional wire-rim glasses. He seemed a perfect example of a plainclothes cop. I gave him a cold dirty look and kept walking.

I was afraid he was going to get out of his car and follow me all the way up to the back door that I used as an entrance to my room. My heart pounded as I unlocked the door; I looked back. He wasn't anywhere in sight.

The next night, though, as I walked past the triangle, he was still there. I gave him the same dirty look, and he unrolled his window.

"Hi there," he said, and gave me a very sheepish smile.

I was equal parts angry and scared.

"I know what you're doing!"

"You do?" He opened the door to his car and got out. I was ready to take off.

"Do you live around here?" he asked.

"That's none of your business," I said.

He looked down a moment at his feet. I'd rarely seen a guy built like that: he was all muscle and beautiful T-square proportions. Suddenly he looked at me, straight into my eyes.

"My name's Len. What's yours?"

Now I saw that he was really nervous, shaking even. I decided instantly he wasn't a cop and put my hand on his shoulder and told him my name.

I got into his car, and we drove the short distance to my room that had parking in the back. He was an ex-lifeguard and football player, living in an adjoining town near his parents, working in insurance. With his clothes off, he was an exquisite lover, tender, soft, a bit sad. He left very early in the morning, but gave me his number at work.

We began "dating," you could say, but mainly just having sex in my room. Out of bed, Len was extremely reserved, hardly expressing any feelings; every time I saw him I was sure it was going to be my last. But it wasn't.

Chapter
21

In May, after I had been working at Pratt & Whitney for about six weeks, I got a notice from the Connecticut draft board to appear for my induction physical. I was told that in a week there would be a bus waiting for me at 7 AM downtown to take me to the Induction Center, and that all I had to do was show this letter to my boss and I would get off from work. Also, if I did not show up, I would be liable for court action—which, after my experience in California, was a very sobering thought.

Mr. Sanders, my foreman, took the letter and shook his head.

"Damn! Well, ya gotta face it. The Army'll do good things for you, Perry. Just don't get ya'self killed in Viet Nam if ya can help it."

I saw Len later on.

"I was in the Army," he said. "I didn't like it, but there was nothing I could do about it. I'm in good shape. I couldn't lie."

I didn't know what to do. I just knew that I had taken ROTC (called derogatorily "Rotcee")—Reserve Officer's Training Corps—both in high school and during my one year at the University of Georgia. I'd hated both of them, but they were good portents of what life in the Service would be: I would be constantly harassed, bullied, and ordered around, often by men with the intelligence of fleas. My high school "Rotcee" instructor, Sgt. Jones, read English on about a fourth-grade level—he could not read any name harder than Smith. Most of the time he just barked at us, and occasionally, while we were working on something, fell asleep in class. I decided I didn't want three years of having stooges like Sgt. Jones over me.

There was also the realization, very real, that they were drafting me only because of poverty: if I'd had money, I'd be back in some school I wanted to be in, not surrounded by rednecks in the South or working in a factory up North.

I really stiffened at the thought of it. I called my mother and told her there was a chance I'd be drafted. As much as we did not get along, that really upset her.

"You should have stayed in school," she said. She went to our family doctor, a profoundly narrow-minded man who was an ardent segregationist, and he told her it would be a good thing if I were.

"It will make a man out of Perry," he informed her.

Since at that point I had already had sex with enough former military guys, I only laughed. I knew I'd make a man out of myself—on my own terms.

At 7 AM there was a line of boys about half a block long waiting in the morning chill to get on buses. They were extremely nervous, many of them holding cups of coffee and cigarettes.

As the buses rolled in, a drill sergeant barked orders at us to get rid of the coffee and the smokes. Most of the kids on the bus—some of whom looked close to twenty, others closer to fourteen—were stony and silent. Some talked though, and a guy sitting next to me talked nervously.

"I don't want to leave my Mom. She's not well. But if I gotta do it, I guess I gotta do it."

At the Induction Center, we were weighed and our height was measured. With our shirts off, a doctor checked our hearts, and in assembly-line fashion, our blood was drawn. An obnoxious, fat Army medic grabbed my upper arm like it was piece of knockwurst, and squeezed it. I was furious.

"Don't do that," I insisted. "You don't have me yet!"

"Well, 'scuse me!" he said, and walked away. Another medic approached, smiled, and put on a quick tourniquet.

After this, we were all seated together in this huge room, and given the Army's quick version of an IQ test, and then a questionnaire to fill out. I decided to mark a check by everything I could. Yes, I had nightmares, wet my bed, had flat feet as well as several maladies I had no idea what they were—and "homosexual tendencies."

I had heard about the "queer box," and now I had no problem at all checking it. There were four men in civilian suits at big desks in front of us. After all the questionnaires were gathered up, my name was called. I had to walk up the aisle, past rows and rows of boys, with everyone looking straight up at me, to the first desk where a middle-aged, Eisenhower-looking man with a faintly pleasant, thin-featured face gestured for me to sit.

He looked over my questionnaire.

"What about these homo tendencies, Mr. Brass? Do you still have them?"

"Yes, sir," I answered. "I do."

"Can you do something to get rid of them?"

I paused.

"No."

"How long have you had them?"

"All of my life," I answered. "I moved to San Francisco, and I got"—I de-cided to use a scientific-sounding word with this guy—"I got 'fixated' there."

Any semblance of cordiality on his face froze. He took out a large red rubber stamp, and marked on my papers: "REJECTED."

"Go into the other room," he said, pointing to a distant door, "and see Lt. Duncan. He'll tell you what will happen next."

I did, with every eye again following me.

Lt. Duncan was a kind of good-looking officer who did not seem as stony as the civilian reviewer in the other room. He asked me to sit down in front of his desk.

"You know why you're being rejected?" he asked me.

"Yes," I said. "I do."

"Do you know what this rejection can mean to you?"

"No, sir. I just know that you are rejecting me."

"It means that no matter what, you cannot volunteer later. You cannot serve your country, you will not be an upstanding part of your communi-ty, and this record is confidential, but if asked the Army can inform courts and other government officials why you've been rejected. You *do* understand this?"

Suddenly any sense of relief I had dissolved. I felt terrible. *They* were re-jecting me, not the other way around.

I hung my head. "I do."

"All right."

He handed me several papers that all said "REJECTED" again and again, and then told me to wait outside by the buses. I did, for several min-utes alone, then this flood of boys poured out of the building, all talking about when they'd be called up. It was like a floodgate of words had opened, and they all had something to talk about. The buses soon rolled up, and I got on one. Several guys asked me when I was being called up, and I just nodded and didn't answer. I felt like the bus ride back took hours; in truth it was only about half an hour. I kept thinking about what Lt. Duncan said: That now I'd really be cut off from the "normal" world.

Len, though, didn't agree.

We were in bed naked.

"You did the right thing," he said. "Why should you put yourself through that if you don't want to? It was bad enough that I *had* to do it. I could never have done what you did—I'd be scared my parents would find out. The truth is, I wasn't even gay then. I just couldn't figure out why girls didn't do anything for me."

I started seeing Len a good bit. If I had been older, I might have thought of him as my "boyfriend," but it was hard for me to think of anyone in that way. Mostly what I thought about was my own survival on an immediate day-to-day or a day-to-somewhat-future date basis: like how I'd pay Mrs. Crawford the rent, or buy paints, or endure another week of boredom at Pratt & Whitney. Since I didn't have a phone, and calling Len was difficult, he usually just popped up at my door, and we'd either stay in and have sex or go out and have dinner. There was hardly time for both. He let out so little of himself though that I felt no emotional connection to him.

My own feelings were always constrained to someplace else; they were still in my childhood in Savannah, or with Rodney. I got several letters from him. He had a job as a veterinarian's assistant a few miles outside of Nashville. He invited me to come visit him—that is, not to actually be with him, since he was still living with his parents, but—

"I'd like to see you again, Perry. I have a job now I like. It's part-time after school, but it pays good, and I'm not doing what I used to do to make money. I can't go back to that. It would hurt my parents and they love me I know it. I've made some changes in my life. I'd like to talk to you about them, but I miss you. Believe me. I do."

I decided I'd do it. I'd go to Nashville to see him. It was the end of June, heading into the Fourth of July weekend. I decided I'd fly to Savannah, to see my mother, then fly to Nashville and see Rodney. I told Mr. Sanders, my foreman, about it. He told me that because I hadn't been at the plant for very long, I had no vacation time coming, but I could just use this as a "leave of absence," and he'd make sure I had my job when I got back.

Flying was very easy then. As a kid, under the age of twenty-one, I could just show up at the airport and get a half-price standby fare to anywhere. It was a program most of the major airlines had instituted to encourage the huge, baby-boom market to start flying early. If you were from "Twelve to Twenty-One," that was all you needed to do. You could check one bag, and if there were no seats in coach and the only seat left was in first class, it was yours. Of course first class then did not cost as much, even in old dollars, as first class does now, and the difference between coach and first class was not that obvious. What was obvious was that I had never flown.

A few days later I was at Hartford's airport to take a small commuter plane into New York's John F. Kennedy Airport, where I'd get on another plane to Savannah. As soon as the small plane left the runway, I thought my heart would rise into my throat—then I just let go, and loved it. I wanted to watch everything as the ground below receded and the houses got tiny.

A young stewardess approached.

"I'm flying!" I said, smiling. She smiled.

"Is this your first time?"

I nodded, too overwhelmed suddenly even to talk.

At JFK I changed to a larger plane that seemed extremely luxurious to me, even in coach. I was offered a cocktail and took it, since once you got on the plane no one knew you were flying standby youth fare. At the small airport in Savannah, my mother was waiting. I kissed her, but I could tell she was not that happy to see me.

"I don't know how you can go up in one of those things," she said. "They scare me too much."

My mother had never flown in her life. She had gained weight, and her face was horribly careworn, like there were things stamped on it worse than the REJECTED on my draft papers. We got into her car, and she lit a cigarette. She was dressed in ugly, ill-fitting slacks and a blouse that looked more like a man's shirt. She drove like a man, too, with her right hand on the wheel and her left hand dangling her cigarette out the window. She was no longer living in the housing project where I had grown up, but she and Esther, the difficult, often overwrought German immigrant woman who had become her partner, had rented a small apartment in an older part of town. On the way in, I looked around at the old cobblestoned streets filled with thick, far-branching live oak trees dripping Spanish moss, and dense, dark rows of azalea bushes; Savannah was gorgeous. There was no denying it.

She took another deep drag on her cigarette, letting the smoke curl out of nostrils.

"Why did you decide to come back?" she asked. "I thought you hated Savannah?"

"I wanted to see you."

"Why? You never loved me. You never did."

I couldn't say anything. I knew this might be a difficult situation—my mother and I had never talked about the "big thing": that I was as queer as she was. The difference was I could face it. After I had tried to kill myself at fifteen, after the worst year of my life in continuous war with her—when she made it plain that she took "no prisoners"; she was either going to control me completely and use me my whole life, or destroy me in the process—I could face it.

She had said to me, "Only one of us is going to be left standing when this is over, Perry. And it's not going to be you."

"I wanted to see you," I repeated as we slowed down and then parked. "I thought it was time."

"You didn't have to do me any favors," she said, and cut off the ignition. I got out with my small suitcase. Inside, the paintings I had done as a high school student were on the walls. There were also photographs of me and my sister Nancy, and of Esther and her little girl from a former marriage. Esther was dark-haired and definitely *zaftig,* with a large, rouged, florid face. She waddled over to me and kissed me.

"It's so nice to see you, Perry," she said brightly. "Helen and I were looking forward to you coming."

Chapter

22

The next several days were extremely difficult. Helen and I could barely talk to each other. Sometimes you have the ghosts of the living as well as the dead. There was the constant pain she had inflicted on me in my childhood, when in moments of becoming a "real boy" I had stopped taking care of her. With her endless stream of maladies real and imagined, she was constantly breaking up, falling apart, and having violent temper tantrums in which I was the victim. Her numerous, often wealthy relatives in Savannah knew about this, and pretended to look the other way. "Mental illness" was not something you talked about, nor was lesbianism. She was described as being "emotionally fragile," and "unusual." She did not dress like Southern women did, in demure "tasteful" little dresses. She was tall, strident, and assertive when not being destroyed by her mental problems, and, "like a man," wore pants most of the time when good Southern ladies did not.

She had met Esther in group therapy. They had become close. Esther had had a very hard time growing up in Berlin as Hitler came to power. She was not Jewish, but at a young age had married a Jew, a fact that protected him and allowed the two of them to immigrate, as he had relatives in America. They were lucky; neither of them had been jailed or kept in a concentration camp, though her husband had been sent to one briefly.

She had been able to get him out; she felt actually guilty about it.

"Sometimes people think I'm a *Jew*," she told me. "I have dark hair, and I married one. But I didn't want to be a Jew. I just wanted to lead my own life. Sometimes, though, you can't do that. There are people who'll take your life away from you. They exist here in Savannah, too. It's a pretty place, but you have to be very careful what you do. It's hard to be yourself here. But, Perry, you know that."

I called up some of my friends from high school. One of them, Steven, a shy, slender guy with wire-frame glasses who was incredibly smart, I'd had a huge crush on. We had even spent a year together at the University of Georgia, where he studied economics and I was studying art, a situation he had absolutely no belief in. "You're talented," he said to me accusingly. "You don't even have to work at it."

It was true. I'd become a "star" in the art department at 17, recognized as a prodigy in this small pond where I took senior painting classes and was on a first-name basis with many of the profs. I'd also had death threats in my dorm, filled with freshmen boys right out of the backwater sticks of Georgia—who were sure I "wuz a queer" who should be killed if he "evuh so much as looked at me," as one kid put it. Then he added: "I wish he wud." For weeks I'd gone into a rock-solid depression that even Steven couldn't pull me out of.

When I first arrived I'd met this beautiful kid who was there on a full tennis scholarship. Most of the boys sneered at him. "Only queers and fairies play tennis." I'd learned that he was "shipped out" after the first six weeks of the term. He had tried to kill himself, but luckily had failed at that.

Now, Steven picked me up in his father's car and we drove out to a woodsy subdivision just out of town. He wanted to walk around.

"You became like a myth at Georgia, the way you left school. People talked about it. They envied you that you had got away. What did you do?"

I didn't tell him everything, but told him about the life I'd had in San Francisco, going to bars and gay coffeehouses and being free, finally. Steven had a girlfriend who was completely in love with him, although he was not that much in love with her, but was trying to be. At Georgia, he was scared he was going to "end up gay," like I had. There was no way he could even imagine himself doing what I did—in any kind of circumstance. His father, a retired Army colonel, would have disowned him.

"I'm going to stay at Georgia," he'd said, "and get my degree, and then apply for a graduate program at a real school—like Columbia or Princeton. My dad will go for that. He'll pay for it, but he had to know I was going to do OK at the state school first."

I saw several of my high school friends; they were interested that I had left the South. Savannah was still being wracked by civil rights tensions. You could feel it in the air; that Old School Southern veneer of charming gentility—the "sit down and set a spell" graciousness that most people put on—

now had clearly visible cracks in it.

Finally, I called Terry Loewenthal, one of my few gay friends in Savannah. He was six years older than I, a good-looking, dark-skinned guy with a lean, athletic body as well as both a Southern accent and high-born affectations you could cut with a knife. This was common with Southern queers who aspired to the upper classes, because only up there could you be afforded some shelter from the redneck violence below. Savannah had a very strict class system, and you were either to the manor born, or Jewish, or . . .

He was very glad to hear from me. He was working at an antique store but agreed to pick me up at 8 when he got off, and we could go out for a drink. He had just bought a house, his first in Savannah, on an old square in downtown. I told Mother that I was going out for the evening. She wasn't happy about it. She had become more morose and resentful every day I was there. It was my last night in Savannah, but she and Esther had not included me in any plans.

Terry and I went to a bar by the river that had been created out of old warehouse space. It was very air-conditioned and dark, the way that Savannah bars tended to be, especially if any part of the queer population might frequent them.

I asked him if it was a gay bar.

"Well, Savannah always has a floating gay bar, because the cops close them down in about six months. So you have the same customers, but a different bar in a different location. This one is not really *that* gay but it's gay enough, you could say."

He smiled at me, and after a few gin and tonics he invited me to see his new house.

It was amazing, immense, and incredibly beautiful, dating back to the 1880s, with original silk wall coverings, parquetry, French doors with beveled glass in them, and a gorgeous room at one side of the house all covered with beautifully cut-glass panes.

"It was the *orangerie*," Terry said. Some of the glass had fallen out, and the floor was warped from being open to the elements. I could see a crescent moon floating above, and the pungent sultry air of Savannah at night, filled with night-blooming flowers and bathed in humidity, wafted in. The house had been vacant for several years and finally sold for a pittance. "The bank said if I could fix it up, I could have it. It's that way with these old houses. The families die out or no longer want them. It's also in a neighborhood that has become pretty black, so that doesn't help."

He opened up his refrigerator. There was some cheese, bread, and cold wine in it, so he made us some cheese sandwiches. After another glass of wine, he asked me if I wanted to spend the night. I nodded. I was fairly drunk, and the house, despite the floors with nails popping out of them and plumbing that barely worked, was romantic in every sense of the word.

I woke up early the next morning in Terry's bed, with him snoring badly beside me. He had to get to work in the antique shop—because of the bad plumbing, there was no water in the shower; he had to wash quickly in the kitchen sink.

"I'm going to fix that as soon as I get some money," he promised. I felt really grungy and desperately needed to brush my teeth. He drove me back to my mother's apartment. I knocked on the door. She was furious.

"You didn't come back here to see me," she screamed. "You only came back to renew old acquaintances!"

"They're my friends," I said. "I wanted to see them, too."

Esther was beside her.

"You've made your mother really upset, Perry. We were worried about you. There's no telling what could have happened to you. You didn't call."

Suddenly I realized I hadn't. I apologized—after living completely on my own for more than a year, the idea of calling hadn't even occurred to me.

My mother turned away from me.

"It's too late now," she said. "It's just too late."

"Yes," Esther said. "Get out, Perry. You've upset your mother enough."

My plane, to Nashville, was going to be leaving at 3 PM. I took a very quick shower and packed my bag. When I came back into the living room, only Esther was there.

"You're not a very nice boy," she said to me. "You've been an extremely bad son. Your mother's very sick. You don't even know how sick she is, and all you do is hurt her."

Suddenly I hated Esther. After what I had been through as a child, with my mother's recurring violence toward me, how could she say that? I turned around, and walked out the door without saying goodbye.

Chapter
23

I took a cab out to the airport, and there I got a real shock—basically, the airport was shut down. On the day I arrived for a flight to Nashville, July 8, 1966, roughly 35,000 airline workers walked off their jobs to bolster their demands for pay raises after the major airlines went from conventional engines to jet ones and profits climbed. I was told there was no flight out of Savannah to Nashville, or any place, as the only airlines that serviced the city were on strike. I asked at the ticket counter what could I do, and was told that there was a Greyhound station close by, and I should go there.

I did. Buses were packed, but I managed to get on one for Nashville, with a change in Atlanta. The bus ride was miserable; it was not air-conditioned, and the temperature was sweltering. I arrived in Atlanta about four hours later, and from there at another counter was told that the connecting bus for Nashville was filled, and I would have to wait for eight hours for another bus.

I went ballistic, screaming at the young polite Southern kid behind the counter.

"They promised me in Savannah I could get on this bus!"

"Suh," he said. "There's an airline strike on. We're overbooked. People have been waiting here for hours for another bus. There's nothing—"

"You don't give a *damn* about us, about promises, about—"

He looked mortified with shock.

"Suh," he said. "There are ladies present. Please watch your language."

I was now furious.

"You're going to have more than my language to deal with—"

Suddenly he changed. He realized I meant business, and obviously I had lived in the North long enough not to care what kind of ladies were around me. He wrote out a ticket for me, and walked me to the bus. I thanked him courteously, and got on it.

A Real Life • Perry Brass

The bus was not all that filled, but it could have been that other people were getting on at various stops. I now had some time to think and all
I could think about was seeing Rodney. I was still so smitten with him; I
remembered the way he looked and his beautiful eyes and face and body. Everything now seemed like a dream that I was in. The bus was going through
this hilly Southern countryside approaching Nashville, Tennessee, and his
face was all over it. All I had was his telephone number at home; I decided I
would call him as soon as I got there.

The sun was setting as the bus stopped at the station in Nashville. I retrieved my small canvas suitcase and hit a payphone. A woman answered,
and she turned the phone over to Rodney. I said hello, and he answered.

His voice sounded very flat, guarded, but I understood. His mother must
have been the one who answered, and she was right there. I asked if I could
see him. He told me no.

"I can't see you tonight, Perry. But I can tomorrow. Can you stop by the
vet's office where I work? There's a kennel behind it, and we can talk to each
other there. There's something I need to say to you."

"OK." I asked him for directions how to get there, and he told me. It was
"a small piece out of town, but you can catch a city bus that will take you
right there."

Next to the Greyhound depot was a group of small, cheap hotels, and I
found one. I was getting low on money and I decided I had to keep enough
cash for a plane ticket back to New York. A few airlines were not experienc-
ing the strike, and one must have been flying out of Nashville. My hope was
that Rodney might have a friend I could stay with, or know about a spare
couch someplace, even in his garage, that I could land on. I wanted to see
him, to spend time with him, to hold and kiss him.

That night I walked around downtown Nashville. It seemed more like a
small town than a larger Southern city, certainly bigger than Savannah. At
the center of downtown was the Grand Ole Opry at the Ryman Auditorium, an ungainly, almost comic-looking building in a mishmash, kind of
Southern-Gothic-Moorish style. Outside were posters advertising stars like
Cousin Minnie Pearl, Loretta Lynn, and Tex Ritter. There was no show that
night, but I walked into the lobby and got to peek inside the auditorium.
The place was huge; I was no country music fan, but I could see why people

194

were taken with it. Stars were made there.

I got up the next morning, had breakfast, and left my suitcase with the hotel clerk. At about 11 o'clock, I got off the city bus and walked several blocks from the bus stop through a beautiful, leafy residential area to Truman's Veterinary Hospital and Kennel, where Rodney worked. I was perspiring from the damp heat, but my hands felt cold from nerves. I kept rubbing them together, while perspiration ran down inside my thin, white cotton short-sleeve shirt. I had wanted to look good, but now I felt nervous and disheveled.

A pretty blonde girl in her late teens was at the desk. I asked for Rodney, and she called him on an intercom system. I waited for a second, then he came out.

He looked different. He had gained weight, and was more muscular and glumly sad looking. He shook my hand, and asked me to come to the back, into the kennels where he had work to do.

"I'm right glad to see you," he said formally with a heavier accent than I remembered him having. "It's been a long time. I never thought I'd ever see you again."

We were now alone. It was just the two of us and all those cages of dogs, most of them eating contentedly or sleeping.

"I thought about you constantly," I said. "No matter where I was."

Suddenly his head went down.

"You shouldn't. You should just leave me in the past. I'm not the same person I was last year in LA. I don't do what I did before."

"I understand. You're not hustling anymore. That's good."

He looked at me directly in the eyes.

"I'm not *gay* anymore. Maybe I never really was. I have a girlfriend. I been seein' her. I like being straight. I like being like other kids. I like it that I don't have to lie to my parents anymore. I had to lie to them about everything in LA."

Suddenly I could barely breathe. All I had wanted to do was hold him and kiss him, and now I knew I'd never get to do that again. I could hardly keep from crying.

"Why did you want to see me again? Why did you write me those letters?"

He paused.

"I don't know. I did feel something for you, Perry. You know that. You're a really nice guy. You weren't like the other hustlers I knew. You were like . . . a real guy. But the truth is I don't like boys anymore. Not in that way. I want to get old and be normal." His beautiful face looked suddenly like it was crushed. "Maybe you should just go now."

I did. I didn't even say goodbye. Not a real kind of goodbye where you embrace. I felt like the sky was crashing in on me. Suddenly the dogs started barking loudly after everything had been so quiet. For a moment I turned and looked back at him. He was crouching down, petting them. He looked up at me for a second with that same pained look. I left.

By the afternoon, I was at the airport in Nashville. Things were totally crazy because of the strike, but there was an American Airlines flight to New York, and I was able to get on it. I was tired but managed to sleep on the plane, where I was also given a nice meal. I now had almost no money and no way of getting more. There were no cash machines then, and I had no credit cards. We arrived at John F. Kennedy Airport about 7 at night. It was sweltering. I discovered there was a way to go by public transportation into the Village. I knew I could find my way to Julius's, the bar I'd been in before. With a little luck, someone might pick me up and give me a place to wash up and stay for the night.

I placed my suitcase in a locker at the West Fourth Street subway station, and then ventured out. Because of the weather there were tons of people all over the place on the street.

I found Julius's and managed to buy myself one beer. I started cruising madly and making it pretty obvious that, at eighteen, I was available for the night. Nothing happened. Several guys came up to me, but after a couple of minutes they walked away. Suddenly hours slipped by.

I ended up spending the night in Sheridan Square, close to the location of a bar that three years later would make history—the Stonewall Inn—nodding off several times on a bench. At about 6 AM I asked a cop what would be the easiest way to get back to Hartford, Connecticut?

He told me there were buses to take or trains. When I told him I had no money, he smiled. He'd heard it before.

"Whatcha need to do is get a subway out to Pelham in the Bronx. It's the end of the line. From there, you can find the Interstate, and you can hitch on one of the ramps. But be careful. You can't hitch on the Interstate itself in Connecticut. They'll arrest you for it."

I thanked him and did what he said. First I got my suitcase back, then got on the subway and rode it out to the end of the line. I kept falling asleep, but woke up when the train made its last stop.

Around 3 in the afternoon I was finally home, so exhausted I could barely breathe. I took a shower. It felt absolute wonderful, like I had not had one in a week. I got into bed, and there was a knock at the door.

I got up in my underwear. It was Len. I told him how exhausted I was and went into some of the story of the trip.

"That airline strike is really screwing up everything," he said as he took off his clothes and got into bed with me. Suddenly I was very glad to see him. He held me in his large, muscular arms, and I responded. This was what I had wanted from Rodney, but would never get.

Chapter

24

Shortly after I got back from my difficult trip to Savannah and Nashville, Pratt & Whitney's school for sheet metal apprentices started a new mid-summer session. I would be in classes from 9 in the morning until 4 in the afternoon, and be paid for it. The term went on for 9 months, at the end of which I would receive a certificate and then be eligible to go on for advanced training in more specialized forms of metalwork, such as direct repairs on engine parts. Finally, after two years, I could be certified as a master crafts-man, qualified to do exacting tool-and-die work.

Since the war, and thus the draft, was heating up further, finding young men—and they were all young *men*—to be in these classes was becoming difficult. Pratt & Whitney had tried to get young sheet metal craftsmen mil-itary deferments, with little luck. Whereas I had found working on the fac-tory floor kind of fun, a lark, say, I found being in the classes more difficult. I couldn't disappear in them. I was different from the other guys—quieter, less open, less *overtly* working class, although I had come from deep poverty in the Deep South, and that in itself became contentious. Being Southern made me suspect too. It was like they expected me to be something out of *Gone with the Wind*, and even though my class was all white, the attitude was that deep-down, inside, as a Southerner I just had to be genuinely *stupid*.

Our instructor, a kind of slobby, middle-aged guy with a huge stomach and glasses that always looked dirty, immediately made fun of me.

"What are y'all doin' up here?" he asked me, grinning, when he learned where I was from.

I told him that I needed a job.

"Why Pratt & Whitney? Don't y'all have jobs down there?"

I shrugged. I decided the less I said, the happier I was going to be. I was actually good at the classes; there was some math involved, but it was ba-sically on about a seventh-grade level, so I could do it. I also became good at welding, both with an oxyacetylene torch and with a tungsten arc heat source. After working with art materials for so long, I had no fear of the tools and materials involved, even with the danger they entailed—from extremely high, focused temperatures, or the threat of electrical shock from tungsten arc welding.

I had no idea what I was going to do with this skill, because I was certain that I was not going to stay at Pratt & Whitney much longer. I saw a notice in the *Hartford Courant* that Cooper Union down in New York's East Village was accepting candidates for its free art night school. I called the admissions office, and a very polite woman told me that there was no formal application at all for this class: the entire class would be made up of people who had passed an entrance exam given at Cooper the next weekend.

"We judge you entirely by your drawing skills," she said. "But remember, we have close to three hundred applicants trying for about eighteen places."

On the next Saturday I got up before dawn and took a bus in to Manhattan. The exam was at three in the afternoon. She was right: about three hundred people were there for the exam. It consisted of drawing a still life of an inanimate display that had been set up; of drawing from "life" a draped female model; and of drawing, from pure imagination, a scene of a couple ice skating. Applicants were given a drawing board with newsprint paper attached to it and charcoal and pencils, and told when to start each of the three projects.

I found the still life the hardest because in the setup were a plaster cone, a sphere, and a cube. The question was how to make these look interesting. I decided not to worry about that, and just draw them as they were. Drawing from the draped model, a young woman, was easy for me. I had drawn from models before. I was not sure how well I did; I was younger than most of the applicants, but again I just drew what was before me.

Then, strangely, in the third project, I just took off. I'll never forget it. I remembered from previous art classes the idea of "kinesthetics," the idea that movement has an aesthetic of its own that you can feel with your own body. Suddenly I felt ice skating. I could feel it in my body, even though I had *never* done it. The drawing I did of a man and a woman ice skating really worked. It was jazzy, fully formed, and real; I could tell it. I smiled and then handed the three sheets with my name on them to one of the proctors, along with an actual application form that had my contact information on it.

I felt happy leaving, but realized these were still pretty stiff odds. I took the bus back to Hartford, and the next day told Len about it.

"I hope you get in," he said. "You need to get out of here. You need to have some goals in your life besides just surviving."

Two weeks later, I got a formal letter in the mail telling me that I had been accepted. I was overjoyed, though I had little idea how I was going to do this—move to New York. Classes would begin the second week in September, at night, three nights a week. It was a certificate program that would last for two years, at the end of which I could apply for the day school.

We were approaching the last week of July, and I knew I'd be quitting Pratt & Whitney and moving to New York the first week of August.

I told Len, and he said we should have a celebration. "There's a gay beach in Rhode Island. Let me take you to it."

The following Sunday, Len picked me up in his open two-seater roadster and we drove out, on a gorgeous day, to Rhode Island. I had never been to a "gay beach." The whole idea seemed novel and almost scary to me. Like, what would you *do* at a "gay beach"? The beach was very isolated and almost deserted, except for a few scattered families and teenagers on it. Then suddenly this other couple, two men who looked like they were either hairdressers or very flamboyant window decorators, arrived wearing very colorful "beachy"-looking clothes and carrying a small, white, yappy dog and a huge, very deluxe, reed picnic basket—the kind you'd find with inside leather fittings for champagne glasses, sterling silver tableware, small plates, and of course a loaf of French bread and a jar of pâté. I thought: So this is what goes on at a gay beach? You have these queens who bring champagne and pâté. It seemed almost comical.

Len and I went into the water. He was a fantastic swimmer—he had been a lifeguard—and I loved oceans so I swam with him. Afterwards we drove to a seaside restaurant, and he treated me to lobster. It was the ending to a beautiful day—until, driving back in heavy traffic toward Hartford, we came to a stoplight near a mall. A Pontiac full of teenage boys pulled up next to us. Suddenly I could feel them all looking at us in Len's open roadster.

Every nerve in me tightened up.

"Are you two queers?" the kid next to me shouted out his window, with that leering smile carrying a razor blade inside it.

I didn't say anything. I didn't want to look at him. I could see the color in Len's face drain. It was like this big guy with his huge shoulders had become terrified.

They blew the horn, the light changed, and they headed off.

Neither of us could speak for several minutes. I had no idea what to say; I only knew that I wanted to get the hell away from Hartford as soon as I could.

Chapter
25

I arrived in New York by bus in August, exactly one month before my nineteenth birthday. Again, I had almost no money—about $80 in cash. I had seen ads in New York papers for several cheap hotels on the Upper West Side, and decided to look around there. I left my suitcase and a few boxes with my paints and some artwork in Greyhound's baggage claims office, and approached a subway entrance to get up there from Forty-Second Street. The subways were cheap, hot, and bewildering. When I asked a fat, middle-aged clerk at the token booth what was the easiest way to get to West Seventy-Second Street, he replied: "Take a cab."

With the use of a map, I did figure it out, and soon I emerged on Seventy-Second Street and Central Park West. There was air from the park around me, and tons of dog shit on the sidewalks. Every step I took seemed to land me in it, and I'd have to go back into the park to wipe my shoes off on the grass. After doing this three times, I resolved to watch every step I took, and visited some hotels. The clerks were brusque and looked at me like *I* was covered in dog shit myself, but after a few tries I found a place with a nice room on the 6th floor overlooking the street and a barely functional elevator for $14 a day.

I went back to the Port Authority, got my things, and managed them upstairs in the elevator. I kept thinking this hotel reminded me of the one in *The Catcher in the Rye* where the bellboy got Holden Caulfield a date with a whore. It had a kind of raw charm to it; now I didn't have to worry for the next day or so. At the beginning of the week, I had an appointment with Cooper Union; the head of admissions wanted to meet me. I didn't have a job or a real place to stay, but none of that bothered me.

At Cooper I met with a woman in her thirties who greeted me courteously. She told me that I had done very well on my admissions test, and Cooper was *very* happy to have me. She asked if I were staying with my parents, and I told her no. I was staying in a hotel and looking for a job.

She skipped over everything I said and continued smiling mechanically.

"I'm sure you'll do beautifully, Perry," she said. "You're a *very* talented young man, and New York has so much to offer you."

When I left her office, I kept hearing her words in my head—"You're a very talented young man." I had heard those words before, and later I would hear them again, usually as a prelude to being fired.

I walked away from Astor Place, where Cooper was, and quickly found myself in Washington Square. There were folksingers strumming guitars all over the park, waiting to be discovered like Bob Dylan. I was listening to one when I became aware of a good-looking young man a few years older than I who had jet-black hair and dark eyes but very pale, clear skin. He was taller than I was by a few inches and in short sleeves had a lean, muscular body. He smiled at me.

"She's great, isn't she?" he asked about the singer.

I agreed, and a couple of minutes later we started walking together. His name was Frank Abollio, and he was warm, nice, and smart. He read poetry and liked talking about it. He asked me what kind of bars I went to, then casually he mentioned Julius's in the Village, which was like a dropped clue to tell me he was gay. I looked into his eyes and smiled. Shortly afterwards we were taking a subway together back to my hotel.

"This is a real dump," he said, entering the room. "You've got to get out of here." He was staying in New Jersey with his parents, and I asked him what should I do.

"There are lots of 'Roommates Wanted' ads in the *Times*, but you have to be careful. A lot of them are dirty old men looking for boys like you"— he smiled as he started to unbutton my shirt—"you know, cute ones from Georgia?"

I nodded my head. "OK."

"There's usually a kind of code in the ad," Frank explained. "They use words like 'looking for congenial roommate,' or 'seeking friendly, like-mind-ed guy.' That kind of stuff."

The next day I got a copy of the *Times*. Frank was right: there were several ads calling for "congenial roommates," as well as "like-minded," "open spir-ited," and one that said he was a "classical music lover." Using all the dimes I could get, I started making calls.

The first man I reached was very friendly. He asked me where I was from, and he said, "Good! I love Southerners! Can you come by right now?"

He gave me his address, and I had no idea how close it was—he was just on West 66th Street, off of Central Park West. I had a map of New York, and got into a cab outside the hotel. The cab driver saw my map, and turned around and went west. Suddenly, using my map I realized we were going in the wrong direction completely. I told him we were.

"It ain't the wrong direction. It's the direction with the least traffic. I live here, kid. Let me drive."

By the time we got to the address, the fare had gone up ridiculously and I knew it.

"Next time, kid," he said. "Don't carry a map wit' ya. That's my advice."

I figured that was worth the ride, and got out in front of an attractive brownstone. Bob Miller, the man I was seeing, was on the third floor. He came to the door wearing shorts, flip-flops, and a very tight shirt unbuttoned halfway down. He was short, muscular-stocky, in his mid-forties, and waving a cigarette, with two very barky little Chihuahuas trailing behind him.

He extended his hand, gave me a very firm handshake, and ushered me through his apartment. It had been the formal parlor floor of the brownstone, with two large rooms connected by a narrow tiled hallway, the second room leading into a closet that had been converted into a galley kitchen, and then a bathroom. Both of the rooms had tall windows that looked out on a small garden below bearing mimosa trees. The front room had been painted in a gloomy, deep Venetian red with the once-beautiful formal details of the walls and ceiling plasterwork picked out in cheap gold paint. It contained a large couch and several chairs. Thick shag, red, wall-to-wall carpeting was on the floor.

"Like the décor?" Bob beamed. "I did it myself!"

I smiled. It was hideous, but I told him I liked it very much. He offered me coffee and a cigarette. I told him I didn't smoke. He was a waiter from a small town in Massachusetts. "I couldn't wait to get outta there," he said. "Although New York is hardly anybody's cup of tea now, with the blacks and Puerto Ricans taking over. One guy answered my ad and told me he was only into black men and I said, 'I'm sorry, but that just won't work here.' Not that I have anything against blacks—they have their place, it's just not with me. By the way, what kind of guys do you go for?"

He said that so fast without batting an eye that I was taken aback. No one had ever asked me that. I had to think about it.

"I guess guys like myself," I said.

"Oh, I get it. You mean young and good-looking?"

I felt myself blush. He looked at me like he was going to take every strip of clothing off me.

"Ah, don't worry, pal," he said reading my face. "I always come off like that. You'll have your own room—it's the front room, the best one really. The couch opens up. It's quieter. I go for straights—y'know, married men? I find 'em sexy. You're not my type actually. I like 'em butcher than you, and not quite so . . . well, you come off a little standoffish. I guess it's that Southern thing. You been taught to be a lady, I can see that. But I like you. The place is yours if you want it. The rent is only $18 a week. That comes to, like, well, close to $69 a month. Lots of guys find that funny."

I told him I wanted to think about it.

He nodded. "OK. Just don't think too long. I can keep it open for a day for you, then after that—well, it's a great location in a brownstone. Remember that."

I went to check out another ad. This guy was worse than Bob; he was older, very jowly, and dressed in a tie and jacket. He had a prissy apartment, and treated me like I was trekking mud on his floors. He immediately asked me what kind of job I had. Bob had never even mentioned a job. I left the second apartment, and called Bob and told him I'd be happy to move in.

Bob was happy, too. He said I could move in that evening. I did. Since he wanted to be paid by the week, that left me more money to live on until I found work.

The next day I looked through the *New York Times*. They had postings for "Art Jobs"; most of them were with agencies, but I had no fear of going in at all. I figured that if I could get a job in an aircraft factor and lie about everything, I could get a job in the "art field."

I put on a clean white shirt, a tie, and my jacket. I had no résumé. All I had was a portfolio filled with sketches, mostly of landscapes and flowers. I tried several tony, snotty agencies where women looked at me and shook their heads. Then I tried an agency that was not specifically an art agency. A very wiry, middle-aged Jewish man spoke to me.

"So you wanna work in art?" I showed him my portfolio. He smiled. "I have just the job for you. You won't be doing art, but you'll be around artists, and if you're good, they may try you out on the board and teach you stuff."

It was my first job in New York, as a messenger in a commercial art studio. The pay was less than $70 a week. When I told Bob that he smiled.

"Honey, you're gonna have t' get yourself a dinner job. That's waiter talk for working two shifts. It ain't much money—but hell, you're so young and good-looking. Sooner or later something better will come along."

On September 15, I told Bob that I had just turned nineteen. I had lied to him and told him I was nineteen when I had moved in.

"Jeez-Louise," he said, puffing on a cigarette. "You done a lot for a kid who's only eighteen."

True. I had; it was hard even to imagine it. I still felt very much alone. I'd not really found myself, or love, but I was coming closer to understanding some basic elements of both of them. First that I had to be authentic to myself. I didn't really even have a choice; it seemed to be a part of my own makeup. No matter how many lies were told around me—lies about my own people, "queers" as they were called; lies about the South and the lies that the South told; and all those lies "necessary" to keep so much of life in America going—I had to give myself one thing. The truth. It was a gift to me, and it would arm me. It was the only thing I had really: my own truth. I thought about Blake and the terrible time he had, having his boys taken from him, and Rodney, the boy I'd fallen so passionately in love with at seventeen; and about being in Juvenile Hall, and then in San Francisco. Somehow my survival and the truth always seemed to be entwined.

And now I was in New York, newly nineteen. What an odd dream it all seemed, as I began a life and an adventure that I would later call, simply, "Lost Gay New York," after a series of blog posts that I wrote in another time. But for now the adventure was just beginning, and waiting for me to recollect it later.

Perry Brass

Born in Savannah, Georgia, and currently living in New York City, groundbreaking author Perry Brass has published 19 books, including poetry, novels, short fiction, science fiction, plays, and bestselling advice books (*How to Survive Your Own Gay Life, The Manly Art of Seduction, The Manly Pursuit of Desire and Love*). He has been a finalist six times for Lambda Literary Awards, has won five IPPY Awards from the Independent Publishers Group, and was a finalist for a prestigious Ferro-Grumley Fiction Award from New York's Ferro-Grumley Foundation. He has had a hundred poems set to music by composers who include Chris DeBlasio, Ricky Ian Gordon, Fred Hersch, Christopher Berg, Paula Kimper, Gerald Busby, Judith Cloud, Mary Carol Warwick, and Scott Gendel. His collaboration with DeBlasio, the song cycle "All the Way Through Evening," concludes with "Walt Whitman in 1989," a song featured in Will Parker's groundbreaking "AIDS Quilt Songbook," that has become an internationally performed anthem of the AIDS crisis.

Active in the movement toward lgbtq rights since 1969, Brass's work deals with issues of sexual freedom, spirituality and personal politics coming out of his involvement with the Gay Liberation Front directly after the Stonewall Rebellion. He has written about and anticipated in his work much of the progressive change we see today throughout the world—around same-sex marriage, economic justice, gender equality, reproductive freedom, men's health issues, especially aging and prostate cancer, and transgender rights. In 1972, with two friends he started the Gay Men's Health Project Clinic, the first clinic specifically for gay men on the East Coast in America. It actively advocated for the use of condoms a decade before the AIDS crisis. This clinic still operates as the Callen-Lorde Community Health Center. He is also a co-founder of the Rainbow Book Fair, the largest lgbt book event in the U.S, and has written extensively for the Huffington Post, the Good Men Project, Gay City News, and other venues.

For more information: www.perrybrass.com

Other Books by Perry Brass

Sex-charge

"... poetry at its highest voltage ..."

—Marv. Shaw in Bay Area Reporter

Sex-charge. 76 pages. $6.95. With male photos by Joe Ziolkowski.
ISBN 0-9627123-0-2

Mirage *groundbreaking science fiction*

An erotically-charged gay science fiction classic! An original "coming out"
and coming-of-age saga, set in a distant place where gay sexuality and ro-
mance is a norm, but with a life-or-death price on it. On the tribal planet
Ki, two men have been promised to each other for a lifetime. But a savage
attack and a blood-chilling murder break this promise and force them to
seek another world, where imbalance and lies form Reality. This is the planet
known as Earth, a world they will use and escape. Finalist, 1991 Lambda Literary Award for Gay Men's Science Fiction/Fantasy. This classic work of gay
science fiction fantasy is now available in its new Tenth Anniversary Edition.

"Intelligent and intriguing."

—Bob Satuloff in *New York Native*

Mirage, Tenth Anniversary Edition. 230 pages. $12.95. ISBN 1-892149-
02-8

Circles *the amazing sequel to* Mirage

"The world Brass has created with Mirage and its sequel rivals, in
complexity and wonder, such greats as C. S. Lewis and Ursula
LeGuin."

—*Mandate Magazine*, New York

Circles. 224 pages. $11.95. ISBN 0-9627123-3-7

Out There *Stories of Private Desires. Horror. And the Afterlife.*

"... we have come to associate [horror] with slick and trashy chiller-
thrillers. Perry Brass is neither. He writes very well in an elegant and
easy prose that carries the reader forward pleasurably. I found this
selection to be excellent."

—*The Gay Review*, Canada

Out There. 196 pages. $10.95. ISBN 0-9627123-4-5

Albert *or The Book of Man*

Third in the *Mirage* trilogy, and decades ahead of its 1995 publication date, *Albert* predicted gay marriage and the division of America into progressive "blue" states and conservative "red" ones. In 2025 the White Christian Party has taken over America. Albert, son of Enkidu and Greeland, must find the male Earth mate who will claim his heart and allow him to return to leadership on Ki.

"Brass gives us a book where lesser writers would have only a premise."
—*Men's Style*, New York

"If you take away the plot, it has political underpinnings that are chillingly true. Brass has a genius for the future." Science Fiction Galaxies, Columbus, OH. "Erotic suspense and action . . . a pleasurable read."
—*Screaming Hyena Review*, Melbourne, Australia

Albert. 210 pages. $11.95. ISBN 0-9627123-5-3

Works *and Other 'Smoky George' Stories, Expanded Edition*

"Classic Brass," these stories—many set in the long-gone seventies, when, as the author says, "Gay men cruised more and networked less"—have recharged gay erotica. This Expanded Edition contains a selection of Brass's steamy poems, as well as his essay "Maybe We Should Keep the 'Porn' in Pornography."

Works. 184 pages. $9.95. ISBN 0-9627123-6-1

The Harvest *a "science/politico" novel*

From today's headlines predicting human cloning comes the emergence of "vaccos"—living "corporate cadavers"—raised to be sources of human organ and tissue transplants. One exceptional vacco will escape. His survival will depend upon Chris Turner, a sexual renegade who will love him and kill to keep him alive.

"One of the Ten Best Books of 1997,"
—*Lavender Magazine*, Minneapolis

"In George Nader's Chrome, the hero dared to fall in love with a robot. In *The Harvest—a vastly superior novel,* Chris Turner falls in love with a vacco, Hart256043."
—Jesse Monteagudo, *The Weekly News*, Miami, Florida

Finalist, 1997 Lambda Literary Award, Gay and Lesbian Science Fiction

The Harvest. 216 pages. $11.95. ISBN 0-9627123-7-X

The Lover of My Soul *A Search for Ecstasy and Wisdom*

Brass's first book of poetry since *Sex-charge* is worth the wait. Flagrantly erotic and just plain flagrant—with poems like "I Shoot the Sonovabitch Who Fires Me," "Sucking Dick Instead of Kissing," and the notorious "MTV Ab(solutely) Vac(uous) Awards," *The Lover of My Soul* again proves Brass's feeling that poetry must tell, astonish, and delight.

"An amazingly powerful book of poetry and prose,"
—*The Loving Brotherhood*, Plainfield, NJ

The Lover of My Soul. 100 pages. $8.95. ISBN 0-9627123-8-8

How to Survive Your Own Gay Life *An Adult Guide to Love, Sex, and Relationships*

The book for adult gay men. About sex and love, and coming out of repression; about surviving homophobic violence; about your place in a community, a relationship, and a culture. About the important psychic "gay work" and the gay tribe. About dealing with conflicts and crises, personal, professional, and financial. And, finally, about being more alive, happier, and stronger.

"This book packs a wallop of wisdom!"
—Morris Kight, founder,
Los Angeles Gay & Lesbian Services Center

Finalist, 1999 Lambda Literary Award in Gay and Lesbian Religion and Spirituality

How to Survive Your Own Gay Life. 224 pages. $11.95. ISBN 0-9627123-9-6

Angel Lust *An Erotic Novel of Time Travel*

Tommy Angelo and Bert Knight are in a long-term relationship. Very long—close to a millennium. Tommy and Bert are angels, but different. No wings. Sexually free. Tommy was once Thomas Jebson, a teen serf in the violent England of William the Conqueror. One evening he met a handsome knight who promised to love him for all time. Their story introduces us to gay forest men, robber barons, castles, and deep woodlands. Also, to a modern sexual underground where "gay" and "straight" mean little. To Brooklyn factory men. Street machos. New York real estate sharks. And the kind of lush erotic encounters for which Perry Brass is famous.

Finalist, 2000 Lambda Literary Award, Gay and Lesbian Science Fiction

"Brass's ability to go from seedy gay bars in New York to 11th century castles is a testament to his skill as a writer."

—*Gay & Lesbian Review*

Angel Lust 224 pages. $12.95. ISBN 1-892149-00-1

Warlock *A Novel of Possession*

Allen Barrow, a shy bank clerk, dresses out of discount stores and has a small penis that embarrasses him. One night at a bathhouse he meets Destry Powars—commanding, vulgar, seductive, successful—who pulls Allen into his orbit and won't let go. Destry lives in a closed, moneyed world that Allen can only glimpse through the pages of tabloids. From generations of drifters, Powars has been chosen to learn a secret language based on force, deception, and nerve. But who chose him—and what does he really want from Allen? What are Mr. Powars's dark powers? These are the mysteries that Allen will uncover in *Warlock*, a novel that is as paralyzing in its suspense as it is voluptuously erotic.

Warlock. 226 pages. $12.95. ISBN 1-892149-03-6

The Substance of God *A Spiritual Thriller*

What would you do with The Substance of God, a self-regenerating material originating from Creation? The Substance can bring the dead back to life, but has a "mind" of its own. Dr. Leonard Miller, a gay bio-researcher secretly addicted to "kinky" sex, learned this after he was found mysteriously murdered in his laboratory while working alone on the Substance. Once brought back to life, Miller must find out who infiltrated his lab to kill him, how long will he have to live—and, exactly where does life end and any Hereafter begin?

Miller's story takes him from the underground sex scenes of New York to the all-male baths of Istanbul. It will deal with the longing for God in a techno-driven world; with the persistent attractions of religious fundamentalism; and with the fundamentals of "outsider" sexuality as both spiritual ritual and cosmic release. And Miller, the unbelieving scientist, will be driven himself to ask one more question: Is our often-censored urge toward sex and our great, undeniable urge toward a union with God . . . the same urge?

"Perry Brass has added to the annals of gay lit."

—*Book Marks*

The Substance of God. 232 pages. $13.95. ISBN: 1-892149-04-4

Carnal Sacraments *A Historical Novel of the Future*

In the last quarter of the 21st century, Jeffrey Cooper has made a Faustian pact with the global economic system running the world. No matter what age he is, the system will secretly keep him young and razor-sharp, as long as he can stay on top of his job and keep profits high. But Cooper has a problem: work stress and the congested, hyper-competitive life around him is killing him. Can he keep his stress level a secret from the system itself, his co-workers, and even his own seductive "daddyish" German therapist who has told him that when all else fails there are "angels" in the world who can save him, and often we don't know who they are?

But one, in the most violent form, will appear in Jeffrey's life. At first, he seems to be the Devil himself, offering every kind of excitement, even offering Jeffrey back his own lost soul—but will this younger, extremely mysterious and attractive man end up killing Jeffrey, or saving him?

> "Layered with philosophical elements, fascinating descriptions, and a clear focus on character overall, Brass' latest work is one of the most unusual novels I've read in years."
> —*Bay Area Reporter*, San Francisco

> "Exotic locations, high-powered wheeling and dealing and excursions into this new world's dark underside ... make this a book that captures the imagination and will not let it go until the last page."
> —*Out in Jersey Magazine*

Carnal Sacraments. 312 pages, $16.95, 2008, ISBN 978-1-892149-05-3

King of Angels *A Novel About the Genesis of Identity and Belief*

Set in the haunting, enchanting landscape of Savannah, Georgia (Midnight in the Garden of Good and Evil), during the tumultuous early 1960s (the Mad Men era), King of Angels differs greatly from most novels with an lgbt theme: it is about a significant and extremely compelling relationship between a father and son—told from the bond that both father and son feel, despite differences in generation, the many secrets that separate them, and barriers of temperament but not of basic character. This nourishing father-and-son relationship is something many gay men (as well as straight men) seek, but it has been sadly missing, and missed, from most literature.

King of Angels explores this bond as part of a re-examination of the male gender and role. As Benjamin Rothberg, the half-Jewish, 12-year-old protagonist of King of Angels says about Robby Rothberg, his very tragic but heroic Jewish father, he was the "closest thing to a brother I'd ever have, even though I didn't know it then."

Finalist, Ferro-Grumley Award for Gay and Lesbian Fiction, winner Bronze Medal IPPY

Award for Best Young Adult Fiction. 2012.

King of Angels, ISBN: 978-1-892149-14-5, $18.00 370 pages

The Manly Art of Seduction *How to Meet, Talk to, and Become Intimate with Anyone*

Winner Gold Medal Ippy Award from Independent Publisher, Gay and Lesbian Non-Fiction, 2010

"Men are not supposed to be seductive."

Perry Brass heard this while young, so of course it gave him an open field in a kind of behavior that can be exciting, fulfilling, and satisfying. If you feel you're always waiting for someone else to make the first move—if you're traumatized by your fear of rejection and don't have a clue how to open a conversation or expand the terms of a relationship, *The Manly Art of Seduction* is a must-have. Brass explains male territorialism, and how it keeps men locked inside themselves. He talks about making decisions yourself, and how these decisions can be used to make seduction possible—even easy. He deals with the monster of rejection, and how to use mind pictures and exercises to rejection-proof your psyche. At the end of most chapters are questions you can use to tailor this book to your needs, seeing your own progress as you come to master this art.

Although seduction is a part of our commercial environment, Perry Brass has brought it to a place where we can find spiritual and inner nourishment, and where the chronic aloneness of much of life can be changed into a state of delight and deeper sexual and emotional connections.

"Relationships between men can run the gamut from brief connections to long-lasting commitments. This book demonstrates how to break through fear and old patterns to increase your seduction skills and decrease missed opportunities. No matter what kind of connection you might be looking for, the advice offered here is helpful, sharp, and pulls no punches. But the tough love is served with style and humor."

—Dave Singleton, author of
The Mandates: 25 Real Rules for Successful Gay Dating

"A first-class primer for every taste,"

—Richard Labonte, *BookMarks*,
nationally syndicated column about LGBT books

"Filled with useful, practical advice, this guide is likely to make gay men feel more in control . . . Although he touches on common advice like tapping into shared interests, Brass also explores deeper concepts like valor and territorialism, and his stunning chapter on rejection should be a must-read for everyone in the dating scene."

—Elizabeth Millard,
ForeWord Reviews, January, 2010

"What Brass does so well is guide a man in how to get from the initial meeting all the way to the first date and beyond. But the brilliance of the book is that you can actually read it from the perspective of the person being seduced. The 'seductee' can see just how open and vulnerable the person approaching them is being, and also see what types of responses they might end up getting back. The seductee might then see himself and begin to understand how his behavior might be affecting the situation. And in that, he might learn how to let down his own guard, and allow that connection to take place."

—Kevin Taft, *Edge Magazine: Boston*, March 1, 2010

The Manly Art of Seduction, 200 pages, $16.95, ISBN: 978-1-892149-06-0
Ebook ISBN: 978-1-892149-10-7
Also available in a SmashWords edition.

All Perry Brass Titles Are Available At Your Bookstore, Or From:

Belhue Press
2501 Palisade Avenue, Suite A1
Bronx, NY 10463

E-mail: **belhuepress@earthlink.net**

Please add $2.50 shipping for the first book and $1.00 for each book thereafter. New York State residents please add 8.25% sales tax. Foreign orders in U.S. currency only.